How Now, Mad Cow?

Mad Cow?

The Second Year in Rural Galicia

Liza Grantham

For Mum

CONTENTS

Thanks to the Varela family for sharing their wisdom
and making us welcome in their world.

Chapter 1

Red or Black?

It's April, and the early morning drizzle threatens a downpour typical of Galician spring. A blackbird pecks amongst the bowed wildflowers beneath the fig tree, and slugs slope languidly through the damp clover. Staccato raindrops patter on the barn roof, seeping through to the rafters and dripping a syncopated rhythm onto the earthen floor. Intermittent gusts of wind strew clouds of blossom from the apple trees, yet the chestnut with its majestic strength remains still.

I peer out from beneath my umbrella and gaze out across the valley, where the far-off mountains are crowned with pine. There was a time when paradise had seemed as distant as the horizon, but Fate had led us, hoping, trusting, believing, to Galicia, our home.

I hoisted the waterproof trousers up above my waist and gripped them firmly, annoyed that the drawstring had disappeared into the waistband yet again. Trudging across the threshing floor, I cursed as the soles of my wellies slid on the lichens that dappled the stones. I squelched over the sodden grass down to the chicken run, where a cacophony of clucking inside the henhouse signalled the first egg of the day. Puddles were already forming in the hollows where, only yesterday, the hens had taken dust baths in the afternoon sun. This was typical of the weather in Galicia; it had a habit of changing in the blink of an eye. Of course, it no longer surprised us; it was exactly a year since we'd made the house of José Val our home.

Moving from the oppressive heat and bustle of Las Palmas, Gran Canaria to a peaceful hamlet in lush, green Galicia had seemed like stepping into paradise; it was a dream come true. The first year had been eventful, to say the least. Our new lifestyle was every bit as rewarding as we'd hoped, but nothing could have prepared us for the challenges and surprises we'd face along the way. It had been a steep learning curve: we were dyed-in-the-wool townies with no experience of country life in England, let alone in a Galician *aldea*. Over the last twelve months, we'd begun to shuffle off our naivety; we now had a better knowledge of local customs and practices and were becoming accustomed to the ups and downs of village life.

Over the last three weeks I'd come to dread opening the hen house; the cockerel, Rufo, had taken to attacking me savagely with his beak and his claws. My efforts to thwart his behaviour had thus far been unsuccessful. My most recent failure had been a cardboard cylinder; when I stood inside it, it came just above my knees. I'd been confident that the ingenious creation would confound him but, alas, I couldn't have been more wrong. Instead of resolving my predicament, my masterpiece had only exacerbated the situation. Rufo had hurled himself at the cardboard and, realising that it was impenetrable, had launched himself up above it; I now sported scabs and bruises on both thighs, as well as on my calves and shins.

Anxo, our German shepherd pup waited restlessly by the fence.

'Good boy, Anxo,' I told him. 'Wait nicely.'

It was a waste of time, and I knew it. The flapping and squawking of the hens as they left the house sent him into a frenzy every morning. He'd bark loudly and hurl himself at the fence, and no amount of chiding could dissuade him. At first I'd told myself that he'd grow out of it in time, but I was deluded. We'd had the chickens for over two months now, and Anxo was no longer a tiny puppy; at almost six months old he was a strong young dog. The fencing around the chooks' pen was flimsy in places and he still had a lot of growing to do. I wondered how much longer it would withstand the daily bombardment and feared the worst.

I took a deep breath and steeled myself for Rufo's onslaught as I tugged at the door. To my surprise, none of the birds made any move to leave the house. One of the hens was busy clucking over the egg that she'd laid, but everyone else, including Rufo, remained on the roost. The weather, it seemed, had deterred Rufo's determination to maim me; there was an advantage to the downpour after all.

'Raining,' yawned Gary, as I came back into the kitchen,

'Never,' I grinned. I yanked off my wellies, showering mud onto the floor.

'*You* sound cheerful. It can't be because of the weather, what's happened?'

'Actually, it *is* because of the weather. I don't think Rufo likes it – he stayed on the roost.'

'Crikey, that's a first. No wonder you're smiling. Perhaps you should take the watering can with you every morning. A good drenching might just sort him out.'

'It's worth a go,' I nodded, giving it genuine consideration. 'I've tried just about everything else. You don't think it's a bit cruel though, do you?'

'For God's sake, Liza! After the damage he's done to your legs! Anybody else would have wrung his neck by now.'

It was true. Rufo's future lay in the balance, and I was already preparing myself for what seemed the inevitable outcome.

Anxo was growing restless. Thanks to the weather, the energy he usually expended down at the chicken run was still pent up inside him and needed to be unleashed.

'He's ready for his walk,' said Gary.

'I *know*,' I scowled. It was easy for *him* to sit there stating the obvious; *he* wasn't the one who had to trek over the fields for an hour in the rain. 'He hasn't had chance to vent spleen on the chickens. I'll take him down past the spring, through the woods and into the five fields for a good run.'

Out in the open, Anxo was in his element. The wind and showers had brought forth a host of new smells and he was keen to explore. As we turned onto the track to the side of the barn he bounded ahead, while I trod cautiously between the cow pats and stones. Eventually the track sloped downwards and became a shallow stream, sourced by a natural spring. Along the side of the stream. I picked my way over the higgledy-piggledy pathway of slippery boulders which served as stepping-stones. Once back on *terra firma*, I noticed Anxo worrying at something in the bramble. I didn't have to wait long to find out what it was. Within seconds he trotted towards me with his prize.

'It's beautiful, Anxo!' I said, with as much enthusiasm as I could muster. The sodden body of a squirrel hung lifeless from his jaws. He wagged his tail proudly, before trotting off up the slope into the woodland. I resigned myself to the fact that the squirrel would be joining us for the rest of the walk and thanked my lucky stars it hadn't yet succumbed to the early stages of decay.

'Don't think you're taking it home, though!' I called after him.

'Anxo found a squirrel,' I told Gary at coffee break.

'A grey one?'

'No, black.'

'*Black*? Are you sure it was a squirrel, not a mole?'

'*Gary*, it had a big bushy tail and tufty ears. I know a bloody squirrel when I see one.'

'Did he eat it?'

'No, thank goodness. He carried it round for half an hour then dumped it under the chestnut tree at the top of Field Two. Hopefully it'll have gone by tonight, a fox or a buzzard or something's bound to take it.'

'Clever boy, Anxo,' said Gary, bending down to give him a fuss. 'God, he stinks! It must be the squirrel!'

'No,' I giggled. 'I meant to warn you. José Manuel's been manuring. Anxo's been having a jolly good roll.'

At that moment Anxo rushed towards the back door barking a greeting.

'That'll be Tom,' I grinned.

Tom had been living in the *aldea* since summer. The house belonged to his friend Paul, in England, who only came over now and again for a holiday. For the last eight months Tom had been looking for a place of his own. So far, he'd been unsuccessful, but he was spending increasingly less time in the village. He'd fallen in love with a Spanish woman who lived an hour's drive away.

I went through to the entrance passage and opened the door. 'Morning,' I said. 'Come in.'

Tom ambled into the kitchen followed by Maud, his faithful, feisty old brindle dog. His other dog, Ali, wasn't with them. This was ominous; she was fifteen and had recently been having problems. She'd become incontinent in the night and was struggling to get up from her bed in the morning. It was clear that she wasn't going to get any better and I wondered how Tom would cope when the day came.

'Coffee?' I asked, filling the kettle before he could answer; Tom was never one to decline a brew.

'Yes, please. Shit, what's that smell?'

'You've just answered your own question!' laughed Gary.

Tom looked puzzled. I grinned; Maud was sniffing Anxo as if her life depended on it.

'Ignore Gary. He's trying to be funny. Anxo's been writhing about in manure.'

'I could say the same,' he sighed.

'Bad night with Ali?'

''Fraid so. I've spent half the night cleaning up after her, poor old girl.'

'Look, I know it's none of my business, but don't you think it might be time...' my voice tailed off; it was wrong to offer an opinion in such sensitive circumstances, and anyway, I already knew what the response would be. Tom had many strongly held principles. He had an 'issue' with veterinary treatment.

His answer surprised me. 'To be honest, I've been thinking about it, but... I don't know.'

'Look Tom, this isn't about principles, it's about what's best for Ali. It doesn't make you weak-willed or a sell-out if you change your mind.'

'I know that, Liza, but... we'll just have to wait and see how it goes.'

'What news of the leaky roof and the dripping ceiling?' asked Gary, in an attempt to change the subject and lighten the mood.

'Not too bad this morning. The downpour didn't last long enough to cause a real problem. Hopefully it'll be sorted out soon. Actually, that's what I came round to tell you, I had a text message this morning: Paul's coming over next week, he arrives on Tuesday.'

'*Tuesday*!' I exclaimed. 'But it's Saturday *now*! And he's only just told you?'

'He only booked it this morning. Paul's like that, very impulsive.'

So, we'd finally have the pleasure of meeting our mystery neighbour. Tom had told us a lot about him; It sounded like Paul might be quite a character.

'So he's getting the roof done while he's here?' asked Gary.

'No, not this time, he's only coming for a week. He's hoping to get the ball rolling; get a quote and sort out a date for the summer, you know. Once it's organised, he'll fly back out and stay for a couple of months.'

'That's great news,' I smiled. 'Is he going to use Pepe? I could give him a ring this week and see if he's got much work on. I'm sure he'd be able to come round and measure up for a quote.'

Tom laughed. 'That's good of you, Liza, but I don't think Paul's budget will stretch to the roof job you pair have had done. It looks amazing, though. Worth every euro. Those boys really grafted, didn't they?'

'Not half,' I nodded.

It was true. The job had cost twelve thousand euros, and Pepe and the gang had worked solidly for almost six weeks. The dust and the noise had been a nightmare, but it had been well worth enduring. The end result was nothing short of fantastic. Our neighbour, Másimo, said our house was the palace of Cutián.

'Has he got someone in mind then?' asked Gary.

Tom nodded. 'Remember I told you I'd met a Belgian chap at the ex-pats' get together? He knows an English builder somewhere near Monforte. He reckons he's a bit strapped for cash and will jump at the chance.'

By lunchtime the rainclouds had blown over. It was going to be a pleasantly warm afternoon.

'So number ten's finally having a new roof,' said Gary. He sucked the last traces of chicken fat from his fingers and proffered me the plate of bones. 'Anxo can have these.'

'He most certainly can't,' I frowned, tipping them straight into the waste bin. 'As for the roof, I'll believe it when I see it.'

'Don't you think this Paul's going to turn up, then?'

'Oh, it's not that, I'm sure he'll be here. It's just… well, he's had the house for five years and done nothing about it, and even if it *does* happen, it sounds like it might be a bit of a cowboy job, to me.'

'I know what you mean, and anyway, it's too late now for Tom to feel the benefit. The worst of the weather's over 'til autumn; by then he's bound to have moved into a place of his own.'

'Ooh, that reminds me: you know the old tiles from *our* roof that we stacked in the animal pen?'

'Ye-es,' he eyed me warily.

'Don't worry, I'm not going to ask you to build something else for me.'

His relief was visible. 'Good. Go on.'

'Is it okay if I take a couple of dozen or so?'

'What a daft question! They're not *my* tiles…'

'Well, you might have had them earmarked for something…'

'Trust me, I haven't. What's your plan?'

'I'm going to make a raised bed, a little way along from the herb garden. The border catches the sun all morning and afternoon; I thought it might be a good place to grow tomatoes.'

'I doubt the soil's much good there; it's known nothing but weeds for at least ten years. Still, no harm in trying, I suppose.'

By mid-afternoon I'd dug out an area in front of the standing stone wall which served as the primitive border between our garden and that of our elderly neighbour, Carmen. The herbs seemed to be thriving in the bed I'd created a year earlier; despite Gary's misgivings there was no reason why tomatoes shouldn't do the same. I'd just begun to unload the tiles from the wheelbarrow when I stopped suddenly. I could have sworn I'd heard someone speaking English somewhere close by. I listened more intently; the voice seemed to be coming from the other side of our garden. I dashed across the lawn and peered over the brambles, down onto the track that Anxo and I had followed that morning. Sure enough, a middle-aged couple and a black and white dog were approaching from the direction of the stepping-stones. They certainly *looked* English. I hurried over to the barn where Gary was sitting at the work bench sifting through packets of seeds.

'Gary!' I whispered. 'There's a couple walking down the track. I think they're English.'

'Are you sure?'

'Almost certain. Perhaps they've heard about us on the grapevine and come to have a look.'

Although the Galician *aldeas* are often several kilometres apart, news travels quickly. It hadn't taken us long to learn that the local rumour mill was a highly effective means of communication.

'Could be,' he nodded. 'Or perhaps they're visiting Tom? He met loads of people at the ex-pats' thingy. Let's go and see.'

We hurried down the steps to the ground floor and stepped out into the lane.

'We can't just go and accost them,' I whispered. 'It'd look cheeky. Anyway, we don't want to seem desperate, let's hover until they turn the corner.'

Before Gary could reply, Anxo tore off around the side of the barn, barking exuberantly. Within seconds there was a deeper, gruffer barking and the sound of surprised laughter.

'It's alright, Bob, it's a puppy.'

Seconds later, Anxo reappeared with his new friends.

'Hello,' I called cheerily.

'Hello!' they chorused. There was no mistaking the surprise on their faces; they obviously knew nothing about us after all.

'Do you live here?' asked the man.

'Yes,' I said. 'We bought it a year ago and moved in at Christmas. Are you local?'

'We are,' smiled the woman. 'We live in *aldea* not far from here.'

'Barreiro,' said the man. 'It's on the left as you drive into Antas.'

'Barreiro!' I exclaimed. 'Fancy that!'

'Oh, do you know it?'

'No, but one of your neighbours was especially kind to me back in December. It was a freezing cold morning, and I was walking into Antas. He pulled up in his car and offered me a lift. His name was Manolo.'

They both chuckled, then explained why.

'There are three Manolos in the village,' said the woman.

'Ah,' I nodded. It didn't surprise me. On high days and Holy days there were two Javiers, three Josés and two Antonios in Cutián.

'I'm Jane, by the way.'

'And I'm John.'

'Gary,' said Gary.

'Liza. And that's Anxo.'

Jane smiled. 'That's Bob.'

Bob was sniffing Anxo with great interest.

'That's *most* unlike him,' said Jane.

'Bob doesn't usually like other dogs,' explained John.

'Manure,' I grinned. 'Do you want to have a look at the house?'

Twenty minutes later we were sitting in the kitchen drinking coffee.

'We have a long walk at least once a week,' John told us. 'You can buy ordnance survey maps of the area from a bookshop opposite the central *plaza* in Lugo. There are hundreds of them, showing the public walkways through all the rural territories in Galicia.'

'Public walkways?' I repeated, puzzled.

'Oh, yes. There's a whole network of pathways over the countryside and it's the council's responsibility to keep them clear.'

'Sometimes they don't though,' Jane reminded him. 'There have been times when we've followed a route only to find we can't go any further because it's completely overgrown with bramble or filled with rocks from a collapsed stone wall.'

'That's amazing,' I said. 'I had no idea. I walk for miles with Anxo, but we just trek over the fields. He found a dead squirrel this morning. It was very unusual. It was black, and much smaller than the squirrels in England.'

John nodded knowingly. 'That's a red squirrel.'

'*Red*?' I thought of Anxo's dark, bedraggled trophy. It was a far cry from Tufty[1] or Squirrel Nutkin[2].

John registered my confusion. 'It's the same species as the English red squirrel, but its coat's a different colour – it varies throughout Europe, according to the habitat and climate.'

'So, do the Spanish call it the black squirrel?' I asked, intrigued.

'No. It's still the red squirrel. The *ardilla roja*.'

'Oh, how odd.'

'Aren't they supposed to be endangered?' asked Gary.

'Not in Spain. In fact, they seem to thrive out here – there are no grey squirrels, you see.'

'Have you come across the roe deer yet?' asked Jane.

'*I* have,' said Gary, 'and so has our neighbour, Tom. Liza hasn't, she's not very observant, you see.'

It was true, but I certainly wasn't going to admit it. 'My mind's always on other things,' I protested.

'She's always in a hurry; she needs to slow down.'

'I'd really love to see a *jabalí*,' I enthused, pointedly ignoring him. Wild boars were in abundance all over rural Galicia. Over winter, the hunt had often passed through the woodlands that border the village. It thrilled me to think that these magnificent creatures were living close by.

'We've seen a few since we've lived here,' said John. 'Usually when we've been driving in the early morning. You often hear people say they've seen them crossing the road.'

---

[1] Tufty: the red squirrel mascot of an English road safety campaign for young children which ran through the 1960s and 1970s.

[2] Squirrel Nutkin: the red squirrel character in the illustrated children's books by English author Beatrix Potter.

'They come into the forest at the end of our garden,' added Jane. 'We haven't actually seen them, but we know when they've been; everything gets flattened under their bulk.'

'Backing directly onto woodland must be lovely,' I sighed.

'We back onto Paul's,' laughed Gary. 'It might as well be a wood, it's so overgrown.'

'You'll have to come over and see it,' said John.

'Thank you,' I smiled. 'We will.'

Liza Grantham

The Spanish Squirrel

It's called the Red Squirrel, but it isn't.
Well it is, but it's not 'cos it's black.
It's not the Black Squirrel, it's the red one,
Did you get that? Okay, let's go back...

The Red Squirrel – that's just its name, right?
But the fur can be red, brown or black
On the tufts of its ears and its long bushy tail,
On its head and its legs and its back.

In England there really are red ones,
So the name fits – it's totally cool,
In Poland and Finland they're brownish,
But in Spain they are black as a rule.

The Spanish don't call them black either,
They still call them red, just the same.
It isn't the Ardilla Negra,
The Ardilla Roja's the name.

They're all the same genus and species –
sciurus vulgaris – it's true,
But I think Red Squirrel sounds nicer
(for red, brown or black ones), don't you?

Chapter 2

Strange Goings-on

'Why are you wearing waterproof trousers?' asked a voice, as I closed the garden gate behind me.

'Crikey, Tom! You didn't half make me jump! You're not usually up and about at this time of morning! How's Ali?'

'About the same, I've left her sleeping. I thought I'd walk Maud early; I want to do some spring cleaning today.'

You could have knocked me down with a feather, this wasn't the Tom I'd come to know. It didn't take long for the penny to drop. 'Ah,' I nodded. 'For the landlord's visit, I presume?'

'Yes, I thought I'd better show willing. I mean, it's not as though it's filthy or anything…'

I bit my lip.

'…it's just that, well… Paul's quite a tidy bloke and I'll be the first to admit I'm not. I wouldn't want him to think…'

'That you weren't looking after the place properly? For God's sake, Tom, it's falling to pieces! If he was *that* particular he'd have got his finger out by now.'

'I know. But that's it you see, it could be a ruin, but he'd still want everything in its place. Anyway, you've not answered my question – why are you wearing those trousers? There isn't a cloud in the sky.'

'Long story,' I grinned. 'Tell you what, why not drop in for a cuppa on your way back and you can hear all about it.'

In the kitchen I took off the waterproofs and rolled a cigarette. A loud thud overhead heralded signs of life in the bedroom above us. Anxo's tail started wagging; he'd recognised the sound of our cat, Scholes, leaping from the bed. Moments later the pans hanging from the ceiling began to jiggle as heavy footsteps thumped across the floor. Gary was getting up.

'Morning,' he yawned, as I handed him his cuppa. 'It looks like being a nice day.'

'Hope so,' I nodded. 'Oh, Tom'll be round shortly, when he's walked Maud.'

'Tom? At this time of morning?'

'Preparations,' I grinned.

'Ah, the visit.'

'Yes. He mentioned spring cleaning.'

'Bit late for that, he's only got today and tomorrow, the place is a pig-hole.'

'Well, it's so dark and dingy in there, maybe Paul won't notice. Anyway, Tom wanted to know why I was kitted out for a downpour earlier on.'

'A downpour? You mean you had your brolly?'

'No, I was wearing the waterproofs.'

There was a knock at the door.

'Ah, that'll be him. Come in!' I called.

'Morning, Tom,' said Gary.

'Morning, and a warm, sunny one at that. Which is why I'm rather concerned about your wife, Gary, skipping down the lane dressed like a deep-sea fisherman at sunrise. Is she okay?'

'Daft bugger,' I laughed. 'I'll make you a coffee, while Gary explains.'

'Actually,' said Gary, looking puzzled. 'I can't. I've absolutely no idea….'

'*Honestly* Gary! Your memory gets worse! I was going to try the new Rufo strategy this morning, remember?'

'What strategy?' he paused for a moment. 'Oh, yes, I've got it, the watering can!' He turned to Tom. 'You know how the cockerel's been attacking her? Well, yesterday when it was pouring down, he stayed on his perch. I told her to chuck water over him when he runs at her, it might ward him off, you know?'

'Right,' said Tom. 'Good idea, Gary. And the trousers were to stop you getting drenched?'

'Yes,' I nodded.

'So, did it work?'

'Not exactly. The hens flew into a panic, so I ditched the idea. I didn't want them all flying over the fence with Anxo on the other side. Anyway, Rufo charged at me as if to punish me and…' I paused to draw on my cigarette.

'Go on,' urged Gary impatiently.

'Well, as I shuffled sideways to dodge him, my trousers crackled…'

'*Crackled*?' frowned Tom.

'Okay, rustled… swished… you know the noise waterproof stuff makes… Anyway, he stood still for a second, so I rustled again and bingo! He turned tail!'

'Never!'

'On my life. The sound seemed to alarm him.'

'It ruffled his feathers,' chuckled Gary.

'Trust you.'

'Well, fancy that,' said Tom. 'So you'll need to wear them every morning?'

'Looks that way. But it might save his life.'

On Monday morning, I said a silent prayer as I opened the door of the hen house. Despite yesterday's success I was feeling apprehensive; would my rooster-proof trousers continue to deter Rufo's attacks? Ignoring Anxo's raucous barking and the discordant clamour of the hens as they jostled their way out into the sunshine, I focused on my nemesis. He was already giving me the evil eye. As he fluffed out his neck feathers, I shuffled towards him. The result was nothing short of a miracle; he scuttled meekly over to the feeder to join the hens. I breathed a sigh of relief and turned towards the fence, which was now shaking alarmingly as Anxo leapt up again and again. If Rufo was now the model of compliance, Anxo most certainly was not.

'We're really going to have to think about reinforcing the chooks' fence,' I told Gary as I handed him his cuppa.

'I hope you're not serious. What did I tell you back in February?'

'I don't remember.' Of course, I remembered perfectly well. When we'd first introduced our new flock to their enclosure, the hens had been escaping each day to lay eggs. Gary had made the fence higher, and the problem was resolved for a while, until they began flying into the trees and hopping over onto Paul's land. Eventually we'd clipped their wings, and Gary had sworn it was their last chance. If it happened again, they were destined for the freezer.

'I said I'd raise the fence another couple of feet and bodge up the gaps, and after that I wasn't prepared to spend another *céntimo*. I meant it.' He looked at me sternly.

I countered with an icy glare. 'But this isn't *about* the chickens!'

'Well, of *course* it is! You said…'

'Oh, for God's sake stop being such a grouch and hear me out!'

He looked at me for a moment. The chooks had caused far too many arguments already, he seemed prepared to avert a further blazing row. 'Go on then.'

'The chickens aren't the problem, it's Anxo. He's been jumping up at the fence since he was tiny, and no amount of training will stop him. I've remonstrated with him, ignored him, praised him…'

'*Praised* him?'

'Yes, while he's been sitting nicely before I've opened the door.'

'Okay.'

'The fact is it's all too exciting for him, the flapping and screeching and squawking … he's beside himself.'

'Can't you leave him in the kitchen until you've let them out?'

'I think I'm going to have to, but he won't like it. I'll start from tomorrow morning.'

'Well that's sorted then.'

'Not quite. He sometimes does it during the day. Not often, granted, but now and again, if they're squabbling, or Rufo's chasing them round. It'd give me peace of mind, that's all.'

'And now I suppose you're going to tell me it won't cost anything?'

'It won't. Let me make you another brew and I'll tell you what I have in mind.'

By lunchtime the job was finished. The fence looked like a military blockade.

'It looks like a scrapyard,' said Tom, sceptically, as he peered down from Paul's garden into our chicken run, where three metal bedframes and an old window grille added a whole new dimension to the fence.

'Actually, it looks very Galician,' I said, pleased with the result. 'Javier's got an old bedstead across the entrance to the farmyard. And there are two or three more down on the *fincas* to keep the cows out.'

'She's right,' nodded Gary. 'You see them all over the place. You must have noticed?'

'Well,' said Tom. 'Now you come to mention it, yes… yes, I have.'

'There you go then,' I grinned. 'It means we're *bona fide* villagers. We're fitting in.'

Next morning, I left Anxo surprised and disgruntled in the kitchen when I went to let out the chooks. I was no longer apprehensive about the fence collapsing, but now that there was no risk of being gored to death, it would be nice to stand watching them for a while in peace. I strode confidently down to the run and, for the first time in weeks, I was able to enjoy my hens.

I hurried back up the garden, eager to share the good news with Gary over a fag and a brew. I was about to open the gate when I noticed movement down past the barn. At the corner, the lane narrowed into a grassy track which ran past the garden of Másimo and Solina and into the woodlands beyond. I stopped and stared in amazement. An elderly woman was about to scale the fence. I watched transfixed, as Carmen, our neighbour, paused and looked round furtively. Apparently satisfied that no-one had seen her, she climbed up onto the *hórreo* and stepped boldly over the chain-link fence onto the wall before dropping down into the garden, where she disappeared from view.

'You'll *never* guess!' I announced breathlessly, as I dashed into the kitchen. 'I can't *believe* it!'

'Liza, stop shouting. Has he attacked you again?'

'Not Rufo,' I said impatiently. 'It's Carmen.'

'*Carmen's* attacked you? For God's sake Liza, what are you saying?'

'No, no,' I giggled. The very idea was preposterous. 'Of *course* she hasn't! What she *has* done is climb over the fence into Masi's garden.'

'Never!'

'I kid you not.'

'Perhaps she's had permission.'

'I don't think so, Gary. She looked decidedly shifty, glancing over her shoulder as if she was afraid of being caught red-handed. And what about the timing? She knows full well there's nobody about at that time of the morning.'

'I see what you mean,' he nodded. 'I suppose it does seem suspicious. But what could she possibly have been after? If there was anything worth nicking, Masi certainly wouldn't have left it lying around.'

'Ah,' I said. 'But Carmen's idea of what's "worth nicking" isn't necessarily the same as everyone else's, is it? What about all the stuff she's hoarding in the garden, for a start? There's that bloody big road sign saying: "no right turn", plastic flowers, the rubber chicken...'

'Rubber *chicken*?'

'Haven't you seen it? You must have. It's hanging over the back of the garden seat.'

'I didn't even know there *was* a garden seat, it's all so overgrown. Still, you *have* spent hours on end kneeling in the herb bed peering through the gap in the wall. Talk about Carmen being shifty!'

'Gary!' I exclaimed. 'That's different! I was watching her ducks and hens!'

'Do you realise this is the longest we've gone without rain since St. Patrick's Night?' I said, as we sat on the bench for a fag break late in the afternoon.

'It can't be,' frowned Gary. 'It rained on Saturday morning. Today's only Tuesday, that means we've had three clear days.'

'Exactly. You might not have realised it but up until now it's rained every single day since the middle of March.'

It was true. Galicia is renowned for its rainfall. Over the last month, not a day had passed by when there hadn't been some precipitation. Granted, it hadn't always amounted to much; sometimes there had been an hour or so of mizzle in the early mornings, or a light pitter patter after dark, but at others it had poured down in torrents for several days at a time.

'It'll have done the garden good,' said Gary. 'The soil was dry and powdery in summer, but with all the digging and the rainfall it should be moister now. I just hope our veg will do well.'

Neither of us had any previous experience when it came to growing vegetables, so this first spring would be pretty much down to trial and error. However, with heaps of enthusiasm, a seed parcel from a friend in England and a gardening book we'd been given for Christmas, we were determined to give it our best shot and, with my usual cheerful optimism, I didn't doubt for a moment that we'd succeed.

Gary had been turning the soil every day since the new year, even when the afternoons had been bitterly cold, and we'd spent many a happy hour scraping up the trails of cow muck left by our neighbours' herd along the lane. In February, Gary had sowed some radish seeds and he'd finally harvested the crop of perfectly formed, shiny radishes a few days ago. I wasn't really keen on radishes but eating food from our own garden had been gratifying, even if there *had* been only half a dozen of them.

'It'll be so exciting,' I enthused. 'By summer we'll be filling the freezer with our own produce. With the eggs *and* the veg we'll be a lot further along the road to self-sufficiency.'

'You sound very confident,' said Gary. 'But you mustn't build your hopes up *too* much. I've been thinking...'

I didn't find out *what* he'd been thinking; at that moment Tom came strolling down the lane. Although it was only a little after five, he was carrying his striped lawn chair and a six-pack of beers. To my surprise, both Maud *and* Ali were with him.

'How long's she been up and about?' I asked, bending down to give Ali a fuss.

'Since mid-morning. She seems to have rallied with the warmer weather. I think the damp really set her back.'

'That's wonderful news,' I smiled. 'Mind you, if the damp's a problem Paul's house isn't really the best setting for her, is it?'

'Talking of which,' said Gary, 'shouldn't he have arrived by now?'

'His plane wasn't due to land in Santiago 'til just after three. Then he was getting the bus to Palas de Rei, and they only run every couple of hours or so. From there he was going to walk the rest of the way.'

'Walk?' said Gary. 'It'll take him at least three hours from Palas, he's crackers.'

'It has been said,' laughed Tom. 'And of course, he's bound to stop at a bar or two on the way. I reckon he'll be here around eight.'

'So, did you get the cleaning done?' asked Gary mischievously, once we'd been coerced into joining Tom for an early beer.

We could both guess the answer.

'Not exactly. I gave up, to be honest – it would've been a hell of a job. I did cycle into Antas though, for provisions. He'll definitely be expecting a meal after all that walking, and he's a big bloke.'

'What are you going to cook?' I asked, aware that time was ticking away.

'I've got some spuds and veg and a chicken. I was going to do a roast dinner, but I don't know if there's enough butane left. I'll probably do a curry and cook it over a fire outside.'

By six o'clock we'd all moved across the lane and into the garden, where the early evening sun was still casting a surprising amount of warmth. Although Tom appeared jovial, I sensed that he was slightly on edge. I supposed it was due to Paul's impending arrival and wondered if he was regretting not finishing the cleaning after all. Despite the fact that he had culinary duties to attend to he had insisted on nipping back to number ten to replenish the beers.

'You're going to be cutting it fine if you're still planning on cooking that chicken,' I reminded him.

'You're right, Liza,' he nodded. 'I might just use the potatoes and veg and do a soup tonight. There's plenty of bread to go with it, we can save the chicken for tomorrow.'

I looked at Gary, who winked sagely. We knew Tom pretty well by now and could see where things were heading; it would only take a couple more beers and the weary, hungry traveller would be arriving to bread and cheese.

'Listen, Tom,' I ventured, 'why don't you leave the cooking until tomorrow? We've got plenty of home-made ready-meals in the freezer: there's soup, curries, quiches…'

'And pizzas,' hinted Gary, hopefully.

'If I take something out now it'll be ready in plenty of time.'

'Are you sure, Liza? Gary? It's very generous of you to offer, but I don't want to put you to any trouble...'

'You wouldn't be,' I assured him. 'My motive is purely self-serving. We've heard so much about this chap, it's my crafty way of finally getting to meet him. If he's only here for a week he'll be swept up in a tide of boozing and reminiscing, not to mention getting the roof job sorted out. If we don't get in quickly, we might not get to see him at all.'

Eventually the sun began to sink behind the house and Gary went inside to light the range. It became clear that Tom wasn't planning to go back to number ten to wait for his visitor, so I suggested pinning a note to the door so that Paul would know where to find him.

By eight thirty there was still no sign of Paul, but Tom and Gary had already polished off large bowls of soup and were now digging into the second meat feast pizza. I slipped through to the pantry and took out another; if I put it straight into the range it would thaw quickly. Once Paul arrived, I'd shove it into the butane oven on high.

Tom seemed unaware that evening was fast becoming night-time, but I was beginning to feel uneasy that Paul still hadn't appeared. At last I thought it might be time to raise the subject.

'Aren't you feeling a bit anxious that Paul has turned up yet?'

'No,' Tom laughed. 'When I said eight o'clock, it was only a guess. It could easily be nearer to nine.'

'It's actually ten to ten,' I frowned. 'Perhaps you ought to walk up to the church to check your phone.'

'Shit!' exclaimed Tom. 'I had no idea. I'll do it now.'

As Tom's footsteps faded out of earshot Gary and I looked at one another.

'He's pissed,' said Gary.

'Hmm,' I frowned. 'I don't know what Paul will think. Poor bugger's come all that way…'

'But at least he'll be arriving to a hot dinner.'

'That's not the point though. Tom's supposed to be one of his closest friends and he's been living in the house rent-free for almost a year. It does seem a bit bad-mannered, don't you think?'

'Well, yes, but maybe Paul won't see it like that. Perhaps he's really laid back; or just too bonkers to care.'

'Listen!' I said.

Sure enough there was the sound of heavy footfall outside.

'He can't have been to the phone and back already…' I whispered.

There was a rap at the door and Tom walked in followed by a tall man of about fifty, clutching a wine box and a glass that was half-full. He was athletically built and quite smartly dressed; not how I'd imagined the owner of number ten to look at all. Furthermore, he really didn't seem happy.

'Hello,' I smiled, 'Come on in and have a warm. You must be ready for a sit down.'

'Thanks,' said Paul, parking himself on the bench and setting his drink down on the marble surface in front of him.

'What time did you arrive?' asked Gary.

'I've been here since about quarter past eight,' he said pointedly, whilst avoiding Tom's gaze.

Oh, dear, I thought. We weren't wrong then; he's miffed for certain.

Tom was quick to defend his actions. Rather than speak directly to his friend, he turned to me. 'I've just explained to Paul that you'd kindly invited us both for supper, and rather than wait at number ten in the cold, it made sense to come round here. There would have been little point in lighting the range for a couple of hours.'

The white lie tripped effortlessly off his silver tongue, but it was clear that Paul wasn't taken in. Neither of them spoke for a moment.

'Would you like some soup, Paul?' I asked, breaking the pendulous silence.

'I'd love some, thanks.'

As Paul dug into his soup he still said nothing. He was obviously famished and was soon mopping the traces from the bowl with warm crusty bread. 'That was excellent,' he smiled. 'Thank you.'

By the time he'd eaten his pizza and quaffed a second glass of wine, Paul's mood was much brighter. Whether his earlier reticence had been down to Tom's devil-may-care attitude or simply hunger, it now gave way to an eagerness for wine and conversation. We were finally going to get to know our mysterious neighbour. It looked like being a long and boozy night.

Paul explained to us that he'd experienced his first taste of Galicia when he'd walked the Camino de Santiago five years earlier.

The history of this world-famous pilgrimage dates back to the ninth century, when the supposed remains of the apostle, Saint James, were discovered in an unmarked tomb in western Galicia. Although there was no historical or archaeological evidence to support the claim, somehow the discovery captured the imagination of the Christian world. [3]

The Christian church was quick to promote the idea that by enduring the hardships of the perilous journey, the pilgrims would better understand the suffering of Christ and thus be drawn closer to him. Even in

---

[3] Sharif Gemie, *A Concise History of Galicia*, (Cardiff: University of Wales Press, 2006) p.17

medieval times not all of the *peregrino* fraternity joined the pilgrimage out of religious devotion. Amongst their number were Protestant heretics fleeing from the Catholic authorities and convicted criminals ordered to endure the journey by way of penance. Finally, there were those driven merely by curiosity – the ramblers and sightseers of the Middle Age.[4]

Over a thousand years later, Santiago de Compostela is considered to be the third most important city in Christendom, outshone only by Jerusalem and Rome.[5] Modern day pilgrims flock from all over the world to make the long trek for a host of reasons. Of course, the heretics and criminals are no longer in abundance, and the thousands of religious devotees are not quite as likely to fall prey to wolves, bears or bandits along the way. Paul had met pilgrims of all ages and nationalities, and from all walks of life. In addition to the faithful, some were seeking a spiritual experience or looking to spend time in quiet contemplation away from the roller coaster ride of twenty-first century life. There were also many who simply wanted to enjoy a walking holiday through breath-taking scenery and others who'd gone along just to see what all the fuss was about. Paul's decision to walk the Camino had, in fact, been a combination of them all, but regardless of his reasons, Galicia had made a profound impression on him; so much so, he'd since walked the Camino a further five times.

On his return to England, he'd set about looking for houses. Like us, he'd been so enchanted by the region that he'd acted on impulse, and in haste, to buy a house. This in itself was not unusual; after all, Gary and I had been similarly rash in our compulsion to relocate. We

---

[4] Ibid., p.21

[5] Antón Pombo, Xosé Manoel Santos Díaz and Segundo Saavedra, *Guía Viva: Galicia*, (Madrid: Anaya, 2010) p.308

had, however, been realistic in our expectations. We'd known that we'd have our work cut out and that we'd face hurdles and disappointments along the way. Above all, we hadn't invested our entire life savings into the project; we'd retained a reasonable nest-egg and wouldn't be destitute if our dream fell through. Paul, on the other hand, gripped by a rose-tinted, almost childlike zeal, had sunk every last penny into number ten, Cutián.

Paul was a dreamer, an idealist. Here in Galicia, he'd found his Utopia and he lionised its charms to a delusional extreme. He seemed to believe that the region held an almost magical capacity; it was a place that would afford him protection from the outside world and guide him towards some kind of inner peace. Furthermore (as we would soon discover) he also thought that whilst whiling away his days out in the middle of nowhere, he'd be able to please himself.

On Wednesday morning the sun was shining, and the merest dapple of fluffy white clouds drifted steadily across the sky.

At breaktime we took our coffees out to the bench by the kitchen door to enjoy what was already promising to be the perfect spring day.

I was about to light a cigarette when I stopped suddenly. 'Listen,' I said. 'Did you hear it?'

'Hear what? I heard Rufo a minute ago, is that what you mean?'

'No, don't be daft. Rufo's always crowing. This is something quite different. Be patient, let's see if it comes again.'

Gary sighed impatiently. Thankfully, he didn't have to wait long. The unmistakeable sound of a cuckoo rang out with crystal clarity from the direction of the oakwood.

'A cuckoo!' He exclaimed. 'I don't think I'd ever heard one before we came here.'

'Nor me,' I frowned, trying to remember, 'Ah, there it goes again.'

I lit my cigarette and inhaled contentedly. 'It's amazing, isn't it? There's something new going on all the time.'

'I know what you mean,' he agreed. 'You miss out on all this when you live in a town.'

'And there's so much you'd go through life without ever knowing. Out here we're always learning: the climate, the trees, the birds, the wildlife...'

'And the garden.'

'The garden?'

'Yes. *That's* something we've still got lots to learn about, and we won't really know 'til the end of summer whether we've got it right.'

'I must admit, I hadn't thought of it like that.' I paused for a moment. Even though it was all very new to us, the thought of failure hadn't crossed my mind. Of course, I was expecting us to make mistakes, I'd even imagined lengthy discussions on how to improve our harvest in future years – "We'll have to put the carrots in later next year" or "Perhaps the peppers would have got more sun over there" – that sort of thing. 'Well,' I began, determined to stay positive, 'you've been digging and weeding and manuring for four months now. As far as the preparation goes you couldn't have worked any harder. We've got top quality seeds, thanks to Paula – she's been growing off her own veg for years. We've had plenty of rain – you said only yesterday how much better the soil will be for it. Now it's lovely and sunny, so it's ideal, I've every confidence we'll do well.'

'You're right,' he nodded. 'I wasn't being negative, just cautious, I suppose. I tell you what, I'll go down past the spring and look for some branches that'll do for bean sticks. I'll start putting some seeds in this afternoon.'

'Brilliant,' I grinned. 'I'm going to start collecting firewood again. We've not fetched any since New Year. The woodlands will have started to dry out a bit now and the beams you've sawn up won't last forever. I don't suppose we'll be lighting the fire at night for much longer; it'll give us at least six months to build up a good supply.'

'Good idea.'

'I'll take Anxo with me, the extra walk should do him good.'

'See if you can get him to take a dip in the *río* on the way, will you? He smells even worse this morning, surely the manure should have worn off by now?'

'Oh, *that's* not manure you can smell, it really *is* the squirrel this time.'

'It's disgusting. More like a skunk than a squirrel. You didn't tell me he'd found another one.'

'He hasn't.'

Gary's face was a picture. 'You don't mean…'

'Yes, it's the one he found on Saturday. He's carried it proudly every day. This morning he rolled on it.'

'*Rolled* on it? It's been dead for five days! Christ, no wonder he stinks!'

'It won't be for much longer, there's not much left of it to be honest.'

'I don't think I want to hear any more.'

'Good *tortilla*,' said Gary, as he polished off his last mouthful of lunch. 'It's not like the ones they serve for *tapas* though. I know you put extra stuff in it like *chorizo* and peppers, but it's more than that, it's different somehow and I can't work out why.'

'I'll let you into a secret, then, shall I?'

'Go on.'

'It's not really a *tortilla*, it's a *frittata*.'

I waited for the look of enlightenment to spread across his face. It didn't. I'd have to explain.

'When you make *tortilla* you fry the spuds and add the beaten eggs and cook it through in the pan. The trouble is you need to stand over it 'til it's done. If you don't watch it, it'll burn. With a *frittata* you follow the same procedure, but you cook it in the oven. It's far easier and doesn't waste valuable time.'

'That's clever. And it's Spanish?'

'No, Italian.'

'Right. What's the other egg thing we used to have in the Canaries? It wasn't solid like a *tortilla*; it was just slopped onto the plate.'

'Sounds gorgeous, you have a way with words. I think you're talking about *revuelto* – like scrambled eggs, but with things like spinach and bacon in it?'

'That's the one.'

I started grinning.

'What's up?'

'Do you remember the menus they used to translate into English for the tourists? *Revuelto* always came out as "smashed eggs".'

'So it did,' he chuckled. 'I'd forgotten that. Crikey, it seems like a lifetime away.'

Suddenly the latch on the back door began to rattle loudly. Not one of our Galician neighbours had ever knocked; each had their own unique way of getting us to come to the door. Másimo would pace up and down by the barn, whistling. Maruja would stand opposite the kitchen window and call, 'Elisa!' from the lane. Solina would venture right up to the doorstep and shout '*Dónde estás?*' at the top of her voice.

The latch rattled again. There was only one person it could possibly be.

'I wonder what Carmen wants,' I said, getting up from the bench to let her in.

Carmen stood on the doorstep, clutching a sheet of scrunched up newspaper in both hands.

'Come in, Carmen,' I smiled.

She followed me through to the kitchen and set the mysterious gift down on the marble surface.

'It's just a few peas,' she told me, in a half whisper. 'Just a few peas. It will save you buying them. You'll need to soak them in water before you plant them.'

'Oh, thank you, Carmen. It's the perfect time, Gary's going to start putting seeds in this afternoon. He can soak them overnight and plant them tomorrow.'

'No, Elisa, he mustn't.' She looked troubled. 'He mustn't put them in yet, it's April.'

Her earnest tone made me feel as though we'd been about to become the victims of some terrible disaster and she'd managed to catch us just in time.

'Oh,' I said, falteringly, before deciding it was best to look well-informed; Carmen liked to chatter, and a lengthy explanation might keep us in the kitchen for the best part of the afternoon. 'Oh, yes, April, of course.' I hadn't a clue why April was of such significance, but it clearly wasn't the time to be sowing the humble legume.

'Not until the first day of May,' she continued, as if to make doubly sure we wouldn't make a *faux pas*. 'After the first of May, it's fine.'

As I showed Carmen out, I thanked her again and was about to close the door when I heard laughter coming from further up the lane. I stepped out and looked in the direction of number ten. Paul was heckling Tom, who was bent over his bicycle, cursing. Judging by their raillery, the dicey start to Paul's holiday was water under the bridge.

'Afternoon!' I called.

'*Hola*,' said Paul, obviously keen to get into the swing.

'Off on a bike ride?'

'Hopefully,' frowned Tom. 'If I can get this tyre pumped up. Here,' he said, thrusting the pump towards Paul, 'You have a go, otherwise it'll be closing time before we get there.'

Paul took the pump from him. 'Tom's taking me to the pub,' he grinned.

Back in summer, Tom had cycled out to the neighbouring *aldea* of Santa Mariña where he'd discovered a tiny pub-cum-village shop. Gary and I had been incredulous. It was called the Black Eagle.

'You're going to the Águila Negra?'

'Yes,' nodded Tom. 'Paul's never been to Santa Mariña, I thought we might carry on to the river beach after – if it stays like this we can go for a swim.'

I wished them luck and went back into the kitchen.

'What on *earth* was Carmen talking about?' asked Gary. 'My Spanish can't be that bad, she *did* say I can't put the peas in 'til the first of May?'

'Absolutely.'

'But how can it make a difference? It's the twenty-fifth now, I'd only be six days early.'

'It doesn't matter,' I said, feigning earnestness. 'Just *one* day early could spell disaster.'

He looked at me as if I'd lost my marbles.

'I'm *joking*!' I giggled. 'Seriously, though, I reckon it's that ancient rural tradition thing – planting by the stars and the phases of the moon.'

'Like when Masi told us you shouldn't plant if there's been a mist in the morning?'

'No, that's different. They say it brings the *bichos* with it, you know, insects that'll eat the seeds and young plants. The lunar stuff goes way back to the year dot, don't you remember – we read about it in *Brave Old World*?' [6]

'I do remember, yes. I also seem to remember the conclusion being that it was all a load of old cobblers.'

'That was Tom Hodgkinson's conclusion, yes, but these ideas have endured down through the centuries, you can't help but wonder...'

Throughout the afternoon the sky was completely cloudless, and the temperature had risen considerably. It felt as if the good weather was here to stay.

By five o'clock, Gary had put up the bean sticks and poked the beans into the soft, damp soil. He'd sown rows of carrot, beetroot, cabbage and cauliflower seeds in neat rows, and set the larger courgette and pumpkin seeds in pots. He'd watered everything in and covered the newly sown beds with remnants of chicken wire. My efforts seemed pitiful in comparison. I'd been wrong to assume that the woodlands would be drier after only four days of sunshine. My collection of damp branches lay sprawled across the threshing floor.

'You've done wonders,' I told him. 'Pity I can't say the same.'

'Never mind. The branches will dry out eventually on the threshing floor, they've got all summer. Come on, let's grab a bite to eat and settle down with a beer.'

As we came through the gate, Gary peered up the lane towards number ten.

'No sign of the holidaymakers,' he grinned.

'I shouldn't think they'll be much longer. The dogs will need to be let out for a wee.'

'*We* ought to do it one afternoon, you know.'

'Do what?'

---

[6] Hodgkinson, Tom, *Brave Old World* (London: Hamish Hamilton, 2011)

'Have a trip out to Santa Mariña.'

'It's hardly a *trip*, is it? It's only about three kilometres down the road.'

'Exactly. We've known about it since summer and we still haven't been.'

'You're right. We were so busy in August though, and to be fair we haven't really had the weather for it until now.'

'True enough. Why don't we go this Saturday? Lunchtime down the Black Eagle, what do you think?'

'Sounds like a marvellous idea.'

After a shower and a late tea of cheese and onion butties, we took our beers out to the threshing floor to enjoy the last hour of sun before it sunk behind the rooftop. We drank and smoked and chatted and listened in amusement as Carmen chided her ducks and chickens on the other side of the standing stone wall. Scholes was curled up in a ball, dozing beneath the fig tree, while Anxo lay on the warm stones, snapping at the occasional fly. Suddenly a succession of alien sounds shattered the early evening calm. The holiday makers had returned.

I dashed over to my lookout post in the herb bed. Hidden by the cascading broom, I shifted and strained to find a view through Carmen's wilderness and into Paul's garden beyond.

'Where's the corkscrew? Come on, it's no good without the corkscrew... ah, that's the way!'

A creak. A scrape. A flash of white, as a plastic sun-lounger was dragged into the sunshine.

A pop. A glugging. A clink.

'Cheers!'

I turned, aware that Gary was now standing behind me. 'They're back then?'

'Shh! They'll hear you. Anyway, what are you doing? I thought you didn't hold with lurking in the herb bed.'

Satisfied that nothing of any real interest was about to happen, we returned to our beers. For a while the sound of chatter and laughter carried across the gardens until a voice declared:

'Music! We should have some music!'

We heard footsteps and the creak of Paul's gate. Shortly after, music started to boom from one of the upstairs windows. Laughter was one thing; a nineteen eighties' disco was another. Someone else obviously felt the same. A discordant clanging began in Carmen's garden.

'Whatever's that?' I frowned.

We dashed back over to the herb bed. Carmen was standing by the opposite wall, bashing a tin plate with a spoon.

'My God, she's joining in!' I exclaimed.

I stared harder. Carmen looked angry. She started to bash her plate more wildly than ever. She certainly wasn't trying to keep time.

'She's not joining in,' said Gary. 'She's cross about the music. She's protesting.'

Tom came to the wall. 'Carmen, Carmen. It's okay. I'll sort it out.' He loped towards the gate and a couple of minutes later the music halted abruptly.

Carmen looked visibly relieved, but Paul, obviously keen to build bridges, rose from the lounger and began to make his way over to the wall.

'Christ almighty!' said Gary.

We looked at each other, astounded. Apart from his flip-flops, Paul hadn't got a stitch on.

Liza Grantham

The Celestial Gardener

He wanted to plant
In the soil he'd been turning,
Though totally green
He was eager for learning.

He purchased a guidebook –
His neighbours were cynics:
'Ignore what the book says,
The answers aren't in it!

To work with the earth
You must look to the Heavens.'
(There's so much to learn,
He's at sixes and sevens!)

'It's all in the stars
And the phase of the moon,
Your crops won't fare well
If they're planted too soon.'

He read Virgil's 'Georgics',
Translated from Latin,
(The bloke knew just when
To put this or put that in).

But even in English
The task was demanding –
The dates were all weird,
Way past all understanding.

When it said 'Ides of March' –
He was left none the wiser,
He tried Columella,
The farming advisor.

How Now, Mad Cow?

'Sew six grains of hemp
When Arcturus is rising...'
He hadn't a clue
What the bloke was advising.

'The Kalends of March...'
Well, he just didn't get it:
'Farewell, Columella,
I think we'll forget it!'

He turned to Tom Tusser,
To see what he'd *written*
(The words might make sense,
He was from Tudor Britain.)

He caught on at once
To what Tusser was saying,
He'd soon have those seeds in,
With no more delaying.

'When full moon has past
Then the pease will need sowing,
But drill other seeds
While the moon is still growing.'

He waited 'til nightfall
And stared at the sky
But there was a problem,
'Oh, mercy! Oh, my!

Dear Tusser, I wanted
To do as you'd bidden,
But rain fell for weeks
And the moon remained hidden!'

He'd heeded the scholars
And, begging their pardon,
They'd been of no help
In his vegetable garden.

'I'll use common sense
And suffice it to say,
I'll leave it to luck
At the end of the day.'

Chapter 3

Alien Invasion

I sat out on the bench as the sun rose, drinking a strong black coffee and smoking my first cigarette of the day. The air was fresh, and the pink tinge along the horizon morphed subtly to an almost perfect blue, marred only by an aeroplane trail which was breaking into fluffed out patches across the sky.

The call of the cuckoo seemed intrusive amidst the familiar crowing of cockerels, and I wondered how long it would take before it ceased to be remarkable, blending comfortably into the auditory canvas of the village at dawn.

My gaze drifted up the lane as I thought about the events of the previous night. The episode in the garden had left me feeling annoyed and indignant; some sounds must *never* become part of the everyday background noise.

I was lost in contemplation when Anxo leapt up from the mossy flag stone beneath the kitchen window. I glanced round to see another German shepherd emerging from the corner field. The dog was smaller than Anxo, lighter in colour and painfully thin. It was Pastora. She belonged to Tonito who lived at the top of the *aldea* between the farmhouse and the church. We'd first made her acquaintance back in summer when she was only a puppy, scrawny and ridden with ticks. We'd fed her and treated her for parasites, and by the end of August she was a picture of health. When we finally moved into the village at Christmas, Pastora looked just as bad as she had before. Her poor condition hadn't dampened her spirits; she'd taken an instant liking to Anxo and the pair of them would play for hours. Now that she was an adult, we rarely saw her; she spent most of her days and evenings minding Tonito's cows. This morning's visit was particularly surprising. We'd seen neither hide nor hair of her for over two weeks.

'Pastora!' I called.

She gave a short bark of recognition and hastened her pace towards us. Anxo sniffed her thoroughly before leaping sideways, inviting her to play. Pastora wagged her tail half-heartedly before heading off up the lane.

Just then the back door opened, and Scholes ambled out. Pausing only to give Anxo a cuff and a warning grumble he strode across the lane and slinked under the door of the barn.

'Morning,' yawned Gary, who'd stepped out behind him.

'Morning. I didn't realise you were getting up; I'd have put the kettle on. You'll never guess who's not long been to visit?'

'Go on, surprise me.'

'Pastora.'

'Get away. I was beginning to think we'd never see her again. It must be over two weeks now. How did she seem?'

'Thin, obviously, but she wasn't her usual sprightly self, she seemed... I don't know... jaded, somehow. I wasn't imagining it, Anxo was dancing round her, and she didn't want to know. It was as if she was saying, "Not now, Anxo, I'm not in the mood today." It was strange.'

'Poor fella,' said Gary, stroking Anxo's head. 'You're banned from letting the chooks out and now your best mate won't play with you. Never mind, at least you've got your walk to look forward to.'

'It'll be an adventure for him this morning, we're taking a different route.'

'Because of the squirrel?'

'Don't be daft, I'm not squeamish like you. We`re going on a reccy to find a new patch of woodland for collecting branches. We'll have a meander and if I find a spot that looks promising I'll go back with the builder's bucket after break.'

'That sounds fun. I'd join you but I want to get the rest of the seeds in before lunch. There's the broad beans, sweetcorn, swedes…'

'Not the peas, though.'

'Definitely not. Now I've seen Carmen in a rage I wouldn't dare.'

I set off with Anxo in the direction of the oakwood. As we passed Masi's *hórreo* I paused to look through the fence, half-expecting to see Carmen poking about in the garden. A short distance ahead of me Anxo stopped and gave a low growl. I caught up quickly and traced his gaze up into the field to the side of the *río*. I realised at once what had unnerved him.

'Good God!' I breathed, as I stared in horror. An array of wet clothing was draped along the entire length of the ramshackle stone wall. A terrible thought crept into my mind. Campers! It had to be! But where had they come from? Had a hapless band of pilgrims lost their way along the Camino? I'd read in the local paper about farmers who were tearing their hair out over the number of *peregrinos* traipsing over their land, and the

Xunta was always under pressure to improve the route and put up more signs.

Still feeling piqued by Paul's transgressions, I stomped up into the field ready to take issue with whoever had invaded Cutián. Beyond the wall, a second field stretched back as far as the *fincas*, intersected by a clear, fast-flowing stream. It was the perfect campsite, but as I scanned the expanse of pasture there wasn't a single tent to be seen. I crossed over to the wall and stared at the laundry splayed over the stones: black sweaters, black leggings, a garish tunic and plastic feed sacks. The answer suddenly became clear.

'You'll never guess,' I said, after I'd called Gary in for a coffee break half an hour earlier than usual.

'Ah, something's afoot,' he teased. 'I thought there must be a reason why coffee break was on time.'

'Cheeky bugger,' I giggled. 'I'm always punctual. But you're right, it's early because there's something I can't wait to tell you.'

'Is it to do with Tom and Paul?'

'No, I haven't seen either of them yet this morning. Given that they've both been pissed for two nights running I'm guessing they're having a long lie-in.'

'The longer they're out of the way the better as far as I'm concerned. I bet poor Carmen's had enough already.'

'Ah, yes. Carmen. That's what I wanted to tell you. It looks as if she's done a month's laundry all in one go, and you'll never guess in a million years where she's hung it.'

'On the trees?'

'Don't be daft, she always hangs it on the trees. It's somewhere bizarre.'

'Go on then.'

'You know the field behind the *río* with the crumbling old wall?'

'Where the blackberries grow in summer?'

'That's the one. Well, she's got clothes and bags and all sorts draped from one end to the other. I panicked at first; I thought a tribe of holiday makers had descended on the village. I'm glad I was wrong.'

A smile began to spread across his face. 'Perhaps you weren't.'

'What do you mean?'

'Perhaps Paul's invited a crowd of naturist friends to join him. They've all stripped off and left their clothes on the wall and gone off for a hike over the fields; that'd be why you missed them. They're probably down there now, skinny-dipping in the *río*.'

The heap of branches on the threshing floor had more than doubled by lunchtime. From the lane my hoard looked impressive, but closer inspection told a different tale. Much of the wood was aged and hollow, or completely rotten after lying for months on the forest floor. The chances of it being any use as firewood seemed doubtful; with the changeable weather I wondered if it would ever be dry enough to burn.

After lunch I took the rubbish up to the village wheelie bin, accompanied by Anxo, of course. These brief jaunts had become something of a ritual, and he seemed to enjoy them almost as much as his evening walk. There was always something exciting to grab his attention outside the farmhouse: dogs to greet, hens to chase, clods of manure to writhe in or lunchtime leftovers to steal. As we went past Maruja was standing on the doorstep. I'd first met her back in the summer and since then she'd taught me a lot about the *aldea* and the cows. Anxo adored her. Now he ran up to her, wagging his tail.

'Anxo, *amigo*,' she laughed, patting the top of his head. '*Buenos días*, Elisa.'

45

'*Hola*, Maruja. *Buenos días.*'

Anxo shifted his attention to Pastor, Maruja and Javier's old cow dog. Pastor had the basic shape of a German shepherd but was shorter and stockier, with tattered ears and round bobbly eyes. He reminded me of a moth-eaten old teddy bear. Although his herding days were over, he still made a feisty guard. He gave Anxo a warning growl.

'No Luna today?' I asked Maruja. Luna and Pastor usually lay out in the lane together, while the youngest farm dog, Res, went out with the cows.

'We've shut her in because she's in season. Bitches are hard work at this time of year, you can't watch them all the time, it's easier to lock them away.'

I didn't bother to ask if they'd thought about spaying. Rural people did things differently to townsfolk and it wasn't my place to interfere.

'Pastora's been in season as well,' she continued. 'Tonito tried to keep her in the cowshed, but she kept escaping. She's bound to be pregnant; Res and a couple of other dogs were always hanging about outside.'

Poor Pastora. She was just over a year old and had barely enough meat on her to cover her bones. The thought of her enduring a nine-week pregnancy and then feeding a hungry litter filled me with despair.

'The postman came while you were walking Anxo,' said Gary, on Friday morning. 'I think you'll be really surprised.'

He handed me a postcard. It was a typical beach photo: blue sky, blue sea and hundreds of people crawling like ants over an expanse of yellow sand. There was, however, something about the hackneyed image that seemed familiar. Eventually I twigged.

'My God!' I exclaimed. 'It's Las Canteras!'

Las Canteras beach spans the length of the city of Las Palmas, Gran Canaria and it's reputedly one of the best city beaches in the whole of Spain.

I flipped the card over.

'Just to remind you of what you're missing!
Hope you're both well and enjoying the weather,
Sandra xx'

Gary was right, the postcard was, indeed, surprising. Once we'd made the decision to move to Galicia, we'd turned our backs on the Canarian social scene, determined to stay in and save every *céntimo* for the inevitable outlay that comes with renovating a two-hundred-year-old house. As our time on the island was nearing its end we were practically hermits. Apart from a handful of very close friends, I'd assumed that everyone back in Las Palmas had forgotten us.

'Well I never, after all this time. What we're *missing*? If only she knew!'

I looked again at the photo; it only served to remind me how much I'd grown to loathe those visits to the beach. By mid-afternoon it was always so noisy and crowded. Despite the breeze coming in off the Atlantic, the heat was usually stifling; the only respite was to plunge into the sea, but at the water's edge the waves rolled in so forcefully that I didn't dare go in deep enough to cool off.

The photograph was cleverly done. It showed nothing of the urban sprawl of Las Palmas which stretched back beyond the *paseo* towards the port, where the sun rose every morning in an eerily radioactive-looking orange glow. There was no hint of the ugly grey apartment blocks with thick hunks of electrical cable looping from building to building like hangmen's nooses or the lines of nose-to-tail traffic belting out the relentless chromatic symphony of revving engines and beeping horns.

After lunch I shut Anxo in the garden before taking the rubbish up to the wheelie bin. If strange dogs had been hanging about when Pastora was in season it was highly likely that they'd be lured back by the prospect of getting up close and personal with Luna. Although Anxo wasn't sexually mature, he was full of enthusiasm and curiosity; I didn't want him mauled by malingering males because he'd overstepped the mark.

By the time I reached the wheelie bin the only dog I'd seen was old Pastor. Chiding myself for overreacting I strode back down towards the village, but as I neared the farmhouse, I became aware of light, rhythmic footsteps behind me. I turned round and was surprised to see that I was being followed, uncomfortably closely, by a large dog I'd never seen before. It was a Spanish mastiff, with a dense white coat patched with ginger, and feathering on the legs reminiscent of a Springer spaniel. The dog was whining, and its proximity was making me feel ill at ease. Under normal circumstances I was confident around dogs, but I was unfamiliar with the *mastín* and knew nothing of its temperament. It seemed that my earlier apprehension about canine invaders had been well-founded until the dog, in a desperate attempt to gain my attention, rushed in front of me. Only then did I realise that it was a female. It was also desperately thin. It wasn't about to attack me – it was weak and desperately hungry. Perhaps Maruja would know who it belonged to. I stopped at the farmhouse and rang the bell.

'I don't know where she's come from,' said Maruja. 'She's been hanging around since early this morning, crying for food. She must have lived in an *aldea*; even though she was starving she didn't go for the hens. I gave her some *sopa de leche* left over from breakfast, but now she's hungry again.'

I looked at the dog. It was going to take more than hunks of bread soaked in milk to sustain her. Still, I reasoned, if Javier and Maruja had ditched their time-honoured rural Galician breakfast in favour of eggs and bacon they might have been less willing to share.

'José Manuel knows a lot of people. He's been putting the word out, but I doubt anybody will come for her. People drive out into the country to abandon dogs all the time.'

'I'll take her with me and give her some of Anxo's *piensos*. I'm sure someone will turn up eventually. If she's wandered some distance, it could take a while for word to get round.'

'*Ven*,' I told the dog, who was still whining. 'Come on, let's go and get you something to eat.'

The dog followed me willingly. As we turned the corner, I bumped into Carmen pushing a wheelbarrow up the lane.

'*Buenos días*, Carmen.'

'*Buenos días*, Elisa. It's a nice dog, isn't it? It's very affectionate. I gave it some bread this morning, it looks like it's hungry again.'

Outside number ten, Tom was smoking and drinking tea. There was no sign of Paul, but music was blaring out into the courtyard from the kitchen window.

'She's a smasher,' said Tom, after I'd explained the predicament of my companion. 'I saw her hanging about this morning, but I didn't realise she was a stray. If I'd known, I'd have given her some food.'

'José Manuel's asking around, apparently. Maybe her owners will turn up.'

'Let's hope so,' Tom nodded. 'She's far too nice to be abandoned. If I didn't have a two-dogs-only policy I'd take her in myself.'

Back at the House of José Val, Gary and Anxo were in the garden. I repeated my story once more.

'She's a lovely looking dog,' said Gary.

Anxo obviously thought so too; he was desperate to come into the lane to say hello.

'Don't open the gate just yet,' I warned. 'I need to feed her first and you know what dogs are like when there's food around. We don't want them to get off to a bad start.'

Once our guest had devoured a good-sized portion of Friskies, Gary opened the gate. Anxo bounded into the lane, but the dog backed away nervously, startled by his exuberance. Anxo gave a low whine and hung his head. I had to smile; it looked for all the world as if she'd hurt his feelings. Cautiously, she came forward to sniff him and seconds later her splendid plume of a tail was wagging from side to side.

'I know she's thin,' said Gary, as we stood watching to see what Anxo would make of her. 'But I'm guessing that's only because she's wandered. She looks in good condition, if you know what I mean.'

'Yes,' I agreed. 'I think she's been well cared for. Maybe the owner died or couldn't afford her upkeep; she'd take some feeding. If she's had a good home, she'd have needed a good reason to stray.'

As Anxo's evening walk drew near, the dog was still with him. The pair were lying together in front of the barn.

'Looks like you're taking both of them,' grinned Gary.

'Thanks,' I frowned, feigning indignation. 'Cutián dog charity, all mutts walked for free. Come on then Anxo, you can bring Rubia with you I suppose.'

'Is that her name then, Rubia?' asked Gary. when we returned from the fields.

'Rubia?'

'Yes, that's what you called her earlier.'

'Oh, I see. I hadn't really thought about it. It was the first thing that came into my head, because her patches are the same colour as the cows, I suppose.'

In Galicia the most popular breed of meat cattle are *rubia gallega*. Javier and Maruja had a herd of two dozen, their colours ranging from a deep rust through gingery orange to creamy apricot. The word *rubia* describes their colour perfectly: it can mean red, reddish or blonde.

'It's quite a pretty name,' I mused, 'but it's Castilian. It ought to be something in *galego*, like Anxo. Perhaps we should look it up.'

According to my well-thumbed dictionary, the *galego* equivalent for *rubia* was *roxa*.

'That's nice,' nodded Gary.

Finally, our new arrival had a name.

At dusk I shut the hens away and made my way back to the kitchen, looking forward to relaxing with a beer by the range. Gary was already sitting with a glass of wine and Anxo had taken up his place on the warm concrete above the vent that ran beneath the floor. Roxa, however, did *not* want to join him. It soon became clear that she wasn't going to settle inside once the back door was closed. Finally, I let her out to sleep in the lane, leaving the barn door open for her in case it rained.

Roxa was still lying in front of the barn when I opened the back door on Saturday morning. Anxo charged out to greet her and I sat on the bench to watch them, with a fag and a brew.

Their play was rougher and livelier than yesterday, but they were well matched. Anxo seemed dwarfed by Roxa, but what he lacked in size he made up for in tenacity. Satisfied that no harm would come to either of them, I sat back to listen to the cuckoo. This morning the call was more frequent and persistent and seemed to be coming from several directions. I focused more intently. There wasn't just one cuckoo, there were three.

By the time I'd finished my coffee, Anxo and Roxa had bounded into me several times. It seemed a good idea to get them out into the open. Gary would have to make his own cuppa today.

Half an hour later, I plodded back up the track, perspiring. The dogs charged up to greet Gary who sitting on the bench, yawning and drinking tea.

'Good walk?' he asked.

'It was for *them*,' I sighed.

'Oh,' he said, puzzled. 'What happened?'

'It was dangerous. They were belting about all over the place and nearly had me over God knows how many times. It wasn't what you'd call pleasurable. I gave up and stood clinging to a tree in the end.'

'Morning!' called Tom, who was heading down the lane with Maud. 'Any news?'

'Yes,' grinned Gary, 'The wife's converted to tree-hugging.'

'It's not funny,' I scowled. 'Ignore him, Tom.'

'I meant any news about the ox?'

'What ox?' I frowned.

'That one,' chuckled Tom, nodding towards Roxa. 'Look at her, she's nearly as big as Javier's cows.'

Gary and I laughed. Tom wasn't far of the mark; she really was enormous.

'She's fine,' I told him. 'She doesn't half eat well.'

'We've named her Roxa,' said Gary.

'But we're not keeping her,' I added firmly.

'Roxa, is it?' Tom smiled at her, ruffling the top of her head. 'You'll always be the Ox to me.'

As Tom and Maud continued down towards the track, Roxa stood up, stretched and fell in behind them. Gary,

Anxo and I watched as the three of them turned at the *río* and disappeared from view.

'Perhaps we should take Anxo with us?' I suggested, as I picked up my bag.

'Better not,' said Gary. 'He'd have to stay on his lead the whole distance. It'll take us a good hour to get there, he's not used to having the lead on that long. *And* we'd have to watch him constantly once we got there. It's not my idea of a relaxing drink at the pub.'

'I s'pose you're right,' I nodded. 'He'll be fine.'

I was locking the back door when Scholes sauntered out of the barn and jumped through the gate into the garden. Roxa made no move to pursue him but thumped her tail as he went by.

'It looks like she's fine with cats,' said Gary.

'We're still not keeping her,' I frowned.

At Gradoi the road forked, and we turned left to follow a sign saying 'Río Ulla'. Thirty minutes later we were approaching the village of Santa Mariña and, much to our surprise, an imposing *pazo*[7] came into view. Surrounded by thick stone walls, it was reminiscent of a small fortress; its dominant presence contrasting starkly to the humble dwellings of the *aldea* which converged onto a well-tended village green.

The Águila Negra was nestled amongst a cluster of stone houses. Had it not been for the English-style pub sign we would never have known it was there. Intrigued, I pushed open the door and stepped into a small, cosy room. On the far side was a bar. Although it was fitted with beer pumps it doubled as a shop counter. Next to bottles of wine and spirits there was an assortment of

---

[7] *Pazos* were built throughout rural Galicia in the 18th and 19th centuries, the dwellings of lower nobility who owned much of the surrounding land.

tins and packets stacked on shelves at the back. On the wall to the side of the bar was the stuffed head of a wild boar. It was enormous: a prehistoric-looking pig with razor-sharp teeth and curved, pointed tusks. The angry eyes and flared nostrils suggested that its rage had endured after death.

'Crikey!' I shuddered.

Gary chuckled. 'And this was the woman that was desperate to meet a *jabalí.*'

The man behind the bar smiled when he saw us marvelling at the monster. 'My grandfather shot it,' he said.

To the left, a door was open revealing a typical Galician kitchen, much the same as our own. The wood burning range was in the centre of the room and an old lady was stirring something in a large saucepan.

We took our overpriced bottles of Estrella Galicia out into the sunshine.

'Whatever was in that saucepan smelled nice,' said Gary. 'Tom didn't tell us they served food.'

'They don't,' smiled an elderly man at the next table. 'That's the family kitchen, it's their house as well, you see.'

We must have looked taken aback because the man started laughing. 'I lived for eight years in England,' he chuckled. 'But it was a very long time ago. I like the fish and chips.'

After two bottles of lager apiece we set off on the winding, uphill journey home.

'I wonder if anyone's been for Roxa while we've been away,' I pondered, as we were walking.

'I doubt it. It's three days now. The more time that passes, the less chance there is, I suppose. Anyway, it's nice for Anxo to have company. He's not had chance to play since Pastora stopped coming round.'

Gary was right. It had been lovely to see Anxo enjoying himself. The walk had been tiresome, but I supposed the initial excitement would wear off in time. Roxa had completely ignored Maruja's hens outside the farmhouse and not batted an eyelid when Scholes had walked by. In many ways she'd fit into our lives perfectly, but I still harboured reservations. Adopting a dog wasn't a decision to be taken lightly; I could only sit on the fence for now.

Back in Cutián, the tractor was pulling up outside the farmhouse. The 'shit chucker' (as Gary so eloquently termed it) was hitched to the back. Our sunny days were obviously numbered; they only ever did the manuring when the forecast gave rain.

'*Hola*!' called José Manuel, as he climbed down from the cab. At only eighteen years old he was able to perform each and every one of the countless jobs around the farm. He had no social life to speak of and seemed perfectly content to spend his days and evenings ploughing, mowing, manuring, herding and milking, whatever the weather or the time of year.

'*Hola*!' we chorused.

'Have you heard anything about the *mastín* yet?' I asked.

He shook his head. 'Nothing. I thought we might have found the owner this morning; José who drives the bread van said a man in Vilane was out looking for a missing *mastín*. I drove over and asked around. It turned out his dog's a brindle male and it had already come home. It must have been out looking for *chicas*; it's that time of year.'

It was becoming clear that neutering dogs wasn't common practice amongst the *aldea* communities. Roxa was already a young adult and likely to come into season at any time. If we *were* to adopt her, we'd be facing a hornet's nest of problems. We didn't want to end up with half a dozen or more lumbering mastiff puppies but, on the other hand, we couldn't whisk her off to be spayed straight away in case her owner turned up. It wasn't unheard of for dogs to climb into vans and be transported miles from home; if Roxa had travelled some distance, it might be weeks before someone finally came to claim her. Whichever way we played it we'd be on dodgy ground.

Much to my surprise, the evening walk was almost serene compared to the morning's rampage. Anxo and Roxa seemed happy to potter in and out of the bracken, breaking into the occasional charge when flurries of small birds flew up out of the long grass.

'Do you want me to come with you?' asked Gary, on Sunday morning, as I pulled on my wellies and grabbed Anxo's lead.

'No thanks. They were a lot calmer last night. Now they're used to each other I'm sure our walks will be quite civilised affairs. They're bound to have the odd game of chase, but that's not a problem. It was all that full-on hurtling I couldn't abide.' A smile played on my lips.

'What?' said Gary.

'Unless you wanted to get in on the tree hugging, of course.'

When we arrived back an hour later, I reached straight for the tobacco. 'God, do I need a fag,' I groaned.

'Same as yesterday morning?' asked Gary, stifling a chuckle.

'Repeat performance, I'm afraid. It must be a pent-up energy thing. They've had chance to get it out of their systems by the time I take them at night.'

I walked over to the cooker and picked up the kettle. 'I need caffeine, are you ready for a brew?'

'Make that three,' said a voice as Tom walked into the kitchen. 'Sorry, I didn't think to knock, the door was open.'

'Don't be daft,' I grinned. 'Not long 'til your visitor goes then?'

'Tomorrow morning. His flight's not until Tuesday but he likes to stay in Santiago the night before. Actually, that's what I've come to see you about. He wants to know if you'd like to come round for a drink tonight to say goodbye.'

'Why didn't he come himself?' asked Gary.

I could already guess the answer.

'He's feeling a bit embarrassed about Wednesday. All the noise and the trouble with Carmen, you know.'

'What's done's done,' said Gary, stoically. 'I'm sure he's learned his lesson.'

On Sunday evening the sun was warm but occasional puffs of grey-tinged cloud were beginning to drift over from the south. With Anxo and Roxa ambling behind us, Gary and I walked down the grassy pathway that led off the lane and into the garden of number ten. I was feeling slightly apprehensive, wondering how the *soirée* would unfold. To begin with the atmosphere was one of polite conviviality and we settled into the white plastic chairs arranged incongruously on the threshing floor. If we humans were guarded, our canine companions harboured no such inhibitions. Anxo and Roxa, forgetting their manners, made straight for a bowl of potatoes and crackling left out for Maud and Ali. Maud dashed over growling, as if taking them to task like a crotchety maiden aunt. The pair, deterred but not yet defeated, hovered persistently, inching forward now and again in the hope that they might avoid Maud's reproachful eye. In no time they had us all in stitches and we were soon chatting easily once more.

I was shocked to discover how little Paul knew about the *aldea* and its inhabitants; Gary, Tom and I were experts in comparison. Apart from Carmen, Paul knew none of the names of our neighbours. 'The Farmer', 'The Farmer's Wife', 'The Farmer's Son', 'The Taxi Driver', 'The Man with Three Cows' and 'The Family Who Come At Weekends' was the best he could do. He had the barest smattering of Spanish and was in no hurry to learn.

His plans for number ten only served to reinforce his limited understanding of the ethos of the village.

'There'll be the tennis court eventually, but I'm starting with a *petanque* court over there.'

'What's *petanque*?' I frowned.

'Like *boules*,' said Gary.

'Ah, is that the same as bowls?'

'Sort of. But it's played on sand.'

It sounded awfully boring. Still, if it was tucked away behind the threshing floor, we wouldn't be able to see it from our garden. After the *petanque* court, there would be a sunken jacuzzi in the courtyard and a billiard table in the *bodega* beyond.

It'll be ages before he gets round to the tennis court, I consoled myself. Odds are the budget will have run out by then.

'It'll be a feature,' Paul enthused, 'a place where people can relax when they're doing the *Camino*. I think it'll do well.'

Tom winked at me reassuringly and I nodded my understanding. There was no need to worry. It had taken more than four years for Paul to think about getting the roof done; Cutián's leisure complex wouldn't be happening any time soon.

'I can't see Carmen playing tennis,' grinned Gary.

I spluttered on my beer.

'I'd be happy to teach her,' said Paul, quite earnestly. 'I'd like us to be friends.'

'I think you might have got off on the wrong foot there,' I frowned. 'What with the music and the… erm… sunbathing.'

'I was upset that I'd offended her,' he sighed. 'I honestly didn't think she'd mind a bit of music…'

And *us*? I thought but said nothing.

'…but I doubt she was bothered about the sunbathing,' he continued. 'She *is* very eccentric after all.'

His dismissive attitude irked me. 'Carmen isn't as doolally as she might seem,' I said, determined that she should have a fair hearing. I wasn't totally convinced about my assertion, but I'd always had a hunch that there was a good reason for most of the strange things she did.

'Well, how do you explain this, then? Yesterday she came home from Antas in a taxi. The driver unloaded carrier bags of shopping and a sack of bread, enough to feed a family for a week. Lovely, it looked. Now I'm assuming the baker gave it to her, you know, took pity on her because she's poor. Anyway, she took the shopping inside and left the bread on the doorstep. It's still there now, all dry and stale. What a waste.'

'You don't know that she's poor, what makes you assume that?'

'Well look at the clothes she wears for a start. Everything's full of holes.'

'That means nothing.' I thought back to last April when I'd emptied the wardrobes of José Val. I'd set aside a few bits and pieces I'd thought would do me for working in. Everything had come up well with a good boil. Since December I'd been getting my wear out of them. Through constant encounters with chicken wire and bramble and branches most were already in holes. It didn't stop me wearing them; I couldn't see the point of ruining something new.

'It isn't right,' said Paul, 'she needs caring for. When I come back in the summer, I'm going to bring her some clothes of my Mum's.'

I thought of the Carmen that *I* knew: the one who dragged cookers into the woodlands, dug for hours over the *finca* and climbed surreptitiously over walls. She was hardly a charity case. Paul meant well, but his attitude was patronising to say the least.

'It's about time I put the hens away,' I said. 'Excuse me, I won't be long.'

I was only away for ten minutes, but hoped it was long enough for the topic of conversation to have moved on. As I walked back towards Paul's gate, Carmen was standing on her doorstep tearing up bread from the sack and cramming it into a bucket of water.

'*Buenas tardes*, Elisa,' she said.

'*Buenas tardes*, Carmen.'

'It's for the ducks and chickens,' she explained, registering my puzzled expression. 'You can buy left over bread from the *panadería* – it's only a *euro* a sack. If you soak it overnight in water, it's cheap *comida*. That way you don't use so much corn.'

'What was Carmen talking about?' asked Gary.

'She was explaining about the *pan* on the doorstep.'

'I s'pose there's a rational explanation.'

'There is,' I grinned.

Paul looked confused. 'A pan on the doorstep?'

I nodded but said nothing. Until he put himself out to learn some Spanish, Carmen's foibles would continue to be way beyond his comprehension. I certainly wasn't going to make the effort to explain.

Toxic Sunrise

*Pink-orange luminescence
above an ocean of grey tongues
lashing black sands.
Oppressive heat
hangs over a stagnant city,
stealing through streets
that will never truly see the dawn,
and where dew-kissed green
is but a memory.
And yet there is the hope
of purity in birdsong:
high up on a balcony,
a canary sings...
in a cage.*

Chapter 4

Feathered Fiends

When I opened my eyes on Monday morning I lay still and listened for the familiar pattering against the window. By the time we'd left Paul's the sky had been heavy with steel-grey storm clouds; I'd been fully expecting to wake up to rain. Even from the bedroom I could hear the hooting of owls in the oakwood, but beyond that there was silence. I eased myself out of bed and padded over to the window. Parting the curtains, I stared out onto the dimly lit threshing floor. The absence of puddles said we'd earned a reprieve, at least for now.

Down in the kitchen I lit a cigarette. I set the kettle on the stove and let Anxo out while I waited for the water to boil. Within seconds Roxa emerged from the barn. She rushed towards us, her tail wagging and, as I bent to hug her, the realisation hit me; I was becoming fond of her. The pair of them mooched off down towards the *río*, and I crept up the lane towards number ten. There were no lights on, and I wondered whether Paul had overslept. He'd told us he'd be setting off at daybreak; it wouldn't be much longer before the sun rose, surely he'd be up by now? As if to confirm that dawn was imminent, I heard the first crow of the day. Up above, the dark clouds were still looming; if Paul was walking to Palas there was every chance he'd be caught in a downpour. I considered knocking, but there was coffee to attend to; he could always thumb a lift if the worst came to the worst.

When I went to let the hens out the garden was teeming with birdlife. Blackbirds were pecking industriously over the lawn, sparrows twittered and skittered in the treetops and a solitary blue tit flew out of the broom. The rich variety of avian visitors to our garden never failed to amaze me. Throughout winter and spring much of the birdlife could just as easily been seen in any garden in England, but during the summer they were joined by a medley of species I'd never seen back home. Most of them still remained nameless to me, but I'd come to love watching the beautifully crested pink hoopoe birds and the aptly named golden orioles with their melodic fluting call.

As I entered the chicken run, scores of collared doves fluttered up into the trees. *These* birds were prevalent whatever the season of the year. With muted grey-fawn plumage and distinctive black neck rings their appearance was undeniably charming; but looks can be deceptive. As far as I was concerned, the collared doves were public enemy number one. They had voracious appetites and were particularly partial to corn, and consequently, the chooks' food was disappearing at a great rate of knots. We'd had the chickens for almost three months now and it was hard to believe they'd caused so many rows in such a short space of time. Gary was like a stuck record when it came to reminding me how much they'd cost us; it was only a matter of time before he noticed how quickly we were getting through sacks of corn. There had to be a way to deter them; I couldn't let the dreaded chicken argument rear its ugly head again.

Rufo barely gave me a second glance as he strode out of the house. It was a week since he'd last attacked me and I wondered whether it would be safe to ditch the waterproof trousers once and for all. I watched as he focused his attention on his harem; those that remonstrated were quickly rebuked with a jab of the beak. As they made their disorderly way to the feeder I cursed with exasperation; the wretched doves had descended again. I looked despairingly at Rufo; what a pity he didn't object to their presence like he had to mine.

Sensing that rain was imminent I decided to take Anxo and Roxa down past the *rio*, through the oakwood and into the field beyond. They'd still have plenty of chance to run off their energy, but the route was shorter, and the canopy of the trees would afford us some protection if we were caught in a shower.

As we strolled home my thoughts returned to our feathered freeloaders. Surely there was *something* I could do? As the track descended out of the oakwood and down towards the village the land to the left fell away steeply giving a breath-taking vista of the valley below. I watched in fascination as a pair of buzzards hovered on the thermals high above the pasture. It was then that I had an idea.

When we came to the *rio* my eyes widened; I couldn't believe what I saw. There was Carmen's laundry, still spread out along the wall. I hadn't been this way since Thursday, and that was four days ago; we'd had nothing but sunshine, why hadn't she taken it in before now?

Gary was standing on the doorstep when we reached the corner. The barn doors were open, and it was clear he was ready to do the weekly shop. He was earlier than usual, and that was a bonus; it would give me more time to pull off my plan.

'Good walk?' he asked, bending to fuss Anxo and Roxa.

'Loads better. They're already improving. I think things will be okay given time. Anyway, you're early this morning, you're not usually so keen to get away.'

'I'm going to buy some lettuce plants from the *ferreteria*. Do you want me to get some tomato plants for your raised bed?'

'It's not ready yet, hadn't you noticed? The tiles are done, but I haven't even started filling it. Anyway, it seems a bit early for tomatoes. I think I'll wait 'til the end of May.'

Once Gary was out of the way it was time to focus on my idea. Until this morning I'd been toying with the option of making a scarecrow, but if *my* presence in the chooks' pen had done nothing to dissuade the doves, I'd only be wasting my time. A human wasn't a threat because it wasn't a predator; they had to see something that would make them think again. Birds of prey not only hunted rodents; they also fed on smaller birds. There was every chance that a giant model of a hawk or a buzzard would do the trick.

Aware that I wouldn't have long to complete the project, I needed to think on my feet. It didn't have to be anything fancy: flapping wings and beady eyes were essential, beyond that, any large dark shape would do. A black bin bag would work a treat for the wings, they'd flutter well in the wind and be waterproof into the bargain. But what about the body? I dashed out to the barn and grabbed a two-litre pop-bottle out of the recycling; with the tapered end for the head it wouldn't look too far off the mark.

Half an hour later I'd covered the bottle with black polythene and was trying to jab the end of a wooden skewer through the plastic to make a framework for a wing. I could've dropped through the floor when I heard the sound of an engine approaching. It could only be Gary. I couldn't let him know the real reason for the bird scarer. There was no harm in telling a little white lie.

'Bloody hell, it's Blue Peter[8]!' he laughed, surveying my materials strewn over the marble surface. 'Do you remember? "Here's one I made earlier", that's what they always used to say.'

'So they did. And then when you tried to make one it never looked quite the same.'

'Crikey, you've even got the German shepherd and the cat. What is it anyway? Is it a witch?'

'Don't be daft, you can *see* what it is.' Actually, you couldn't. I hoped the wings would make it less obscure.

'It's a dove deterrent, Same principle as a scarecrow. except that it's to scare doves.'

'Is it for the veg plot? Oh God, don't tell me they've been at the seeds.'

Seeds? I thought wryly, these doves are *much* more discerning; they've been noshing on chicken feed at fourteen *euros* a bag.

'Calm down,' I said quickly. 'It's for the chooks' pen. I remembered hearing once that pigeons carry diseases. It occurred to me that doves might do the same.'

'Ah,' he nodded. 'Good thinking. Prevention's better than cure.'

I turned back to my conundrum.

---

[8] British magazine-style children's TV programme which was first shown in 1958 and continues to be popular today. Over the years an assortment of studio pets have proved a major attraction of the show.

'Wait,' said Gary. 'You can finish it in a minute. Put the kettle on first, I've got some good news.'

'Here, take this then, I'm trying to bodge this skewer through there. See if you can do it. I'm buggered if I can get it to go in.'

'*Not* so Blue Peter,' he chuckled. 'Are you ready then? This is *big* news.'

'*Gary…*'

'We've had a text message from Ron and Miranda. They want to come over for a week in June.'

'That's brilliant news! June, you say? It's nearly May now, crikey Gary, we haven't got long to prepare.'

'*Prepare*? Honestly, Liza, I don't know what…'

There was a knock at the door, and Tom walked in.

'Morning Tom,' we chorused.

'Morning,' said Tom. 'Ooh. That looks interesting. Is it for Hallowe'en?'

'Not *you* as well,' I sighed. 'I'm making a dove deterrent. It's to scare the collared doves out of the chooks' pen.'

'Ah, yes,' he nodded. 'I've watched them from Paul's in the mornings. Are they stealing the corn?'

I shot him a warning look. 'It's to stop them passing diseases to the chickens.'

He smiled knowingly. I was relieved he'd cottoned on.

'If it works, you should patent it. The Scare Dove. You'd be worth a fortune.'

'That *and* the rooster-proof trousers,' I grinned.

'I take it Paul got off alright then?' asked Gary.

'*Oh* yes. About half past five.'

'Never!' I exclaimed. 'I'm surprised he managed to get up that early.'

'He didn't. He was worried he might sleep through the alarm, so he stayed up all night. He was bumping and thudding about for hours; I don't think I slept a wink.'

'It's a good job he went early,' I said. 'It'll be raining before lunchtime at this rate, but I s'pose he'll be on the bus to the airport by now. Did he sort something out about the roof, by the way? I forgot to ask him last night.'

'He *told* us,' frowned Gary. 'You can't have forgotten? How many beers did you have?'

'She was putting the chickens away,' Tom reminded him. 'Very diplomatic it was too.'

'They're starting in summer,' began Gary.

'They?'

'Paul and Tom and the builder, what was his name?'

'Kev. He came over while you were out on Saturday. He's hoping to start in August and get it done in three weeks.'

'Three *weeks*! That's impossible! Look how long ours took, and Paul's is twice the size.'

'Well, I've told you Liza, it'll all be low-budget. He'll do the bare minimum to stop it dripping and that's about it. The less time he spends on the job, the less it'll cost, you see.'

It occurred to me that Tom didn't do ladders. How on earth was he going to work on the roof? 'Hold on a minute, you're going to be working with them?'

'I know what you're thinking, Liza; don't worry, I've no intention of going up on the roof. I'll be barrowing stuff about and doing the cooking. After this week though I'm not looking forward to it if the truth be told.'

'I thought things were okay between you and Paul? I know there was an atmosphere last Tuesday, but it sounded as if you've been getting on alright since then.'

'Oh, it's nothing major. He was annoyed that he couldn't find things. I'd moved stuff round and he didn't like it. But you saw what it was like when it rained hard;

I had to get things out of the way so they wouldn't get drenched.'

I nodded.

'Actually, there were a couple of things that never did turn up. There was a wooden spoon I could've sworn I'd left on the cart in the courtyard. Then there was a sickle, but that was in the garden... anyway, I was the last to use it, I don't suppose I lent it to you?'

'We've got a couple of sickles...' began Gary.

'This one's distinctive, it's got orange paint on the handle.'

'Can't help you with that one, then. Sorry.'

'It'll turn up eventually, and even if it doesn't it's not a problem. God, there are sickles everywhere.'

'That's true,' nodded Gary. 'I saw Carmen using one yesterday.'

For a split second I thought of Carmen's fence-scaling exploits. Surely she wouldn't... I hastily pushed the thought to the back of my mind.

'Let's tell Tom about our bit of excitement,' I said, to change the subject.

'Excitement?' asked Tom.

'Troglodytes,' I grinned.

'As in cavemen?'

'Exactly. Our cave-dwelling friends are coming all the way from Andalusia to visit Cutián.'

'There you go,' said Gary, at lunchtime. 'It's raining. I planted the lettuces just in the nick of time.'
I stared hard but said nothing as a trail of damp soil fell from his wellies across the kitchen floor.

'I'd better get Anxo in,' I sighed. 'He'll smell if he stays out in the drizzle, he's still wearing *eau de* manure.'

Anxo was already waiting on the doorstep, and so was Roxa. As Anxo trotted into the kitchen she followed. Much to my amazement she didn't bat an eyelid when I closed the back door.

'Crikey,' I said, 'That's progress. She must really be gaining in confidence. She seems to trust us, perhaps she's starting to feel at home.'

I felt in limbo. Roxa wasn't ours, yet somehow I felt responsible for her. The longer she was with us, the more attached I was going to become.

'We always said we'd have two dogs eventually,' Gary reminded me.

'Yes, but we said we'd have another when Anxo was older. When we'd trained him and... well, it's a big commitment, these things are usually planned.'

'As far as commitment goes, we're already tied because of Anxo, not to mention the chooks and Scholes. And as for the timing, well, what does it matter? Anxo's already pretty obedient, and they get on well together. And we know she won't bother the chooks or Scholes.'

I looked at Anxo, then at Roxa. He was enjoying her company and so were we. I didn't suppose Maruja would want her, she'd already got three dogs of her own. Tom was very taken with her, but he was quite determined when it came to his two-dogs-only rule.

'Okay then, we'll keep her. I'll have to let the neighbours know. They'll need to stop feeding her if she's going to be properly ours.'

Maruja seemed surprised when I stopped at the farmhouse to let her know what we'd decided. 'She'll cost a lot to feed if you keep her. And you know what I said about bitches? Dogs have been coming from all over for Luna. Still, it's up to you.'

Tom was delighted. 'That's wonderful news, Liza. She deserves it, she really is a smashing dog.'

By Monday evening the sky was clear once more.

'I hope the rain holds off for tomorrow,' I mused, as I moved around the kitchen picking up the logs and plastic sausages that Anxo had left on the floor. 'It's over a week since I started the raised bed and it's high time I knuckled down to finish it. Crikey, Anxo, you haven't half been busy with your toys.'

'I thought he hid them in his bed,' said Gary.

'He does, yes. But he doesn't usually have this many out in one go. Perhaps it's because Roxa's here.'

Anxo's 'bed' was the small fruit box he'd slept in when he'd first arrived. Lined with a tartan cushion it had been perfect for a two-month-old puppy, but he'd outgrown it within a matter of weeks. By then he'd accumulated all sorts of 'precious things' under the cushion. I hadn't the heart to move them, so the bed-cum-toybox remained.

I took the armful of goodies over to the box and, as I lifted the rather worn cushion, I gasped in surprise.

'Oh, *Anxo*!'

'What?' said Gary anxiously. 'What's he done?'

I dropped the logs and sausages into the box and lifted out the chewed remains of a wooden spoon. I held it up to show Gary.

'Oh, dear,' he grinned.

When our laughter had finally subsided, I shoved the spoon back under the cushion. 'We'll have to tell Tom,' I said.

'Wouldn't it be better not to say anything? There's nothing to be gained by it after all.'

'There is, though, if you think about it. If he's aware of what's happened, he'll know not to leave anything important lying around. I think it's only fair to warn him.'

'Okay,' he nodded. 'Let's hope he sees the funny side.'

Tom's reaction wasn't quite what I'd expected. 'Paul's got loads of wooden spoons, it's not a problem. But I'll say this, Liza, you need to start training him. I've got expensive fishing tackle in the courtyard and if anything happened to it, I'm afraid I'd be disciplining him myself.'

I was too taken aback to answer at first. I was sure Tom hadn't meant to sound threatening, but I felt uncomfortable all the same. If Maud and Ali were in the courtyard and the door was open, how could I possibly deter Anxo from going in? Tom was a good neighbour, and he was also a friend. I didn't want to cause an atmosphere. 'I'll do my best,' I said.

The Scare Dove in the chooks' pen looked wonderful. The wings flapped like billy-o with the slightest gust of wind. Alas, the collared vermin were oblivious. If anything, their number was greater than ever by Tuesday lunchtime; perhaps they were attracted by its spangly silver eyes. It was a rather fetching model and actually *did* bear some resemblance to a bird of prey. Even Gary had been impressed, especially when he'd seen it in all its glory, swinging about in the breeze. It seemed such a pity it had failed to do the job it was built for, and nobody was likely to see it or appreciate its splendour while it was tucked away beneath the trees. I sighed inwardly. Bang went the patent and the fortune; the Scare-Dove was neither use nor ornament after all.

In the afternoon the weather was still fine. I couldn't procrastinate any longer; it was time to start barrowing earth from the far end of the garden down to the raised bed. It would have been far easier to have taken soil from the veg plot, but there were carefully positioned sheets of chicken wire, netting and polythene all over the place. Gary had gone to so much trouble to protect the plantlets and newly sown seeds from birds and other pests, the last thing he needed was a Bigfoot with a barrow rampaging through.

Opposite the chooks' pen was an overgrown area that we hadn't yet got round to using. Shaded for most of the day beneath the canopy of the chestnut tree it wasn't a suitable site to grow veg. Gary had suggested turning it into a shrubbery in the future, but I had other plans. I was secretly nurturing the idea of building a second enclosure and keeping some ducks. I hadn't mentioned it to Gary; I was happy to hang fire until he'd overcome his bugbear about the chickens. In the meantime, it seemed like the perfect place to source my soil. Strictly speaking, of course, I'd be pilfering. The strip of land under the trees wasn't ours. The patch I was about to excavate, along with the space where we'd built the chooks' enclosure, was owned by a woman called Hermitas. It was only a couple of weeks since she'd brought the matter to our attention; we'd assumed, not unreasonably, that it belonged to us. Hermitas was a cheerful, amiable sort of woman. I was sure she wouldn't begrudge us a few barrowloads of soil.

The ground was hard and compacted, and the roots of the chestnut tree spread over most of area only inches beneath the surface. Each time I plunged the shovel in it struck something solid.

It was almost tea-time on Wednesday when I shovelled the last barrowload of soil into the raised bed. My back twinged when I moved, and my arms were aching. What had looked like a straightforward task had turned out to be seriously hard graft. As I rolled a cigarette, I totted up how long I'd spent on the job. The whole project had taken me over nine hours; how I hoped my tomatoes would grow.

On Thursday morning Tom turned up on the doorstep. We hadn't seen him since the confessions-of-a-spoon-stealer incident, and I was beginning to think he'd taken offence.

'I'm going to the ex-pats' get together in Monterroso later. If the goat woman's there, do you want me to get you some cheese?'

I didn't really. Goats' cheese was my favourite, but I'd taken to buying a fresh cheese every week from Maruja in an effort to be neighbourly. It occurred to me that this might be Tom's way of letting us know there were no hard feelings. Under the circumstances I didn't want to rebuff him, I was sure we could manage to scoff an extra lump of cheese.

'Yes please,' I said, 'Hold on, I'll get you some dosh.' I nipped into the kitchen and grabbed a fiver off the telly shelf. 'There you go, are you sure you don't mind?'

'It's no problem, honestly. I thought I'd buy some myself and maybe some ham and *chorizo*. I'm off to Isabel's on Saturday and thought it might be nice to take her a treat.'

As I started to dish up the dinner, I told Gary about Tom's visit.

'It sounds like he's forgiven us then?'

'Oh yes, I think so. He was back to his normal self. I reckon he's got it bad for Isabel, in fact…'

I was interrupted by a knock at the door.

'See who that is, will you?' I said, dolloping a helping of steaming cottage pie onto a plate.

I heard the door open and Gary speaking in the passage.

'Oh, hey up, Tom, Liza said you were going to Monterroso. She's dishing the dinner up, but come in.'

He came back into the kitchen with Tom behind him.

'Hi, Tom,' I said, as I carried the plates over to the marble surface. 'Change of plan?'

'Erm, you could say that.' He was wearing an uncharacteristically grave expression. 'Look, I'll come straight to the point. I need to talk to you both. I know you're about to have dinner, but after what's happened, I felt I should come round straight away.'

A knot was already beginning to form in my stomach. 'It isn't Anxo again, is it? What's he done now?'

'Relax, Liza. This isn't about Anxo, it's about your other dog…'

'But we haven't got… oh, you mean Roxa?' It was early days, and the idea hadn't yet sunk in. 'Sorry, I haven't quite got round to thinking of her as ours, it's all been so sudden, you see.'

'I'm glad to hear that,' he said, looking as if a great weight had just been lifted off his shoulders. 'I want to take her in.'

You could have knocked me down with a feather. I looked across at Gary, who seemed equally stunned.

'This has all come about in the last half hour,' Tom began. 'It's going to sound crazy…'

'Try us,' I said. The news was a bolt from the blue, yet deep down I wasn't disappointed. I realised that circumstances had railroaded me into a decision I hadn't really been ready to make.

'When I locked up The Ox was lying in the lane. I patted her and got on my bike and thought nothing more of it. It wasn't until I looked behind me for traffic as I joined the main road that I realised The Ox was behind me. I stopped, gave her a fuss and told her to *vamos*. When she turned round I set off again. I didn't look round again until I came to Martín. I couldn't believe my eyes; she was still behind me.'

'Good God,' gasped Gary. 'So, you decided to give up and bring her home?'

'No, that's just it, I didn't. At first I wondered if she was expecting me to lead her back to wherever she came from, I just didn't know. I was so sure she'd give up eventually, but once I reached Valdrid, well... I'm absolutely convinced she'd have followed me all the way to Monterroso if I hadn't turned round.'

'Well, I never,' I said. I knew she spent time round at number ten during the day, and that Tom had come to think the world of her. I hadn't realised how strong the bond had grown.

'I know I've got a two-dogs-only policy, but... well, the way Ali's looking I wouldn't be breaking it for much longer...'

I was sure I detected tears welling in his eyes. 'Consider her yours,' I grinned. 'I suppose we'll have to call her The Ox from now on.'

Pink Liza
(4.15pm, BBC 1)

I turn on the telly
At quarter past four,
It's time for Pink Liza –
let's see what's in store...

"This week it's a gadget
That might come in handy,
Look, here's one I've finished –
Now, isn't that dandy?

You'll need a black bin bag,
Some sticks and elastic,
A big empty bottle,
(Just make sure it's plastic).

Some cardboard, some tin foil,
Some scissors and glue,
But please *let your Mum know*
(She might *make one too)."*

I follow each step
As she puts it together.
"Hey presto!" she tells us,
"My, aren't you all clever?"

My Scare Dove looks brilliant,
It swoops and it swings,
Hung up on elastic
With huge flapping wings.

I'll write to the telly,
Tell Liza she's magic:
"Dear Liza, I love
How you make all those gadgets.

I love your companions,
The cat and Alsation,
The cockerel who pecks you
Is such a sensation.

I've watched every programme,
Made every contraption,
And now all my friends
Have got in on the action.

They love your ideas
And the stuff that you've taught 'em,
Yours truly, John Percy,
aged eighty, from Norton.'

Chapter 5

Unexpected Deliveries

I stood on the doorstep at dawn on Saturday morning, breathing deeply as a strong wind from the south-east blew in the bracing smell of manure. Shivering with an inexplicable tingle of excitement, I wondered what the weekend had in store.

It was almost five months since I'd shaken off the shackles of bells and timetables; in theory, Saturdays and Sundays held no particular significance anymore. Gone were the shopping sprees, the minibreaks, the nights out on the town; there were animals, vegetables and everyday household chores to attend to seven days a week. Nonetheless, weekends were something I still looked forward to; here in the *aldea*, the *fin de semana* held an excitement of a very different kind.

On weekdays, there were only seven permanent residents in the village. In addition to us, there were Javier, Maruja, José Manuel, Tonito and Carmen. We could no longer include Tom in that number, he was often away at Isabel's and was likely to be moving out any time soon. All of us went about our business so unobtrusively it was fair to say that the animals made more noise. At weekends, however, everything changed. When Másimo, Solina and Begoña arrived on Friday evenings they brought with them a voluble, hearty, industrious energy which seemed to stir the sleepy village to life. Even Luna and Pastor would be roused from their slumber on the farmhouse doorstep and by late afternoons they'd be installed on the corner, lying in wait.

All weekend we'd hear banging and clanking, raised voices and laughter in the mornings, then the sound of the telly as Solina and Begoña watched soaps in the afternoons. Peace was restored as the daylight faded, but around midnight there would be whistling and singing and the sound of a *bordón* clicking against the shingle, as Másimo weaved his way home from the farmhouse, plied with red wine.

By midmorning the wind had diminished and the barely perceptible floral fragrance of Solina's laundry drifted over on the breeze. With it came Begoña's joyful, resonant cry:

'*Papáa! Papáa!*'

'*Si, mi reina!*' bellowed Masi, from down in the *finca.*

'*Papáa!*'

'*Si!*'

I smiled to myself. It seemed only fitting to join the chorus. 'Coffee, Gary!' I yelled across the lane.

'I've really enjoyed the walks these past two mornings,' I said, as I handed him his coffee. 'It makes such a difference not being jostled and jolted about.'

'It's safer for you, as well,' he nodded. 'I'm surprised how well you've taken it really. I was expecting you to be tearful yesterday.'

'I'd grown fond of Roxa, but I was starting to feel left out, if I'm honest. When she was with us Anxo didn't seem to notice I was there.'

'It's put us back in Tom's good books, that's for certain. Shame about the goats' cheese, but there you go.'

'Don't worry, we'll get some next month. It'll be a treat for Ron and Miranda when they come.'

'I wonder what they'll make of it all. We're very basic. They might be cave-dwellers, but I bet their house is all mod cons.'

We'd become friends with Ron and Miranda while we were living on the island, and we'd shared in their excitement as they'd scoured the Spanish mainland for a cave to convert into a house. Eventually they'd found exactly what they were looking for in a village near Huesca in the province of Granada. It was little more than a grotto full of goat poo, but they'd since transformed it into a beautiful home.

'I *know* they'll adore it here,' I enthused. 'They're very outdoorsy, it'll be right up their street. And as for the house, well, I'm sure they'll find it charming.'

'I reckon you're right,' he nodded. 'Even though it's all higgledy-piggledy and the doors don't fit and...'

'I think they'll appreciate that sort of thing, it gives the house character. Actually, that's something I wanted to run past you. If we're really going to plug the rural charm vibe, I think it'd be fitting to put them in bedroom four.'

'But it hasn't got a ceiling yet, they'd be lying in bed looking up at uralite and rafters.'

I gave him what I hoped was my sweetest smile.

I was peeling potatoes at the low marble sink when the head of a mop bobbed past the window. The frosted glass at the bottom was a constant source of frustration;

determined not to let it stifle my natural curiosity I was forever standing to on tiptoe to peer through the clear panes above.

Intrigued to discover the cause of this most recent phenomenon I dashed through to the passage and opened the back door. The mop was attached to Carmen, who was also carrying a scrunched-up carrier bag.

'*Hola,* Elisa, *buenos días.*'

'*Buenos días,* Carmen,' I replied. I couldn't for the life of me imagine why she'd be taking a mop to the *finca,* what reason could there possibly be? Remembering the bread on the doorstep, I wondered if I might elicit an explanation and peered quizzically at the mop. As far as enlightenment went, today I was out of luck.

'I'm putting the peas in this morning,' she half-whispered. 'Tell Gary today's a good day to put in the peas.'

'Okay,' I nodded. 'Thank you, Carmen, I will.'

I returned to the potatoes and continued to ponder on the riddle of the mop. Perhaps it was in some way connected to the pea-planting? Perhaps she wanted to poke at something high up in the trees? *Surely* she wasn't going to wash the cow poo off the stepping-stones...? No. Even for Carmen that would be taking things a tad too far. However hard I wracked my brain I couldn't conjure up a feasible answer. I resolved to ask Gary when he'd finished faffing about with his measuring tape upstairs.

By the time I'd taken the peelings down to the composter Gary was back in the kitchen. I stuck the kettle on and regaled him with the latest event.

'So,' I said, taking a swig of coffee, 'what do you think?'

'Not a clue,' he mumbled, as he sat scribbling sums in his notebook and frowning. 'You told Paul there was always method in her madness. This time it looks like you're wrong.'

I nodded. I had to concede defeat.

'Right then, on to more important matters.'

As he cleared his throat I sighed inwardly; it was always a bad sign.

'Bedroom four's roughly three times the size of the bathroom, so the wood'll be seventy-five euros at least. Then there's God-knows-how-many nails, a couple of bottles of squirty filler... we'll be looking at a minimum of eighty-five euros...'

'Good,' I nodded, thinking that was very reasonable. 'And obviously I shall need to paint it when you've done.'

'Make that *ninety*-five,' he sighed.

Now that my plans for the fourth bedroom were as good as in progress I could begin to think about the arrival of our visitors. There were places of interest to visit, walks and picnics... it would take some planning and I was keen to get into the swing.

As Gary picked up his measuring tape and made for the doorway, I remembered the peas.

'Oh, I nearly forgot to tell you. Carmen's gone down to the *finca* to put her peas in. Apparently, today's a good day.'

'Too late. It was the first of May on Thursday. I planted ours in the afternoon.'

'No!' I cried, throwing my arms up in mock horror. 'Let's hope you've not been too hasty. Still, Día do an own-brand frozen if all else fails.'

In the afternoon I sat in the garden thumbing through Galicia travel guides and jotting down ideas. The wealth of attractions the region affords amazed me: coastal and river beaches, natural forests, nature reserves, vineyards, cathedrals, monasteries... we could have entertained our visitors for at least month. However, there was Anxo to consider. We had to establish a sensible radius so that he wouldn't be left on his own for too long. Up until now, he hadn't been home alone for much more than three hours. I settled on six hours as the maximum time we could spend away from the house.

I lit a cigarette and was scanning my list of potential outings when suddenly there was a loud thud as something landed on the threshing floor close to my feet. It was a pig's trotter, with a good six inches of wet, greyish-white leg still attached. I looked up in astonishment. A barrel-shaped man of diminutive stature was peering over the gate.

'Másimo!' I grinned. '*Qué pasa*?'

'*Hola*, Elisa!' He gave a hearty rasping chuckle, causing his ample paunch to shake. 'That surprised you! It's for Anxo, it's a pig's foot.'

'Lovely,' I lied. 'I'll call him. He'll be under the chestnut tree watching the hens. Anxo!'

Anxo was delighted. He grabbed his prize and carried it proudly over to the shade of the fig tree where he lay down and began to gnaw.

'You can have this as well,' he continued, dangling a bulging carrier bag over the gate.

'Thank you,' I said.

Whatever was inside the bag was heavy. It also had a rather unpleasant smell. Steeling myself I parted the handles. As I stared at the rolled-up blanket of blubber I felt my stomach lurch.

'Pig fat,' said Masi. 'It's for the chickens. You don't have to cook it, just cut it up into pieces and scatter it on the ground.'

'Lovely,' I lied again.

'It's not staying in here,' frowned Gary, when I took it into the barn to show him. 'God, it's disgusting. I'm glad *I'm* not a chicken. Are you s'posed to cook it?'

'Don't be daft. Apparently, I've to cut it into pieces and throw it down.'

'Do you think the chooks will eat it?'

'I've absolutely no idea, and we're not going to find out.'

'Why not? It might keep the price of the food down.'

'Trust you. I'm going to toss it in the wheelie bin. I don't want raw flesh lying about in the chooks' pen, it might entice foxes, not to mention rats.'

'Crikey, I hadn't thought of that. You're right. Take it straight away then. I don't want the bloody stuff in here.'

'Are you nipping to the woodyard on your way back from shopping?' I asked Gary on Monday morning.

'Don't be silly. I can't clad a ceiling with planks. You *know* the place at Monterroso doesn't sell tongue and groove. *Honestly.*'

'Of course. Sorry, I'd forgotten. You went to Monterroso for the floor in the terrace. The bathroom floor and ceiling came from Lalín. Crikey, it's only three weeks since you finished the bathroom, it feels as though it was months ago.'

'I know what you mean,' he nodded. 'It's been one job after another really. Still, once bedroom four's got a ceiling the inside of the house will be more or less done.'

Strictly speaking, this wasn't true. When Gary referred to 'the inside of the house' he actually meant the living quarters; apart from the kitchen, pantry and entrance passage, our entire ground floor consisted of animal pens. The floors were loose earth, the walls were bare stone and there were rows of standing stones to section off separate areas for cattle and calves. The pens were exactly as they were when the house was built around two hundred years ago. Short of an enormous lottery win, that was the way they were going to stay.

'That's great news. It means there'll be nothing but the garden to work on over summer.'

'Not quite. I've been thinking about pointing the outside of the house.'

'*Really?*'

'Oh, aren't you keen?'

'God, yes, of *course* I am. How many times have I admired Masi and Solina's, and the ones along the roadside on the way to Monterroso? I know you've mentioned it, but it's such a big job, I s'pose I never quite believed you'd get it done.'

'It *is* a big job that's for certain, but it'll be ongoing, that's the beauty of it, you see? It's not as if I'll have to plough on, day in, day out, until I've finished. I can do it a bit at a time, whenever the mood takes me or when I've got nothing else on.'

'It sounds like you're looking forward to it, anyway. It'll be like a new hobby for you in a way. Will it be expensive?'

'Not really. *Mortero*'s only a couple of euros a bag, so...' He paused, as if doing a mental calculation. 'Good God! It's unbelievable! Do you realise, to point the whole house will work out cheaper than doing the ceiling in bedroom four?'

The *magnum opus* was scheduled to begin on Wednesday morning. It wasn't going to be a straightforward job. The ceiling boasted three chunky oak beams and somehow the cladding would need to be fitted up against them. As if the beams weren't enough of a hindrance, there were also the walls to contend with. In the other upstairs rooms, the walls had been rendered with mortar to give a flat though pockmarked surface, but in the fourth bedroom they'd been daubed thinly, leaving the bumpy outline of the stones. The overall effect was attractive but when it came to getting the cladding flush against them Gary wouldn't have a prayer. The job would have been a challenge even for an accomplished carpenter with bags of know-how and a box of state-of-the-art tools. Gary, of course, had neither. He was, by his own admission a bodger, and his tools were basic to say the least. Imagination, optimism and a handsaw he'd bought for two euros were the only credentials he'd be bringing to the job.

By now I'd lived through many of Gary's do-it-yourself endeavours, and it wasn't without good reason that I was feeling on edge. I had every confidence in his workmanship, but the risk of what would happen in the process filled me with dread. After coffee break, I rolled a second cigarette and braced myself as Gary ascended the stairs for his latest foray into the land of DIY.

Two hours later, I placed a plate of chilli and rice on the marble surface, stood at the bottom of the stairs and shouted: 'Lunch!'

The man who walked into the kitchen was a stranger. There was no perspiration, no knitted brow, no sighing. I eyed him warily for a moment before finally plucking up the courage to ask:

'How's it going?'

'Good. I've about finished the level half. I'll be starting the sloping bit after lunch.'

The prettiest characteristic of bedroom four was its quaint sloping ceiling. I could stand at full height in the middle of the room, but at the window my head would be close to the ceiling if I knelt down.

'Can I look?'

'Go for it. I think you'll be pleased.'

The work was perfect. Where the walls met the ceiling the gaps between the cladding and the stones were almost imperceptible. This was one project that was going to run smoothly after all.

By three o'clock I thought Gary deserved a coffee. While I'd been pottering about in the garden, the poor devil had been cooped up indoors.

'Do you want a brew?' I shouted up the staircase. When there was no answer, I shouted again. I went back into the kitchen and rolled a cigarette expecting that, at any moment, Gary would come through the door. Eventually I supposed he hadn't heard me. I set off up the stairs and heard a loud bang from the far end of the house. As I walked through the dining room my worst fears were confirmed.

'For fuck's sake!'

'Are you alright, Gary?' I paused momentarily, wondering whether it was safe to go and see.

'Fucking beams!'

Cowardice got the better of me. 'I've made you a brew,' I called, before doing a U-turn and heading back downstairs.

This time it was the Gary I knew that came into the kitchen. He was ruddy-faced and glaring, and I noticed a trickle of blood congealing just above his brow.

'You're bleeding,' I said, stating the obvious.

'Fucking beams.'

I'd spent most of Thursday weeding the garden; it had made sense to put plenty of distance between myself and bedroom four. By mid-afternoon my knees were aching; I was more than ready for a fag and a brew. As I crossed the threshing floor the backdoor opened, and Gary appeared on the doorstep. He was grubby and perspiring, but his colour was normal. Moreover, he was smiling and holding a beer.

'That's more like it,' I grinned. 'I take it all problems have been resolved?'

'I'm not sure about *that*,' he chuckled. 'I won't know until *you've* seen it. However long I spend I won't get it perfect, but if you're satisfied then I reckon it's done.'

At first glance the ceiling looked super, it was only when my attention shifted to the beams that I could see the flaws. There were intermittent gaps on both sides of the beam that ran across the centre; in a couple of places they were a good two centimetres wide. I thought about Gary: his blood pressure and the gash on his forehead. I thought about my nicotine intake and my nerves.

'What do you think?' said the voice behind me.

'I like it,' I nodded. In the interests of health and safety, it would have to do.

Tom came back from Isabel's late on Friday afternoon. The Ox looked fantastic, groomed to perfection and closer to her fighting weight. Ali, on the other hand, looked thin and fragile. It would take more than the warmth and comfort of Isabel's apartment to ring the changes. Nothing short of a miracle would save Ali now.

During his sojourn Tom seemed to have forgotten Anxo's misdemeanour. I told him about the trotter and the pig fat, and it made him smile.

'Funnily enough, that's something I wanted to ask you about, Liza.'

'Pig fat? I'm not sure I can be of much help…'

'No,' he chuckled. 'Not pig fat. Unexpected deliveries. Someone's left a bunch of plastic roses in Paul's barn. I wondered if it was you or Gary.'

'Plastic roses?' frowned Gary, 'Not me, mate.'

'Nor me,' I said.

'I doubt they'd have come from Másimo and Solina,' Gary added. 'They've only ever given us stuff to eat. Ah, hold on a minute, I think I can guess who's left them…'

'So can I,' I grinned.

Tom looked pensive for a moment. Then the penny dropped. 'Carmen! Of course! I wonder what she thought I'd want with plastic flowers. Paul's got loads of them. He's stuck them all around the courtyard. They're not only ugly they're a pain in the arse.'

'Perhaps she thought you'd find them useful,' I mused.

'Very funny.'

'No, I meant it. She's used a bunch to block up the hole in the upstairs window. You can see them from the lane.'

'True,' Tom nodded.

'I've seen her carrying some on her way to the *finca*,' added Gary, 'flapping them about to ward off the flies.'

'There you go, then.' I grinned. 'In Carmen's eyes they're very versatile. You should be feeling honoured if you ask me.'

On Saturday morning I was ready to paint the new ceiling and I was delegating the role of coffee maker to Gary for a change.

'I'll see you at break then,' I said, as I picked up the paint bucket and brush. 'And beware of pot-bellied men bearing gifts.'

For the next two hours I worked like a Trojan. When Gary finally called me, I was gasping for a fag and a brew.

'You'll never guess what Carmen was carrying down to the *finca*?' he said, as he handed me my coffee.

'The mop again, I suppose.'

'No, you're not even close.'

'So tell me.'

'No, you have to guess. I'll give you a clue: think of something completely weird.'

'A chair?'

'*That's* not weird,'

'Of course it is. I can't think of anyone else who'd carry a chair over to their allotment.'

'Lots of gardeners had chairs at their allotments in England. Try again, think totally bizarre.'

'Oh, *I* don't know,' I frowned. 'An encyclopaedia.'

'Now you're being silly.'

'But you said... okay, a pillow? A saucepan? A llama?'

'A *llama*?'

'I'm getting frustrated. I said the first thing that came into my head.'

'Okay, I'll tell you... Oh, *actually*, a llama's closer than a saucepan and come to think of it, so's a pillow...'

'*Gary*!'

'A duck.'

'You're having a laugh.'

'I'm not. I was coming back down the garden when she went past. She was carrying it under her arm.'

'Ah, so you were some distance away. That's it then, you must've been mistaken. It might have *looked* like a duck...'

'Liza, it *looked* like a duck because it *was* a duck. At first I wondered if I was seeing things, but I could hardly follow her to find out. Instead, I nipped across the lawn and waited under the apple tree hoping she'd turn onto the track, so I'd get a better look. Two minutes later she came walking by, I could see it clearly *and* I could hear her talking to it. It was most *definitely* a duck.'

'I'd love to sneak down there and see what she's done with it. No rest for the wicked though, the paintbrush awaits.'

By lunchtime the ceiling was finished.

'You had enough paint then?' asked Gary, as I stood at the sink washing the brush.

'Only just. I've emptied the bucket. I thought we could give it a good swilling and use it for apples in the autumn.'

'Good thinking. So, are you pleased with it?'

'I am, actually. You'll have to nip up and see what you think. I tell you what though, the paint's given me a rotten headache. I could do with a walk round the garden to get some fresh air.'

Out in the garden, Scholes lay dozing in the herb bed, while Anxo dug fervently under the fig tree, unearthing his trotter again. I wandered along the side of the fence and went through the gate into the *huerta*. Closing it behind me I cast my eyes over the montage of neatly turned soil and netting, So far there didn't seem to be any sign of the peas. I still harboured doubts about Gary's timing, perhaps there *was* a case for planting by the moon? Suddenly a movement under the bramble caught my attention. I stood still and waited. There it was again. I edged forwards hoping to discover what had caused the disturbance. I gasped in surprise as the reason became clear.

'Gary! Are you in the barn?'

'Yes, what's up?'

'There's a duck in the veg plot!'

'A what?'

'A duck!'

'Are you winding me up?'

'No, I'm deadly serious. It must be Carmen's; it's got a length of blue twine tied to one of its legs.'

Footsteps thudded across the wooden boards and the barn door creaked open.

'Where?' He stared hard at the *huerta*. '*I* can't bloody see it.' He started to walk across the garden.

'There look, by the brambles. Oh… well it *was* by the brambles. Look, *there*, where you've stuck twigs in, you can't miss it…'

'The peas!' shouted Gary, 'those twigs are markers! It's where I've put the peas!'

I'd been looking in the wrong place completely, Between the twigs a row of tiny green shoots were poking up above the ground.

As Gary dashed up the garden I strode over and shooed the duck back in the direction it had come from.

'Where is it?' he panted, as he practically threw himself through the gate.

'Calm down,' I said. 'Look, it's back by the bramble. You'll give yourself a heart attack one of these days.'

'Well it can't stay here. You'll have to catch it.'

'*I'll* have to catch it?' I remembered the not-so-happy hour we'd spent trying to catch the hens back in February, I thought again of Gary's blood pressure, He was right, it was definitely a job for *me*.

Unlike our chickens, Carmen's birds were accustomed to being herded. Most afternoons she'd usher them out of the animal pen, through the kitchen and out into the garden to forage amongst the weeds.

'Stand back,' I said dramatically, as I rolled up my sleeves in mock determination. As I weaved my way slowly across the veg plot the duck waddled towards me and squatted compliantly as I bent to pick her up.

'Unbelievable,' said Gary.

'Here,' I said. 'Undo the twine while I'm holding her. I don't like to think of her being tied up.'

The nylon loosened easily and in seconds the leg was free.

'Thanks. I'd better take her back before Anxo catches on.' I looked over to the fig tree. 'Actually, you wouldn't pop him in the house for a minute, would you? I'd hate to return it without its head.'

With Anxo safely deposited in the kitchen, I grasped the duck firmly and hurried across the garden. I hesitated a moment when I reached the threshing floor. Perhaps

Carmen was back in her garden by now? I strode over to the herb bed and called through the foliage. There was no sign of her. I'd have to trudge down to the *finca* after all.

Carmen appeared from round the corner of the barn as the gate clanged shut behind me. Her face lit up when she saw what I had in my hands.

'Elisa, you've found it! I thought the fox had taken it! I didn't think I'd see it again!'

'She was in our *huerta*,' I told her.

'In the *huerta*?' She looked surprised.

'Yes. She couldn't have climbed up; she must have flown.'

'Yes,' she half-whispered. 'It must have flown.'

I passed the duck over when she reached me. 'I've taken the string off, it's dangerous. It could get tangled in bramble. If a fox came, she wouldn't be able to escape.'

Towards evening, dark clouds were amassing above the horizon. The air was hot and humid, and the wind was blowing from the south, bringing with it an ominously humid heat.

'I'm taking Anxo,' I told Gary. 'There's a storm brewing and I reckon there's thunder on the way. That was probably the cause of my headache, I bet it wasn't the paint after all.'

We'd only been out half an hour when the lightning crackled, and the distant rumble of thunder drove us homeward; I wasn't braving Nature's sound and light show from the middle of an open field.

The emulsion bucket clattered, upturned, on the doorstep. It'd be up in the woodlands by morning if I didn't shift it into the barn. I picked it up and was surprised to find a winebox beneath it. I was even more surprised to find that the winebox was full.

'Look!' I announced, as I walked into the kitchen. 'This was on the doorstep.'

'A winebox? Stick it in the recycling. It must have blown in with the wind.'

'Blown in with the wind? No wonder you didn't get O level Maths. A full wine box is carried on the wind and is fortuitously deposited beneath a bucket at the exact moment the said wind lifts the said bucket off the step. On the scale of probability your hypothesis ranks pretty low, if you ask me.'

'You didn't say it was under the bucket. You definitely didn't say it was *full*. Go on then, Einstein, what's *your* hypothesis?'

'It's from Carmen. It's a thank you for finding the duck.'

Liza Grantham

Whodunnit?

There are bags in the treetops,
A duck in the veg,
There are clothes in the field
And a mop in the hedge,

The barn door's left open
Like someone's been spying,
They've left plastic roses
That look like they're dying.

There's bread on a doorstep
And wine in a bucket
The sickle's gone missing –
Perhaps someone took it?

In Másimo's garden
Somebody's been snooping:
Those footprints are new,
And the fence is all drooping.

There's a road sign that warns
'No Right Turn' in the garden,
There's only one culprit,
It has to be Carmen!

Chapter 6

Seeds of Doubt

The storm had finally subsided when I awoke on Sunday morning. I yawned, rolled over and snuggled deeper down in the bed. The thunder had kept me awake well into the early hours; some extra shuteye would be welcome today. Determined to deny me this smallest of comforts, Scholes leapt off the bed, wailed, and leapt back on again. Gary snored on regardless as I roused myself to dance attention on the wilful feline; alas, there would be no lie-in for *me*.

Outside the air felt fresh and welcoming; on reflection I was pleased I hadn't lingered in bed. This morning Scholes padded along beside me as I went down to let the chooks out; the doves fluttered up and away as soon as we approached the run. I still hadn't plucked up the courage to abandon the rooster-proof trousers, but I'd have to bite the bullet sooner or later; I'd sworn to myself they'd be gone before June.

Rufo strutted and postured in an effort to seduce his wives away from the feeder. Alas, they didn't share his ardent libido; breakfast was definitely priority number one. The sound of Scholes sharpening his claws on the chestnut tree drew my attention away from the impromptu floorshow. It was only when I turned to resume my viewing that I realised the doves hadn't returned. The chooks had never paid any attention to Scholes and up to now I hadn't considered his potential. I couldn't wait to tell Gary; I'd found my dove deterrent at last.

'Scholes the Scare Dove,' chuckled Gary, as we went out to the bench with our coffees. 'It's a pity we can't shut him in there. What did you do with Carmen's blue twine?'

'Gary! That's not funny! I'll tell him. He'll probably bite you and it'd serve you right.'

At that moment Scholes slunk out from under the barn door.

We both erupted into laughter, it seemed for all the world as if he'd heard.

'Scholes…' I began.

'No!' Gary protested. 'Don't listen, son.'

We sat there in hysterics, and Scholes walked away. We were still grinning like idiots when Tom came past with The Ox. The frown he was wearing suggested he was feeling annoyed.

'Morning Tom,' said Gary.

I nodded my greeting. I knew that if I tried to speak, I'd only erupt again.

'Morning,' said Tom. 'You two look happy.'

'*You* don't,' said Gary.

'No, he doesn't,' I agreed, regaining my composure. 'What's up, Tom?'

'Maud,' he frowned. 'She went home before we'd even got to the *río*. She was there one minute, the next she was gone.'

'We didn't see her come past,' said Gary. 'We've been out here a good ten minutes now.'

'You won't have, then. It was over half an hour ago. I wasn't prepared to go after her, The Ox needed walking. The courtyard door's open, she'll be fine.'

'Is it because of The Ox that she legged it?' I asked.

'No. She's been doing it on and off for a while now, long before The Ox came. It's since Ali's been poorly. Maud thinks it's okay for her to miss the walk as well.'

'They must be really close if Maud doesn't want to leave her.'

'I don't think it's that,' said Tom, wryly. 'Maud's crafty. Some days she just doesn't fancy it, she's getting lazy in her old age.'

'You could put her on a lead,' I suggested. 'Like we do with Anxo, just 'til you get to the field.'

'I don't think I've got one. My dogs haven't been on a lead in years.'

'We've got some blue twine,' grinned Gary.

'*Pardon*?'

'Ignore him, Tom, he's joking. It's something that happened yesterday. Carmen had her duck on the *finca* tied up with blue twine.'

For the next ten minutes we regaled Tom with our latest adventure, each of us vying to report the best bits like a pair of overgrown kids.

'I must say, I'm hurt,' said Tom, feigning indignation. 'You pair get a winebox, of all things, and *I* get plastic flowers.'

'Quite right too,' I chuckled. 'It's all you deserve under the circumstances. *We* don't run round the village naked and hold discos on the back lawn.'

'Hey, that was *Paul*.'

'Guilty by association,' I grinned.

'Seriously, though,' he said, 'there are times when I feel quite concerned about Carmen. I'd hate to see her come to any harm. Take last night, for instance, before the downpour. She was dragging an old fridge door across Paul's garden…'

'Across *Paul's* garden?' I interrupted. 'I don't understand.'

'Well, you know she's got that little forest behind the village?'

I thought hard. There were little forests all over the place, it was a pity they didn't have names.

'*I* know it,' said Gary. He turned to me. 'It's full of young oak trees. It's off the track that runs level with the Fonfría road. Part of it borders the far end of Paul's land.'

'Ah yes,' I nodded. I pictured the stretch he was describing. The patch of woodland was probably no more than fifty metres from the end of Carmen's garden, but to get to it she would have had to walk up to the farmhouse, through a cluster of outbuildings, then continue for a further couple of hundred metres along the track. The alternative was to nip across Paul's garden and straight through a gap in the tumbledown wall.

'*Now* I'm with you; she was using Paul's as a shortcut. Sorry, carry on.'

'Right. So, she was dragging this door – it couldn't have been easy, mind, there are clumps of grass and roots and stones all over the place. Anyway, she was heaving and tugging for all she was worth. By now the sky was full of black clouds and it was obvious it was going to chuck it down at any minute, why couldn't she have waited 'til morning? Well, she was nearly at the threshing floor when it started coming down in stair rods. Instead of leaving it there and dashing to her back door she soldiered on as if her life depended on it. She looked like a drowned rat by the time she'd done.'

'I wonder what she did with it,' mused Gary.

'*Did* with it?'

'Yes, once she'd got it inside.'

'She didn't take it in the house. She didn't leave it under the overhang. She didn't even stand it up. She left it lying flat out in the open; it's still there now, full of rainwater.'

After lunch I decided it was time for another visit to the herb bed. Unlike Tom, I was still convinced that there was a rationale, however idiosyncratic, behind most of Carmen's curious goings-on. With this in mind I was determined to shed some light on the intriguing adventures of Little Black Welly-Boots and the Fridge Door.

I peered through the gap in the wall. There was no sign of Carmen, but I could make out the sound of splashing further along the garden where the trees were dense. I glanced over to the raised bed and smiled to myself. Regardless of whether it would prove a good site for tomatoes, it would certainly make a great vantage point for now.

The fridge door was just as Tom had described it, lying flat on the ground, with its moulded compartments filled up with rain. The duck waddled about, indifferent to the paddling pool and the effort taken to install it. Eventually Carmen picked up her ungrateful charge and plonked it into the water. The duck quacked a protest and clambered out again.

'I think it's high time Scholes had a cat flap,' I announced, as I handed Gary the shopping list and his cuppa on Monday morning.

'A cat flap? What for?'

'Because it'd make life easier. For us *and* for him. It was different when we first moved here; he only went out under supervision. He's been a free spirit for months now, he should be able to come and go when he likes.'

'But he already does. We open the door every time he sits there wailing, I don't see what difference it'd make.'

I could see that I'd have to work harder to convince him. 'It'd save money for a start.'

'Ah, now you're talking. How?'

'We'd be able to get rid of the cat trays. We'd save a fortune in litter over time.'

'But we'd have the cost of the cat flap, remember.'

'Ah, but we wouldn't. We can give him a cat flap without a flap. Come on, I'll show you.'

He followed me through the entrance passage, and I opened the door to the stairs. On one side of the staircase was a stone wall, on the other a partition of chestnut planks.

'There,' I said, pointing to the bottom step. 'If you cut a six-inch square in the partition, it'll make the perfect Scholes-size door. He can go round to the back lane, under the door into the animal pen, straight through to the pantry and up the stairs. No screws, no nails... I bet it'd be a ten-minute job.'

'And you're sure he'd use it?'

'If you do it before you go shopping, I'll have him trained by the end of the afternoon.'

Back in the kitchen I rolled a cigarette while Gary peered at the shopping list. I said a silent prayer and held my breath.

'Chooks' food? You've got to be *joking*!'

'I'm not. There's enough for tomorrow and Wednesday, and then we're clean out.'

'Well that's ridiculous! Do you realise what these eggs are costing us? You're obviously giving them too much.'

Nothing good lasts forever. The old record had stuck again.

'It's not the chooks, Gary, it's the collared doves. You've seen them down there. They eat like gannets. That's the *real* reason I was making the deterrent. I didn't tell you 'cos I knew you'd kick off.'

'You should have said something sooner, I'm sure I'd have been able to come up with an idea. Now you've told me I'll have a think about it.'

'Thank you.'

'There you go, I didn't kick off after all.'

'It's only soup and crusty bread for lunch,' I told Gary as he unloaded the last of the shopping. 'I've been working on something while you were out.'

'Soup and bread's fine, don't worry. Working on something, hey? No doubt you're about to fill me in.'

'I'll do better than that, I'll show you. Come upstairs.'

Gary looked mystified as he followed me up to the living room. I took a scrunched-up bag of cat treats out of my pocket and opened the window wide.

'Right,' I said. 'Where's Scholes?'

He stared out for a moment. 'There, look, he's having a wash under the broom.'

'*Scholes*!' I called, rustling the packet at arm's length out of the window.

Gary hated my screechy cat voice. He pulled a face.

'*Scholes*!'

Scholes looked up. I rustled the packet again. He dashed across the threshing floor, through the bars of the gate, along the lane and disappeared around the corner.

'Come on,' I whispered. I ushered him over to the top of the stairs. 'Watch!'

Within seconds Scholes appeared through the cat hole.

'That's amazing! I'm seriously impressed.'

'I'm glad about that,' I smiled, 'because after lunch, it's *your* turn to impress *me*.'

'I don't really understand what you want me to show you,' frowned Gary, as we wandered down to the veg plot for my guided tour. 'I only put the seeds in a week ago, I don't know what you're expecting to see.'

'Actually, it's almost *three* weeks. Anyway, it's not so much about seeing, it's about *knowing*. If there hadn't been a duck on the rampage, I wouldn't have known the peas were sprouting. I realised how little I knew about what was happening in the *huerta*. I want to be more involved.'

'But you *are* involved. You've done the herb garden and the raised bed for the tomatoes, and I know you've got plans for rockeries and borders…'

'Yes, but I'm talking about in *here*, about the veg crop…'

'But you'll be involved when it's harvested. You can jam and freeze and pickle to your heart's content.' His voice held the merest hint of desperation. I could twig the reason; he didn't want me to tread on his toes.

'Don't worry,' I grinned. 'I'm not suggesting I want to start working with you, Gary. We both know it'd end in tears. I just want you to show me where you've planted the different seeds. That way I can come and stare at it and share the excitement when everything starts to pop up.'

As we paced around the *huerta* Gary pointed to the different sheets of mesh and polythene and told me what he'd sown underneath. I clutched his arm suddenly when we came to the peas.

'Gary!'

'Steady on, don't *do* that! What's wrong?'

'The peas! There were more than that on Saturday. Look, there are gaps in the rows. Loads of the shoots have disappeared.'

'Good God, you're right. Something must have eaten them. I bet it's the slugs and snails.'

'I don't think so. I reckon it's the blackbirds. They're always hopping about all over the place, pecking at the ground. Never mind, you can still put some more in.'

'I can't. I've used them all. We'll have to make do with these I s'pose.'

The tour over, we walked back across the garden. Anxo was lying with his 'precious things' under the broom. There were pieces of wood, a punctured ball, a plastic sausage and...

'Oh my God!' I gasped. 'Where the heck has he had *those* from?'

'What?' asked Gary. 'What have you seen?'

'There, look. Plastic flowers. It looks like he's been thieving again. What if they're the ones that were left in Paul's barn?'

'Shit. We'd better not let Tom know. The last thing we want to do is give him ammunition. Here, shove them inside your coat.'

'I bloody well won't! I'm not going to skulk about like some kind of fugitive. There's no *proof* that he's nicked them, he could have had them from anywhere. Carmen might have given them to him, they could have fallen out of the wheelie bin... there are dozens of possibilities... Oh, my God!'

'*Now* what?'

'Give 'em here.' I tucked them hastily inside my jacket.

'But you just said you weren't...'

'Listen. Remember what Tom said about Paul's courtyard? He was moaning about there being plastic flowers everywhere. I bet *that's* where they've come from. First the spoon, now these. Oh Anxo, whatever shall we do?'

On Tuesday morning the sun was shining, and the wind was gusting in from the north. I hadn't planned on doing the laundry but, without a washing machine or a tumble dryer, days like these were a godsend; it was only a matter of time before it rained again.

I was pegging the sheets out when, without warning, Carmen's pear tree started to sway. The motion was regular and rhythmic, there was no way it could have been caused by the wind. With clothes pegs still clenched between my teeth I hurried over to the herb bed. The answer soon became clear. Carmen was half-way up the tree going ten to the dozen with a bow saw. The tableau looked more than a little precarious; wellies weren't really the best footwear for climbing trees. I took the pegs from my mouth and dashed across the garden.

'Gary, have you got a minute?' I whispered as I reached the barn door. Through the chestnut slats I could see him sketching something on a torn-off piece of feed sack. He covered it hastily when I pulled the door open and walked in.

'What are you drawing?'

'Nothing.'

'Well you're obviously drawing *some*thing.'

'Okay, I am, but I'm not going to show you. It's the blueprint for a seriously ingenious invention. You'll have to wait 'til it's finished. It'll be a surprise.'

I wasn't at all sure I wanted surprising. Still, if it kept him quiet, I supposed I didn't mind.

'What did you want, anyway, is it time for my brew?'

'It most certainly isn't. I'm still pegging out and it's only half an hour since the last one. It's Carmen. She's up in the pear tree and it all looks very dangerous. She seems to be trying to saw a branch off and I'm scared she might fall. Will you go round and give her a hand?'

'I think I'd better by the sound of it. Do you want to come?'

'Better not, I *must* get the rest of the laundry out. I'm sure you'll be fine.'

While Gary walked up to Carmen's, I settled myself back in the herb bed. The pegging could wait until later, this was certain to be good fun. I peered through the gap between the standing stones. Carmen had ditched the bow saw and was leaning for all she was worth on the branch while Gary stared up at the tree.

'Do you want me to finish sawing the branch off, Carmen?'

'No. I've finished sawing. No more sawing. It's done.'

'I don't think you'll be able to break it off like that, Carmen. Come down and let me have a go. I'm heavier and I might be able to do it. Come down and I'll climb up and see.'

Carmen climbed down reluctantly. 'I want to keep the branch,' she told him earnestly. 'You mustn't break it; it has to bend.'

'Bend?' he repeated.

'Yes, I want to bend it. Look...' She tugged at his sleeve and led him through the bushes to the end of the garden. 'There,' she said, pointing to a tree that was hanging over into ours. I'd assumed it was dead until it had exploded into pink blossom. Now we were waiting to see what fruits it would bear.

'Like that one. Like that one there.'

She ushered Gary back towards the pear tree and showed him which way she wanted it to bend.

Now it all made perfect sense. The tree was shaded by elders. If the branch was re-routed, its fruit would flourish and ripen in the sun.

Gary climbed nimbly into the tree and found a foothold where the trunk diverged. I turned away as he began to lean hard on the branch. Seconds later there was a terrible creaking and the half-severed limb moved slowly towards the ground.

'*Muy bien*,' smiled Carmen. '*Muy bien*.'

'Did you pack my paints when we left the island?' asked Gary, when he surfaced on Wednesday morning.

'Of course I did, they were from El Corte Inglés, They were bloody expensive as I remember. I'd hardly throw them away.'

'I didn't mean the oils and the water colours. I meant the acrylic stuff, you know, the ones that I bought from the shit shop in squirty tubes.'

Gary had spent a lot of time painting when we lived on the island. Since we'd come to Galicia, he'd sworn that the muse had left him and his days as a budding artist were gone. It was a pity really: he'd done some decent pictures; I'd be ever so chuffed for him if his muse had finally returned.

'I'll fetch them down for you after I've walked Anxo. I don't want you ferreting about up there, I know exactly where everything is.'

At breaktime Gary sat down to a brew and a shoebox.

'There you go,' I said triumphantly as he lifted the lid.

'Thanks. Oh, there's more here than I was expecting. Let's have a look, I'll definitely want yellow and red.'

'Are you going to share with us, Michelangelo?'

'I've already told you, it's a surprise.'

'Oh, I see. It's to do with whatever you were doodling yesterday. And there was me thinking you were going to do clouds and cherubs on the ceiling of the barn.'

'Very funny. Anyway, what's this about doodling? I've told you, *that* was the blueprint for a seriously ingenious creation. You won't have to wait much longer. Just steel yourself, you'll be amazed.'

'What news of the "seriously ingenious creation", then?'
I grinned when Gary came in at lunchtime.

'It's finished, but the paint's not quite dry yet. You
can go and have a look though. I've put it out there on
the bench.'

Outside the back door was an orange cat with large
green eyes. It actually *was* rather ingenious, I had to
admit. It was constructed entirely of bits from the
woodstore. The body was a chunky bough which had
been cleverly sawn at the end to form the shape of a
head. The legs and tail were sections of thinner branches
fixed at such an angle that the cat appeared to be ready
to pounce.

'It's *brilliant*!' I enthused, as I came back into the
kitchen. 'As soon as the paint's dry I'll take it down to
the pen.'

'I don't know what Scholes'll make of it,' smiled
Gary. 'I hope he doesn't take offence.'

Next morning, I wavered between apprehension and
excitement as I set off down to the chooks' pen. I so
wanted the dove deterrent to be effective, but deep down
I knew that the chances were slim. As I neared the end of
the garden there was nothing but stillness. I peered
through the chicken wire and then up into the tree-tops;
there wasn't a single dove in sight. Of course, it was far
too soon to feel triumphant, I wouldn't *really* be able to
call it a victory until I'd topped up the feeder and let out
the hens.

I hovered for a while in a state of nervous
anticipation. After ten minutes it seemed safe to assume
that our guests weren't going to show. It had been a shot
in the dark, but Gary had achieved the impossible; *his*
surprisingly ingenious Scare Dove was a roaring
success. I was about to make my way back towards the

garden when something on top of the henhouse caught my eye. I turned and watched as a pale ginger shape disappeared over the fence and into the bracken beyond. Alas, the celebrations were on hold for now.

In the entrance passage I unzipped my fleece and reached for the drawstring of the rooster-proof trousers. I couldn't feel it, surely it wasn't inside the waist band again? I looked down at my waist and started to giggle. There *were* no waterproof trousers. In all the excitement of the dove deterrent I'd forgotten to put them on.

'Well?' said Gary. 'What news of the Scare Dove?'

'I'm not sure.'

'Not sure? Either the doves were there, or they weren't.'

'They weren't.'

'So it works then.'

'I can't say. Scholes was in there. It might have been...'

'Whoa! Hold on a minute, Scholes *can't* have been there. I've only just left him. He's lying on the bed.'

'But that's impossible! He didn't come back in with me. Mind you, now I come to think of it I don't remember letting him out either. I can't see how...'

'The cat flap.'

'The cat flap! Of *course*! Do you know, I'd completely forgotten about it. Well, bugger me. Perhaps I should go into business.'

'You've lost me.'

'Animal trainer extraordinaire. I've taught Scholes to use the cat flap to a high level of speed and efficiency and I've corrected the aberrant behaviour of a cockerel who was as good as on death row.'

'What about the doves, then?'

'That's all in the hands of a surprisingly ingenious inventor. Let's just say the jury's still out for now.'

On Friday morning the doves had returned with a vengeance. When Gary got up, I'd have to give him the bad news. I glanced over to his wooden cat. It wasn't lifelike, but it was certainly eye catching: I had to admit he'd done a really good job. I turned to admire my own creation, jiggling on its elastic and fluttering when the breeze lifted its wings. We'd both worked so hard on our Scare Doves, I couldn't believe they'd been such a flop. It was then that a glimmer of hope stirred within me: the Scare Doves might be put to some purpose after all. I looked through the chicken wire, over into to the veg plot, where a pair of blackbirds were busy doing their rounds. Just because our creations hadn't thwarted a posse of puffed-up pigeons didn't mean they wouldn't work wonders with the smaller birds.

'I've moved the Scare Doves into the *huerta*,' I announced when Gary came into the kitchen. 'They might keep the birds off the seeds.'

'Fear not,' he grinned. 'I've had a premonition. Roll yourself a fag and I'll tell you my dream.'

In the dream, Gary had sown his seeds in the *huerta* and within days all the veg had started to grow. The marrow plant seemed to be bigger and stronger than everything else he'd planted, and eventually it took over the garden and all the other veg died. He wasn't disappointed because the marrows were enormous and there were hundreds of them. He was handing them out around the village so that none of the neighbours would starve.

'Starve?' I frowned. 'Had it killed everyone else's veg as well then?'

'I don't know. It was this village, but there were loads of other houses. I was going round with a wheelbarrow and dishing out marrows and everybody was thanking me. I felt like a hero, it was ever so strange.'

'Hmm,' I frowned again. 'Have you planted marrows?'

'I haven't actually.'

'Perhaps it'd be prudent to get some then, just in case.'

After break I went to see how our erstwhile dove deterrents were adapting to their latest roles. My bird of prey was a winner: there was no sign of avian bandits filching around the peas. On the other side of the *huerta* it was a different story. Two sparrows were hopping about on a thick orange log.

Tom was tapping on the window at sunrise next morning. Something was wrong. It wasn't only his timing that was portentous, it was the look on his face when I opened the door.

'Ali?' I asked gently.

He nodded. 'I think it's time.'

'I'm truly sorry.' I paused for a moment. I wanted to tread softly but beating about the bush would only prolong Tom's anguish. He was here for a reason, and nothing would change that; the best I could do was spare him the pain of voicing what we both knew. 'Do you want me to ring the vet?'

He nodded again.

Poor Tom. My heart went out to him. Even though he'd known that this was imminent, it didn't make things any easier. I struggled to think of some way to console him. No words would be enough to ease his pain. I reached out and squeezed his arm gently. 'Hold on then, I'll get my phone.'

As we neared number ten. Tom paused. 'Do you want to see her?'

The loss of a loved one cuts deep whatever the circumstances but having a hand in their departure is an intolerable burden to bear. I understood what Tom was asking. He didn't need my advice – I was no more an authority on veterinary matters then he was. He wasn't asking for my opinion either – he'd already made up his mind. Tom was seeking reassurance. Even the merest gesture of affirmation would create the sense of shared responsibility that would help to alleviate that terrible, illogical, inexplicable feeling of guilt that would engulf him as he finally accepted that the last vestiges of hope were gone.

When I saw Ali lying on her blanket, I struggled to keep my composure. Her breathing was slow and shallow as if she was in a deep sleep. Tom was right, it was time for closure. Ali was peaceful now: it was better than waiting and watching her struggle again.

All of a sudden, I was overcome with a sense of urgency. Today was Saturday; the vet would be knocking off at lunch. I *had* to make that phone call before he set off on his rounds. José Luis wasn't based in a surgery; he was a farm vet and most of his work was with cows. Once he was out in the villages he'd be without a mobile signal and I wouldn't be able to reach him. I took one last look at Ali and charged off up the lane.

Pausing only to let Tom know that I'd managed to make the phone call, I left him alone with Ali, promising to be on hand to interpret when the vet arrived. When I heard the car pull up an hour later I lit a cigarette, inhaled deeply, then hurried up the lane to number ten.

José Luis was a dour, thickset man who said little and didn't smile. I'd first met him back in December when he'd come to the house to give Anxo his first jab. As it had turned out, it was Anxo's *only* vaccination; one shot would do, he'd told me briskly, before pricking my puppy with a needle made for cows. Back then I'd found his solemn manner irksome. It was only three days since Christmas, but he'd hardly been the epitome of festive cheer. This morning, his grave demeanour was fitting. I was grateful for his air of detachment; somehow it made it easier to cope with what had to be done.

Later that morning Gary went round to number ten with a shovel. Together, he and Tom dug Ali a grave beneath the oak trees on Paul's land.

The Rampant Calabaza

I thought I'd grow some vegetables
Outside my rural casa –
Potatoes, carrots, lettuce
And perhaps a calabaza.

I dug the garden in the spring
And planted a semilla,
I weeded carefully round it
And I watered it each día.

A few weeks passed and then I saw
Some leaves aparecen,
My marrow plant was growing well,
I shouted 'muy bien!'

When summer came I felt such pride –
My plant was bien crecido
Beneath its leaves the other veg
Had desaparecido!

Then very soon the marrows came,
The size of my small dedo,
Then later, bigger than my leg –
Oh dear, tenía miedo!

The marrows flourished, for it seemed
They loved the rain and sol,
And soon my plant was very nearly
Big as an arból!

Eventually, my plant engulfed
The whole of my small huerto,
Potatoes, carrots, lettuce in its shadow
Now were muerto!

Liza Grantham

And now I've marrows in the lounge,
The bedroom and the baño –
Enough to feed the village
For the whole of the next año!

I only wanted vegetables
Outside my rural casa,
But my life's been taken over
By the rampant calabaza!

Chapter 7

Not Guilty

It wasn't long after daybreak when I went out to the bench with my coffee. I could already hear signs of life at number fifteen. I lit my first cigarette and listened as Solina yelled and Begoña chuckled, while Másimo whistled and banged about in the yard. Anxo, in a rush of excitement, charged off round the corner in search of titbits to plunder outside the gate. Leaving my mug on the bench I strode round after him; pigs' trotters were only the tip of the iceberg, there was no telling what Solina might toss out for the dogs. To my relief there were no spoils this morning, it wouldn't be long though; Luna and Pastor were hanging about in the lane. I summoned a deflated Anxo and together we wandered back round to the bench. I sipped my coffee and tuned in to the comings and goings. I wasn't *that* desperate to eavesdrop, it was simply a matter of having no choice.

Solina was shouting. 'Masimiño!'

The whistling continued.

'*MÁSIMO!*'

The whistling stopped. There were footsteps and a door thudded closed. I wondered if Solina had called him in for a brew.

All was comparatively quiet now; only the volley of crowing and the salvo of birdsong peppered the air. I was rolling my second cigarette when I noticed an inexplicable haze swirling over the track down by Másimo's garden. I dashed down to peer through the fence and stared in horror as whisps of pale grey smoke drifted up from inside the chicken run. There was no doubt about it, something was on fire.

I yelled at the top of my voice: '*MÁSIMO!*'

Within seconds Masi appeared on the doorstep. He was wearing a white boiler suit which stretched taut over his belly but puckered all the way down his short, stubby legs. On his hat was a green and white baseball cap. This wasn't his usual get-up; he was obviously dressed for an important job.

'Over here!' I shouted, waving my arms frantically.

Eventually he looked in my direction. 'Elisa! *Qué pasa*? What's wrong?'

'There's smoke coming from the chicken run! I think something's on fire!'

He gave a deep, rasping chuckle as he glanced in the direction of the fog. 'Elisa don't worry. *No pasa nada. I* made the fire – I'm fumigating the henhouse. The smoke gets rid of the *bichos* and the hens stay healthy. They'll lay more eggs that way.'

'I see,' I nodded.

Unlike Gary, Masi obviously thought the hens were a worthwhile commodity. I wondered how many were in there; the run wasn't visible from the lane. It was almost as if Masi had read my mind.

'We've got twenty-four hens and a cockerel. When we go back to A Coruña we take enough eggs to last the whole week.'

I couldn't help thinking that Masi and Solina were on a cushy number where the chooks were concerned. They only had to put them away on Friday and Saturday nights and let them out on Saturday and Sunday mornings. For the rest of the week Maruja saw to everything. What a generous person she was.

'Priceless,' laughed Gary when I told him about my error. 'I wish I'd seen you, flapping your arms about and shrieking through the fence.'

'I didn't shriek,' I grimaced. 'You'd have done the same if you'd been there. I really believed the chooks' pen was a goner, and then Masi stood there all jolly and complacent...'

'There's a line in there somewhere.'

'How do you mean?'

'Remember how he once told you he had Italian ancestry?'

'Yes.'

'Másimo giggled while the home burned.'

'Trust you. That wasn't funny.'

'It was clever. Anyway, joking aside, I bet you felt a right wally.'

'Not really,' I shrugged. 'The neighbours know me well enough now. They realise I'm still quite naïve about rural life and I get the wrong end of the stick sometimes. I think they find it quite endearing. Masi seems to enjoy putting me right on things and answering my questions. I reckon it gives him a sense of importance, as if he's an authority on stuff, you know.'

After lunch my thoughts returned to Másimo. It was a fortnight since Anxo had been given the trotter and he still hadn't lost interest; the wretched thing had been buried and unearthed and carted about the garden a thousand times. Last weekend we'd escaped a second delivery. I prayed that our luck would hold out today.

'I want to nip up to the church to ring Dad,' I told Gary. 'Are you going to be about for a while?'

'I should think so. I'm going to be chipping out ready for the pointing. I thought I'd start at the front.'

'That's perfect,' I grinned. 'You'll be able to keep watch while you work.'

Gary looked puzzled. 'I don't understand.'

'If Masi comes round with a goodie bag I want you to intercept him. The last thing I need is a trotter, or blubber, or any other part of a pig.'

As I opened the back door, I heard a jingling in the distance.

'I'd better go the back way; it sounds like they're bringing the cows.'

Solina and Begoña were coming out of the gate when I turned the corner. Luna and Pastor lay waiting for scraps in the lane.

'*Hola*, Elisa, *buenos días*,' called Solina. She was holding a long cardboard egg box in one hand and a plastic tray of potatoes and bones in the other.

'*Buenos días*, Solina.'

Anxo ran forward to greet them, wagging his tail.

Solina laughed. '*Hola* Anxo. *No tengo nada para ti.*'

I smiled. Like Maruja, Solina had really taken to Anxo. You couldn't blame them, he was such a happy, friendly dog.

Solina set the tray down outside the gate and Anxo shot forward. Pastor warned him away with a growl. Anxo was getting better at minding his manners but on this occasion the sight of the bones was too much to bear. Pastor snarled, sprang forward, and nipped Anxo on the forehead. Anxo yelped and sank back in defeat.

As if to drive the message home Pastor took a step forward to issue a further caution.

'Pastor!' yelled Solina, bashing the eggbox down hard on his snout.

'It's okay, Solina,' I assured her. 'Anxo's still young; he needs to learn. He can't go helping himself to other dogs' dinners. *I* wouldn't like it if someone stuck their head in my food.'

Solina laughed and nodded her agreement. 'Pastor's not a bad dog really, he's grumpy because he's old.'

Poor Anxo. I felt mean, but he had to learn the hard way. A drop of blood was already forming on top of his head.

'Have you planted much yet?' I asked, keen to show there were no hard feelings.

'Everything. What about you?'

'Gary's put all the seeds in. Carrots, beetroots, cabbage, cauliflower,' I paused. It occurred to me I didn't know the word for swede. If I tried to describe it, it might be tea-time before I rang Dad. 'And the peas and beans.'

'Aren't you having peppers and tomatoes?'

'Oh yes, but we were going to wait another week or so, it seems a bit early to put them in now.'

Solina looked at me as if I was hopeless. 'Of course not. They've had the plants in the *ferretería* for weeks. Másimo put ours in last Saturday, Tell Gary to get them from the *ferretería* in Antas; tomatoes *and* peppers, it's only a euro for five plants.'

Ten minutes later I was back in the kitchen.

'That was quick,' said Gary.

'I got that snotty woman on the answerphone. It isn't half annoying. She sticks her oar in way too early and it costs the same bloody price as a full call.'

Gary grinned. 'Hark at your Mum, Anxo. My God, Liza, what's he done to his head?'

'It's only a graze, it's already stopped bleeding. He tried to gate-crash scraps time outside Solina's. Pastor wasn't impressed.'

'Poor Anxo.'

'Poor Pastor actually. Solina bashed him with an eggbox. He was only looking out for his grub.'

'No shopping list?' frowned Gary, lifting the tobacco pouch and the ashtray, and peering behind his mug.

The list had become something of a ritual on Mondays, Gary liked to peruse it over his fag and his brew. He claimed it was to do with getting it right in Spanish, but I knew otherwise. It irked me, the way he'd pore over it, sighing and shaking his head. If I'd heard once about the price of apricots or icing sugar, I'd heard it a thousand times. He wasn't going to have chance to perform like a tightarse today.

'You won't need the list this morning. I thought I'd come with you for a change.'

'Crikey, what's brought this on?'

The look on his face was a picture; would it put paid to the café-bar and the football paper if the wife tagged along? I'd stopped going shopping when we were having the roof done. The work had gone on for so long, I was out of the habit by the time it was done. During that time Gary had developed a routine that he looked forward to. I sometimes wondered if *café con leche* and *Marca* were the highlight of his week.

'Don't panic, I won't be coming every week. We can still stop for a coffee if you want to, and if it comes with a sponge cake you can have mine as well.'

'Is there a reason?'

'I don't like them, they're like sweet sawdust held together with grease.'

Gary grinned. 'I didn't mean the sponge cake; I meant the shopping. Is there a particular reason you've decided to come?'

'There is actually, I want to choose some tomato and pepper plants for the raised bed.'

'I thought you wanted to wait 'til the end of the month?'

'I did, but Solina said they put theirs in a week ago. You get five plants for a euro in Ferretería Patao. It sounds like a good price.'

'Can't argue with that then. Tomatoes and peppers it is.'

'And it's trout season. I thought we could buy a couple for the freezer, to have when Ron and Miranda come.'

'Ooh, good thinking. It'll make a nice change from cod and hake.'

'Oh, and there was something I meant to ask you. Are the beehives still upstairs in the annexe?'

'The beehives? They must be. I'd forgotten all about them, I've not seen them since last April. I suppose they're still there. Why?'

'Because I've found a great use for them. I told you I would eventually. I'm going to put them in the bathroom. We'll have one either side of the wash basin and keep the toilet rolls and bleach and stuff in them. They'll make unusual rustic storage bins. Once they've had a couple of coats of varnish, they'll look great.'

'*Varnish*? It costs a fortune. Won't they do as they are?'

I sighed inwardly. Even without a list he couldn't help himself. It wouldn't be Monday morning if he didn't get to quibble about a price tag or two.

After lunch I was washing the plates up when there was a short, clipped rap at the door. It was Tom, and he wasn't smiling. By the look on his face, I could see he had an axe to grind.

'Come in,' I said, 'Shall I make you a coffee?'

'Forget the coffee, this isn't a social call. You've got to do something about that dog.'

I looked at Anxo, sprawled out by the dresser. Had Tom found out about the plastic flowers? There was only one way to find out.

'Go on then, *now* what's he done?'

'He's tried to dig Ali up.'

'My God!' This was terrible news, no wonder Tom looked angry. To lose her and bury her was bad enough but to come out and find that her grave had been disturbed... A terrible thought struck me.

'Don't tell me he's... I mean, he hasn't... Just tell me what you found.'

'The soil's been disturbed and I could see the blanket through the loose soil.'

My relief must have been visible.

'That doesn't make it any less serious, Liza. I've spent half an hour filling the hole up and covering it with stones.'

'So it's happened this morning?'

'Yes. In the last two or three hours.'

I could have jumped for joy.

'Tom, listen. It *couldn't* have been Anxo. It's impossible. He was locked in the house when we went shopping and I've not let him out since. He's been with me in the kitchen the whole time. I'm sorry about what's happened, but whoever did this, it wasn't Anxo. There's no way you can pin it on *him*.'

'Fair enough then, but that's not all. He's been killing livestock as well. If you don't control him, you'll have the other neighbours complaining before long.'

I stared at him in horror as I reached for my bacca. Stealing was one thing, but if this was true... I scrolled through the events of the weekend, how long had Anxo had been out of my sight?

My hands were shaking as I lit my cigarette. 'I swear on my life I know nothing about this. It'd help if you could explain.'

'Sunday afternoon a duck was killed in the farmyard.'

'And you actually saw Anxo kill it?'

'I didn't see him, no, but all the evidence points to him. I've seen him running up there on many an occasion. I saw Maruja carrying the duck to the wheelie bin. She showed me a rip in its neck and said "*matado*". Anxo was running around her, with blood on his head, excited as hell.'

I drew hard on my cigarette. If I could only remember what we'd been doing on Sunday afternoon. I began to retrace my steps. Dad's phone call, of course! We'd stopped to talk to Solina... *that's* why Anxo had blood on his head! My spirits lifted, Anxo might yet have an alibi after all! We'd walked up the back lane, past the farmhouse... Anxo had bounded forwards to disperse the chickens that were pecking about in the lane. I'd carried on walking – he liked to scatter the hens, but he'd never pursued them, it was always a matter of seconds before he was back by my side. Up at the church I'd dialled Dad's number and waited impatiently; if he didn't pick up in five rings the answerphone would kick in. Sure enough, that God-awful, toffee-nosed woman had simpered the usual guff about leaving a message and... that's when I next saw Anxo! He was charging towards me as I came back past the wheelie bin. How long had he been outside the farmyard? Three minutes, maybe five? A knot tightened in the pit of my stomach. There was a window of time I couldn't account for. Perhaps Anxo was guilty of killing the duck after all.

'And last week there was the chicken.'

This was getting worse by the minute. I wasn't sure I wanted to hear any more.

'What chicken?'

'It was lying dead on the track down by number fifteen's *hórreo*. I didn't say anything at the time though I had my suspicions. Now with the duck incident… well it's pretty obvious really. Anxo's becoming a liability and it's up to you to sort him out.'

By now I was on the verge of tears, but I'd be damned if I'd let Tom see me crying. 'I don't see that anything's *obvious*. We've already established he didn't dig Ali up. You can't just come round accusing him without any evidence. You'd better go.'

I was dabbing my eyes with a tissue when Gary came in from the barn.

'I've mixed the *mortero* and I thought I'd… Crikey Liza, whatever's wrong?'

'Tom's been round to complain about Anxo. He reckons he's dug Ali up, but he hasn't, and he's killed a duck, but he can't prove it and he…'

'Hey, hey, slow down. Let me roll you a fag, then you can dry your eyes and tell me exactly what's gone on.'

As I told Gary what Tom had been saying, his expression gradually turned from disbelief to anger.

'So we know for a fact that Anxo didn't dig Ali up?'

'Yes, I'm one hundred percent certain, and Tom knows that too.'

'So it's only the duck that we're not sure about?'

'Yes, and the chicken.'

'What chicken?'

'I didn't get that far, he…' I paused to dab at my eyes again. 'He says there was a dead chicken on the track near Masi's *hórreo*. Apparently, that must have been Anxo too.'

Gary was furious. 'There are seven dogs in this village, but Anxo's the one that's nicked a spoon so that makes him the culprit. Talk about two and two making five.'

'Well, I don't know what to think about the chicken, but I tell you what, Gary, I'm worried to death about the duck. He was outside the farmyard around the time it was taken. You have to admit it isn't looking very good.'

'Why don't you go up and see Maruja? You can ask her outright if Anxo killed the duck and if he did, we can pay for it. At least that'd go some way to putting things right.'

I blew my nose. 'I'll go now. They eat a lot later than us; I might catch her before she puts the dinner out. Thanks Gary, I knew you'd know what to do.'

Up at the farmhouse Maruja was on her own in the kitchen. Javier and José Manuel were still busy milking the cows.

'Elisa! Have you been crying? What's happened? Come in, come in.'

'Tom says Anxo killed one of your ducks yesterday. Is it true?'

Maruja looked genuinely surprised. 'A duck *was* killed, but we've no reason to suppose it was Anxo, why does Tom think it was him? We don't know *how* it was killed. I found it dead in the yard with its throat ripped open. *I* don't think it was killed by a dog.'

'Really?'

'Of course not. A dog would run off with it and eat it, it wouldn't just kill it and run away.'

I thought for a moment. Maruja was right, It sounded more like the work of a fox to me.

'Do you think a fox might have done it?'

She looked doubtful. 'It *could* have, but I wouldn't think so. We don't usually see them in the day. *We* think it was a bird of prey that killed it. There was one circling over the paddock all morning; we're sure that's how it died.'

'There's more, Maruja. Tom saw a dead chicken on the *camino* near the *río* last week. He's blaming Anxo for that as well.'

To my surprise Maruja started smiling. 'That was me.'

My surprise turned to complete bewilderment. 'You killed the chicken?'

'No,' she chuckled. 'Solina's chickens are getting old. When I find a dead one, I throw it out in the lane for the foxes. We don't eat them unless we've killed them ourselves. Even if it looks like natural causes, you can never be sure.'

I was elated. Anxo hadn't killed the chicken and the chances were, he hadn't killed the duck either. He'd been accused of three crimes and he hadn't been guilty of a single one. There was a reason I'd named him 'Angel' after all.

'Are you having problems with Tom?' asked Maruja when I'd finally stopped grinning.

'No, well, we *hadn't* been, up until recently. It started two weeks back because of a spoon.'

It was Maruja's turn to look surprised. 'A *spoon*?'

I could guess what she must be thinking: 'Elisa must have got her Castilian wrong.'

'A spoon.' I repeated. I told her the full story; she was incredulous.

'You can't train a dog not to go into other people's houses, it's impossible. If Tom doesn't want Anxo in, he should shut the door.'

I nodded, relieved that Maruja saw things our way.

'You've nothing to worry about, Elisa. We like Anxo. He hasn't done anything wrong.'

I walked home feeling much brighter. I quickened my pace as I passed number ten.

'Well,' said Gary, looking up from his pointing. 'Was it good news?'

'Brilliant,' I smiled. 'Maruja's sure a bird of prey killed the duck, and the chicken was dead anyway; it'd been tossed out for the fox.'

'So he's in the clear then?'

'Absolutely. As far as Maruja's concerned, he hasn't put a foot wrong.'

Now that Maruja had set my mind at rest I was ready to work on the beehives. Gary had found them gathering dust in the annexe last April. They looked like two-foot-high sections of tree-trunk but were actually hollow cylinders of bark, complete with lids. We hadn't had a clue what they were until Pepe, our plumber-cum-builder, had told us they were beehives and were probably over a hundred years old. Eager to preserve a rare piece of rural Galician history I'd vowed I'd find a creative way to have them on permanent display.

Once I'd given the hives their first coat of varnish, I was ready for a breather and keen to see how the pointing was coming along. As I stood up and stretched to ease the tension in my shoulders, I could make out a pale ginger shape at the end of the *huerta*. Scholes was raking purposefully at the earth between the lettuces; the scallywag feline was covering a poo.

'Scholes!' I shouted, as I took off up the garden. 'Scholes, don't!'

When Scholes saw me, he shot off through the bramble and jumped down onto the track. It wasn't like him to run off when I called him. The crafty little rascal knew he'd done wrong.

I strode back over the threshing floor and leaned on the gate as I appraised Gary's handiwork. He'd only covered a small area, but I could see that he was doing a top-notch job.

'It looks brilliant, Gary,' I enthused, as I came out into the lane to stand beside him. 'It really enhances the stonework; it'll make such a difference when it's done.'

I stood back and tried to imagine how the house would look when the whole wall was finished. It was then that I noticed Scholes, sprawled out on the bench. It looked for all the world as if he'd been dozing there for ages. I was coming to the conclusion that he was far more cunning than I cared to think.

'Just look at *you*, you monkey. I wonder what Dad'll say when he knows what you've done.'

'Poor Scholes,' chuckled Gary. 'All he's doing is taking a *siesta*. He's not had chance to get up to any mischief, he's just been lying here watching me point.'

'He's also been doing some manuring. He's pooed in the lettuces and now he's sitting here like butter wouldn't melt in his mouth.'

'When was this then, Scholes? Have you been keeping it a secret? It mustn't happen again, you know, it's poor form.'

'It was only five minutes ago. He shot off when I called him. He's got a guilty conscience, haven't you son?'

'Five minutes ago? But that's impossible. He followed me out of the barn as soon as the cows had gone past. He's been with me out here ever since.'

'But he *hasn't*,' I insisted. 'I tell you; I *saw* him. He was scraping at the earth, and it didn't take a genius to work out what he'd done.'

My accusations were futile. As Gary continued to protest Scholes' innocence it was obvious a unanimous verdict would never be reached. Eventually, I retired to the kitchen; my time would be better spent with a fag and a brew.

By Tuesday afternoon the hives were in situ. Antique rusticity against eighties-style wall tiles was an intriguing paradox; the overall effect was just on the right side of kitsch. Scholes examined the hives and was quick to claim one. Its lid had warped over time, leaving a cat-sized dip in the centre. Scholes deemed it the perfect place to sleep.

When I went through to the bathroom on Wednesday morning Scholes was still on his beehive. He showed no signs of stirring; it looked like I'd be doing the chooks on my own today.

Leaving the hens to fuss over their breakfast, I lingered awhile in the veg plot. Despite my earlier doubts there were hopes for a harvest yet. Now that my bird of prey was standing sentry the remaining pea plants continued to thrive. Here and there, tiny specks of green had begun to appear beneath the mesh covers and a couple of courgette leaves had begun to poke through in the pots. I was closing the gate behind me when I noticed Scholes creeping towards a blackbird under the fig tree. The bird took flight and Scholes traced its path over the garden. Strangely enough, he scarpered as soon as I drew near.

As I walked into the passage, Gary came through the stairs door.

'Morning,' I grinned. 'Scholes is back in my good books; I've just seen him stalking a bird.'

'You can't have "just" seen him. He's curled up on his hive, out for the count.'

Scholes might be clever and cunning but even *he* couldn't have achieved the impossible. I knew my eyes hadn't deceived me; there was something weird going on.

'Do you want the good news, the very good news or the great news?' asked Gary, when I called him in for his coffee.

'Oh,' I laughed. 'That's a hard one. Let's start with the good, shall we, and work our way up?'

'I've had a letter from Howard. He's been doing quite well on the horses, and he says my Mum cheats at crib.'

I giggled. 'Good for her. You'll have to read it to me later. Go on then, what's next?'

'I've just seen Tom loading Maud and The Ox into the camper van. I reckon he's off to Isabel's again.'

'That *is* good news. After what's happened, it'll give things a chance to die down. What's the *great* news?'

'We've had a message from Maribel. Cancel all your plans for Friday, we've got an appointment in Lugo. We're off to the *notario*'s to buy Hilda's land.'

If the truth be told I was relieved rather than delighted, it was an extraordinary saga that had gone on for far too long.

When Maribel, the local estate agent, had shown us the house she'd pointed out a strip running straight through the middle of the garden which belonged to somebody else. She'd assured us that it was only a matter of time before we'd be able to buy it and, despite our surprise and confusion, we hadn't doubted her word. Eventually we were approached by a man who was acting on behalf of Hilda, the owner. We'd agreed a price – way too high, thanks to Gary, but the sale had yet to be completed; a peculiar mix-up in the paperwork had put things on hold.

Up until recently, this forthcoming appointment would have been a momentous occasion; every slab, stone and stick in the garden would be our own. Hermitas' unexpected visit and the bombshell about the chooks' land had changed everything. Friday's visit to the *notario*, however welcome, was no longer our final milestone; there was another, greater hurdle ahead of us before we romped home.

When Friday morning dawned, I was in a state of nervous apprehension. When Gary rose half an hour later, I could tell he was feeling the same.

'I think we should leave around nine,' he announced, as I passed him his cuppa.

'I thought the appointment was at half past eleven?' I frowned.

'It is, but it's better to be on the safe side… you never know what the traffic will be like towards the weekend.'

I sighed inwardly. The traffic on the N540 into Lugo was never nose-to-tail whatever the day of the week. I was about to protest but thoughts of Gary's Irritable Driver Syndrome convinced me it was better to save my breath. I nodded my agreement, resigned to an hour in a cheerless café, drinking black coffee and frowning at cake.

It was just before mid-day when we left the *notario*'s office. The sale had gone through with no hiccups, hold-ups or hitches. I breathed a sigh of relief and thanked God it was over; we'd been daft to get so worked up over a few square metres of land.

When I came back from the fields with Anxo that evening Gary was sitting in the kitchen frowning. There was a can of lager in front of him and a pen in his hand. God forbid that it was another of his doom and gloom calculations; up until now I'd had reasonably good afternoon. On this occasion it seemed I'd done him an injustice. There was a paper in front of him and I couldn't see any sums.

'I'm replying to Howard,' he explained when he saw me peering over. 'There's something I'm stuck on. I thought you might be able to give me a hand.'

'I'm all ears,' I smiled, feeling instantly cheerful. 'I'll help if I can.'

'He says here, "Are you self-sufficient yet?" I'm not sure what to put.'

'Well, we're not, are we? So, say that – what's the problem?'

'I want it to sound really positive. The thing is, people at work are bound to ask if he's heard from me, and how I'm getting on with the garden and all that. I don't want to say, well actually, I've not grown anything yet, I mean, it's nearly June.'

'Well you can't lie to him…'

'Of course not, that's not what I'm saying. I just want it to sound more… optimistic. I wondered if *you* could come up with something, you usually have a way with words.'

I put on an earnest expression. 'How about, "Dear Howard, Are we heck as like self-sufficient! Hardly anything's come up in the garden, and what *has* come up the birds have eaten or the cat's shat on. Still, we're laughing all the way to the greengrocer's and our sun continues to shine."'

'Very funny,' he grimaced, though I could see he was fighting a smile. 'Come on, you know what I mean, just give me some ideas.'

'Sorry, I couldn't help myself. Right then, let's see. Instead of telling him what we're *trying* to grow, enthuse about what we've *already* grown *and* eaten – that'll sound positive. Stick it somewhere in the middle, keep it brief and move swiftly on.'

'Ah, *enthuse* – that's clever. I like it. I'll do that, then. So, what have we have we eaten that we've grown ourselves?'

'The radishes. Don't tell him how many though, it sounds a bit feeble. The half dozen we had were perfect… tell him we had a superb crop. Then there's the kale; now *that's* a good one, we've been eating it for months now, and it still keeps coming – tell him we've grown more than we can eat.'

'Solina gave us the plants though, does it count?'

'Of *course* it does. It doesn't matter where they came from, *you* planted them. They've been in for ages and *you've* managed to keep them alive.'

'Okay, what else then?'

'Erm…' I wracked my brain. 'We've used sage and thyme and rosemary…'

'And parsley?'

'It died.'

'Oh dear.'

'Herbs aren't really food though – it'd sound like we're reaching. Better to miss them out.'

I was struggling now; radishes and kale didn't sound like much of a success story however much you dressed it up.

'Eggs!' Gary exclaimed suddenly. 'We've had eggs galore since March. And if I waffle a bit about all the different ways we've used them, cakes, omelettes, *tortillas…*'

'The ways *I've* used them. And it's *frittatas*.'

'Yes, that as well.'

'I must say, *you've* changed your tune. It's the first time you've shown enthusiasm for our egg production. *You* were all for necking the chickens and buying eggs from the shop.'

'Yes, well, I still am, but that's irrelevant. Desperate measures are called for. I'm being… what do you call it… pragmatic.'

I smiled inwardly. He'd obviously changed his tune on my 'pompous' vocabulary as well. 'Okay, leave it at that then: eggs, kale, radishes – that's as good as self-sufficient, isn't it? You could survive on scrambled eggs and greens if push came to shove.'

Liza Grantham

Haiku for Howard

Eggs, kale, radishes –
is that self-sufficiency?
If it is, we are.

Chapter 8

Rivers, Relics and Ruins

I had the distinct sensation of déjà vu on Saturday morning. It wasn't my imagination, there was smoke over Másimo's garden again. This time the fog wasn't wafting gently, it was billowing out of a tractor in dense black swathes. If Masi was whistling I couldn't discern it; the deep, throaty roar of the engine had scuppered my chances of listening in today.

When I came back into the kitchen Gary was making his cuppa.

'Morning,' I grinned. 'To what do we owe the pleasure, so early in the day?'

'I heard the weirdest noise and it seemed to be coming from the bathroom. I thought I'd better investigate in case something was wrong.'

'*That* was Masi's tractor. I think it's poorly. There're clouds of black smoke blowing into the lane.'

'No, no. I didn't mean the engine. This was different, a terrible wailing. I was worried. I thought it must be Scholes.'

'Was he locked in the bathroom?'

'No, that's the strangest thing about it. He wasn't in the bathroom. He wasn't even in the house.'

'It sounds like you were dreaming. Anyway, you need to start practising getting up early; you won't be able to lie in when Ron and Miranda are here.'

'I s'pose you're right. There's ages yet though. It's not even June.'

'They're coming on the sixth. That's less than a fortnight away – the time's flown since we had the message. I've still got *so* much to do.'

'I don't know what you're worrying about; the bedroom's ready and you've made a list of places we can take them. I can't see what else there is to do.'

'Well, there's the food for a start-off. I want to put some meals in the freezer, not all of them, obviously, but when we've been out all day I don't want to be dashing about in the kitchen as soon as we're home.'

'It'd make *my* life easier; you'll be less fractious. I hate it when you run round like a headless chicken; you're hard work when you're tense. Will there be curries?'

'Of *course* there'll be curries. *And* pizza.'

'That's the ticket,' he grinned.

The thought of scoffing his favourites had clearly pleased him. I decided to make the most of his good mood. 'Actually, I've been thinking about the bedroom. It could do with a couple of bedside tables; people need somewhere to put things and it'd look less bare.'

'I s'pose it wouldn't be a problem. I'll see what I can do.'

'There was something else as well.'

He sighed. 'Go on then.'

'I was wondering if you could knock up a table to eat at. I don't mean anything fancy, I thought it might be fun to have a meal in the barn.'

'I don't think *that's* a good idea, Liza. I've got stuff all over the place, it'd take ages to clear it. *And* it'd mean a trip to the wood yard, not to mention more expense.'

It was time to play it shrewdly. 'Never mind,' I smiled airily. 'Miranda and Ron would have loved it. Still, you're better to take it easy for the time being, once they're here you'll have all the driving to do.'

'Talking of which, you still haven't told me the itinerary. I hope we're not spending hours on the road.'

'Don't worry, there's only Pambre, Lalín and Lugo, *and* – this'll please you – you won't even be driving every day.'

His face brightened, but the smile faded quickly. 'Does that mean there's loads of walking instead?'

'Not *loads*. We'll break the week up with a stroll over to Santa Mariña; we can have a drink at the Black Eagle before wandering back. And of course, we should spend the first day showing them the village and the surrounding countryside. We can do a meandering circuit over the fields and through the woods.'

'We can show them where you camped out last summer. And Sacrificial Stone.'

We'd first come across the stone not long after we'd bought the house. We'd been up in the forest collecting damp wood. It was a huge flat slab of granite lying across a low embankment. Gary had decided it was the sort of place that sacrifices would have been made.

'Do you realise we've never followed the track *beyond* Sacrificial Stone? We always turn left to the oakwood when we reach the glade. I've an idea it might lead back to the main road. I might have a wander with Anxo and have a look this afternoon.'

Straight after lunch I summoned Anxo. He was over the moon to be joining me for an impromptu afternoon stroll. At the *río*, Anxo paused to lap water, disturbing the frogs that were basking in the sun. We followed the track until it rose steeply for a short distance before opening out into the glade. Here the sun cast a golden hue over last year's fallen leaves and acorns, but the track soon fell eerily into shadow as I approached the Sacrificial Stone. I shuddered briefly and called Anxo to me; it was time to discover whatever lay in wait beyond.

The track, overgrown on either side with nettles and bracken, descended steeply before levelling out, narrowing and leading us back into the sun. To the left was a coppice of young oak trees, to the right, a stone wall with a small, scrubby field beyond. Much to my surprise, the field wasn't empty. Tonito was lying in the grass, propped up on one elbow, watching his cows who were grazing close by. At the far end, Pastora was snuffling along the hedgerow. Even from a distance there was no mistaking the swollen belly which hung on her emaciated frame. My eyes pricked with tears and I wanted to throttle Tonito; however would Pastora's scrawny body cope with the functions of being a mum?

I hurried onwards, determined not to dwell on the fate of poor Pastora, and was soon distracted by the sound of trickling water somewhere up ahead. As the sound grew louder the muddy track became a pathway of densely packed boulders with a fast-flowing rivulet gushing underneath. Like the *río* in the *aldea*, this tiny stream would race underground and over land all the way to the Río Ulla. It was almost too magical to believe.

Two minutes later the track ended abruptly, and we stepped out into a wide lane. The muddy surface was deeply etched with tractor treads, and I paused to clip Anxo's lead on before setting off along the verge. We'd walked no more than fifty metres when I caught sight of a ramshackle stone hovel tucked into a thicket to the side of the verge. Picking my way through a treacherous mesh of creeping bramble I managed to reach the tiny, windowless building. To my surprise, its only doorway opened onto the very edge of the bank of a wide stream.

'It's a mill!' I exclaimed, although there was only Anxo to hear me. 'It's a lovely old sawmill! All this time and we hadn't a clue it was here!'

We completed our circuit along the main road and up the steep slope that ran alongside the farmyard. The whole trip had taken just over an hour. Our errand had brought better results than I'd dared hope for, and I was satisfied that our local tour would be a success.

When Gary unloaded the shopping on Monday, I was surprised to see three pallets stacked in the back of the car.

'Are they for firewood?' I asked him.

'Don't be daft, as if I'd burn good pallets. These, oh wife-of-little-imagination, are the outdoor dining table you were pestering me to build.'

I grinned at him. 'You're amazing.' I knew I'd get my own way in the end.

'By the way, there's a cheese festival next weekend in Palas de Rei. There are signs up all over the place in Monterroso, it looks like it might be quite a big event.'

'That sounds good, let's go on Sunday. We can buy a couple of top-notch Galician cheeses to share with Miranda and Ron. Even better we can stuff ourselves silly with samples if we act like we're struggling to choose.'

For the rest of the week we beavered away with our preparations. While I made wonderful smells in the kitchen, Gary made an unbearable din in the barn.

On Saturday night we clanked cans of lager in a toast to our labours. The guestroom had two quaint little bedside tables and there were curries and pizzas and puddings in the freezer. Gary had apparently warmed to the idea of an outdoor dining room; not only had he made a half-decent table, but he'd also created an impressive candelabra out of branches and honey jars. We'd be treating our guests to a candle-lit meal in the barn.

We'd worked hard and I was really looking forward to the cheese festival. On Sunday morning it was bucketing down with rain.

'What do you think it'll do?' asked Gary, as I passed him his cuppa.

'The weather, you mean? I doubt it'll brighten up this morning, it looks like the rain's set in. I shouldn't worry though, I bet the *concello* will have a marquee up. It's Galicia, they'll be prepared for this sort of thing.'

As we approached Palas de Rei the downpour showed no sign of relenting. There was an ominous absence of traffic as we drove through the heart of the town.

'There aren't many folks about,' said Gary. 'I bet it's this weather that's kept them at home.'

'It's early yet, they'll all be out later. They'll stop off for a browse and a natter on their way to the one o'clock mass.'

'Right, where are we heading?' he asked, as we drew up at the crossroads.

'I should think it'll be in the square next to the council building.'

'Let's hope we can pull up close by.'

Gary needn't have worried about the parking; in front of the *concello* the kerbside was completely devoid of cars. I was spot-on about the festival being held in the *plaza*; what a shame my marquee hunch was wide of the mark.

'I have a suggestion,' I said, as Gary turned off the engine.

'Go on.'

'Forget about tasting and choosing, we'll stop at the first stall we come to, buy a couple of cheeses and leg it back to the car.'

'You're on.'

Back in the car, I examined our purchases: two splendid cheeses, a string of *chorizo picante* and a kilogramme jar of local honey.

'We've done well,' I said, pleased that we'd braved the elements. 'Let's spend the rest of the day relaxing, we've got a heck of a week ahead.'

'They're not coming 'til Friday, Liza. You'll be able to take it easy 'til then.'

'Take it *easy*! You're joking aren't you? I've only got four days to do the big clean. The windows want doing, I've not dusted the tops of the wardrobes, and have you *seen* the muck behind the cooker?'

'You'll be a nightmare,' sighed Gary. 'Perhaps I should find a hotel.'

By Friday afternoon the house had been scrubbed from top to bottom, and the table was set in the barn.

'Have I forgotten anything?' I mused, glancing anxiously round the kitchen.

'*Liza*,' groaned Gary, 'their plane lands in less than two hours. It's an hour and three quarters to Santiago airport, it's high time we were gone.'

By the time our friends came through the arrivals door my tension had vanished. It was such a pleasure to see them; I was determined to slow down and enjoy their company while they were here. The drive from the airport was so enjoyable. It was a delight to hear Ron and Miranda marvelling at the countryside as we drove through.

'We've passed lots of little buildings on stilts,' said Miranda. 'Are they something to do with the Church?'

'Church?' laughed Gary. 'They wouldn't hold much of a congregation! They're *hórreos* – it's the traditional Galician way of storing the grain,'

'Oh, I *see*,' nodded Miranda. 'But so many have crosses on top, that's why I wondered…'

'I think you're right, in a way,' I told her. 'I have a theory, you see. Right up until the last century rural Galicians were very superstitious; despite their Catholicism they were strongly influenced by their pagan ancestry, I've a feeling the crosses are linked to that strange combination; on the one hand, there's the link between bread and the church…'

'Like "give us this day our daily bread"?' suggested Miranda.

'That's it,' I nodded.

'And "the body of Christ",' added Ron.

'Oh, yes. I hadn't thought of that one. And then there's the mystical side; the cross is there to ward off evil spirits and protect the grain.'

'The design of the legs protects the grain as well,' grinned Gary. I could tell he wasn't impressed with my theory and wanted to change the subject because religion had reared its head.

'The legs?' asked Ron. 'How?'

'Apparently it makes them rat-proof. It's hard for the rats to scale the smooth stone surface, and if they *do* manage it they come to a dead end.'

'Have *you* got a grain-store?' asked Miranda.

'No,' replied Gary, 'I think we're about the only house in the village that hasn't, come to think of it. We've got a threshing floor, though, and two stone tables. Now they *are* unusual, none of the other houses have got those.'

'Every garden we've passed has been chock-a-block with tall cabbages,' said Ron. 'They're a bit like Brussels sprouts plants, are they a type of kale?'

'Yes,' I nodded. 'But they're not like I remember the kale I ate as a kid in England. I'm sure they were smaller with curly leaves. Our neighbours call them *coles* and they seem to be the staple diet in our *aldea*. They feed them to the chickens by the armful as well.'

'Have you got them in your garden?' asked Miranda.

'We have…' I began. I grinned at Gary. 'Go on, you tell them. You're the veg man.'

'We have, but ours aren't *quite* that big yet. They've not been in long, give 'em time.'

The road from Santiago to Antas de Ulla was hardly inspiring, yet our visitors were enthralled by the breath-taking verdure of the backdrop; such a contrast to their arid Andalusian landscape patched only sparsely with green. It was a joy to listen as they gasped and pointed at rivers and valleys and forests. I couldn't wait to see their reaction when we left civilisation behind us and drove the final stretch home.

Gary slowed as we traced the road out of Antas, past the *panadería* with its colossal bread-oven chimney, and the Swiss-style houses on the outskirts of the town. We wove onwards, through stretches of pasture where *rubia galega* cattle still grazed as the sun sank closer to the horizon, past clusters of rambling stone houses and dense forests of oak, chestnut, eucalyptus and pine.

Anxo greeted our guests with affectionate exuberance. Once he'd made their acquaintance, Gary took him out to the garden, while I led Ron and Miranda upstairs.

'Oh, wow!' said Miranda, as we came up into the living room.

'This is amazing,' said Ron. 'It feels like we've stepped back in time.'

The surprise on their faces was a picture; I was dying to show them the rest of the house. Still, it was getting late, and everybody would be hungry; the bathroom and bedroom would be sufficient for now.

'Full house tour in the morning,' I told them. 'Tonight we'll relax outside with a drink and some grub.'

The guest room was an instant hit. The bumpy walls, the chunky beams, the uneven floorboards and the sloping ceiling summed up rural Galician houses to a tee.

As we came out of the back door, I pointed across the lane to the gate. 'That's our garden. It took a bit of getting used to, but in the *aldeas* it's quite common for the *huerta* to be some distance from the home.'

'Shall we go through?' asked Miranda, as Anxo barked a greeting.

'Heavens, no!' I exclaimed in mock horror. 'Tonight's a special occasion; we shall be dining in the barn.'

We crossed the lane, and I swung the heavy door open before waving them in and ushering them up the stairs. The setting was nothing short of perfect. Whilst I'd been showing our guests their accommodation Gary had found time to light the honey-pot lanterns and bring out the food and the booze.

A loaf of *pan de kilo* took pride of place in the centre of the table, with its thick, smoky crust and soft white centre abundant with holes. On one side there were the cheeses we'd almost drowned for in Palas, and on the other a huge basket of my signature chilli nachos with a hot and spicy tomato dip. A dish of cherry tomatoes and a plate of chorizo added an extra splash of colour and, quite unexpectedly, Miranda added fresh olives and almonds grown close to their home. Two carefully selected (and way out of budget) bottles of wine from the Rías Baixas made our humble supper a touch more grand. At one end of the table a six-pack of own-brand lager seemed slightly out of kilter; in this elegant rustic dining room only the hostess could lower the tone.

'The chilli nachos are amazing,' said Miranda, as we all dug in.

'They're cheap and easy,' I grinned. 'And they don't half freeze well.'

'Remind me to jot down the recipe before we go.'

'The bread's gorgeous,' said Ron. 'It's so light in the middle. It's hard to know where to put the butter because of all the big holes.'

'It's baked in Antas,' explained Gary. 'There are two *panaderías*, each with traditional wood burning ovens.'

'But we don't *have* to go into Antas,' I added. 'Bread van delivers on Tuesdays, Thursdays and Saturdays, and shop van and butane van come once a week.'

It wasn't long before our conversation drifted round to the neighbours. When Gary regaled them with the stories of Carmen's antics, they couldn't have been more amazed.

'She sounds so eccentric,' chuckled Ron. 'Do you think we'll see her tomorrow?'

'You can meet her *now* if you want to,' laughed Gary. 'I bet she's out in the garden even as we speak.'

'Really?' Ron looked at Miranda. 'Shall we see?'

'I don't know,' Miranda hesitated. 'We can't disturb her this late, it's past midnight you know.'

'She'll still be about,' Gary assured her. 'I'm sure she'd be over the moon.'

As we crept up the path, we heard swishing and rustling. Carmen was slashing at her vines with a sickle in the shadows cast by the streetlight at the end of the path. She didn't seem at all surprised to see us. Perhaps I wasn't the only one who snooped by the standing stone wall.

'Hola, Carmen, *buenas noches.* These are our friends from Granada. They live in a cave.'

While Carmen was chattering ten to the dozen, I found myself staring at the sickle. Even in the half-darkness the orange stripe on the handle stood out a mile.

I woke early on Saturday morning, jolted from my slumber by a relentless, ear-splitting noise. What could have possessed me to set the alarm clock? It was then I remembered; our guests had arrived! Conscious not to wake them I was on tenterhooks in the bathroom. I tried to move about quietly until I was safely downstairs. While I waited for the kettle to boil I rushed a bemused Anxo into the garden; there was no time to sit out on the bench today. The usual jobs of feeding the hens and dog-walking lay ahead of me; only then could I begin to play the perfect hostess.

Ten minutes later I heard Gary yawning and shifting about in the bedroom. His footsteps thudded above me and seconds later I heard the terrace door bang. If I'd been worried about waking our sleeping *invitados*, my husband clearly had no such reservations; if anything, he was doing his utmost to drag them from the land of Nod.

'Had you forgotten the visitors?' I frowned, as I handed him his cuppa.

'What a daft question! Of *course* not. That's why I've been creeping about like a mouse.'

Ron and Miranda were shattered after the long trip and late supper. Gary's percussion solo had failed to wake them and it wasn't far off lunchtime when our house tour began. Assuring them that they could poke about later at their leisure we whisked them swiftly through the rooms.

There was lots of 'ooh'-ing and 'aah'-ing as they marvelled at the quirky little features, but the thing that most overwhelmed them was the remarkable prevalence of wood.

'The beams are *huge*!' gasped Miranda. 'Everything looks so sturdy, so... enduring...'

'It's that, alright,' smiled Gary. 'It's almost two hundred years old.'

'It feels like the inside of a church,' said Ron. 'It takes me back to my childhood. The floors, the doors, the furniture – it's incredible to see so much wood.'

Down in the entrance, Ron gazed up at the lintel above the back door.

'Just *look* how chunky the wall is!' he marvelled. 'It's easily two-feet thick. The house must be as strong as a fortress. It must have taken such craftsmanship to build.'

Out in the garden, the proliferation of locally quarried stone amazed them. The size of the slabs on the threshing floor and the stone tables caught their imaginations, and they mooted all kinds of theories on how they might have been moved.

'Liza likes the standing stone wall,' laughed Gary. 'She kneels in the herb bed and spies.'

'It's not spying,' I retorted. 'It's a thirst for education. It's a highly efficient way to learn.'

'Your first year here must have been one long history lesson,' smiled Miranda. 'Everywhere you look there are relics and reminders of the past.'

'Talking of which,' grinned Gary mischievously, 'it's time we showed you the hens.'

'What have the hens got to do with relics?' asked Ron, frowning.

I scowled at Gary. 'Ignore him, Ron. He's trying to be funny. If he'd had *his* way the chooks would be history by now.'

After a brew and a butty it was time for some *real* adventure; our tour of the village and its outskirts began.

At number ten the stable door was open; after three weeks away from the village, Tom had returned. I felt a flutter of apprehension; would he let bygones be bygones? When he called out a cheery *'Hola!'* from the courtyard it seemed that things would be fine.

For the next fifteen minutes, *hórreos*, bread oven chimneys, stone troughs and a carved inscription all fell prey to the camera.

'We'd better get our skates on,' Gary reminded them, eventually. 'There's Liza's fields and forests and rivers and mountains trip to do yet.'

'Don't worry,' I assured them. 'There aren't any mountains. There isn't a *real* river either, only the *río*. Come on, I'll show you. Keep walking this way, it's not far past the lane.'

Just as I'd expected, our guests found the *río* enchanting, and found it hard to believe that this was where Carmen still washed her clothes. At the sawmill, they were intrigued by the probability that this wider stream was the next stage of the *río*'s journey. I promised them they'd see the fully-fledged Río Ulla before the end of the week.

When we finally walked up the slope back into the village Miranda was yawning.

'Five more minutes,' I smiled, 'and then you can put your feet up. We'll have a quick look at the calves and then we'll head home.'

As we paused to look in the calf pen, Maruja came out onto the doorstep. Our friends introduced themselves and she was delighted to learn that they spoke Castilian. They asked her about the cows and the *huerta*. She asked them about the weather and the cave. Eventually, she wished them a happy stay in the *aldea,* and they bid her *'hasta luego.'*

'We've got a cow called Miranda,' Maruja smiled, as we walked away.

Back in the kitchen I stuck the kettle on. All four of us were more than ready for a brew.

'The landscape's so gorgeous,' enthused Miranda. 'It seems to go on for ever and ever. If I wasn't so tired I could have walked for the whole afternoon.'

'*I* couldn't,' grinned Ron. 'Look at my boots.'

We all stared as he lifted one foot, then the other, to show us. The soles of his walking boots had worked their way free from the leather and were flapping at the toes.

'Oh, heck,' I said, feeling guilty that our hike had been their undoing. 'Are they your only pair?'

'No,' Ron laughed. 'I've brought some shoes, don't worry. I was going to bin these before we left but Miranda thought they'd survive one last wear.'

After a cuppa Miranda retired upstairs for a *siesta*. Ron went with her to change into his shoes. Eventually, he reappeared, respectably shod and clutching a Wilbur Smith book, along with the conked-out boots.

'I've defrosted curry for tonight,' I told him, 'but I need to sort out the relishes. You won't be offended, will you, if I start to prepare?'

'Not at all,' he replied. 'I thought I might read for an hour. I'll get rid of these boots first though, which way's the wheelie bin?'

'Left out of the back door, straight on past the farmhouse. You can't miss it, it's just before the church.'

I set about chopping onions for a kachumber and sent Gary off to the herb bed to pick some fresh mint.

Five minutes later, Ron was back on the doorstep. He was still holding his boots and wearing a sheepish grin.

'I think I must've taken a wrong turning. I came back when I reached some farm machinery and bales of hay. Is Gary about? Perhaps he could show me where to go.'

'He's making himself useful in the garden,' I grinned. 'Don't worry, though. You can take Anxo with you, he'll show you the way.'

Ron thought I was pulling his leg, He smiled patiently.

'I'm not joking. He's a herding dog. He'll get you there, you'll see.' I opened the back door and called Anxo in from the lane. 'Anxo, to rubbish! To rubbish! off you go.'

Five minutes later Ron was back again. This time he was empty handed.

'Anxo's amazing! When we got to the farmhouse I could see tracks leading off in three different directions; that must have been where I went wrong. I still wasn't sure which was the *right* way, so I said: "Anxo, to rubbish!" He understood perfectly and charged straight ahead.'

Miranda was impressed when Ron recounted the story to her at dinner.

'That's really clever,' she smiled. 'You've done a great job with his training. He's lovely company, and so is Scholes.'

'I forgot to tell you,' said Ron. 'I saw Scholes up by the farmyard when I went to the bin.'

'That's impossible,' frowned Miranda. 'He slept on the bed while I had my *siesta*. You couldn't have seen him – he was with me the whole time.'

'The cat flap,' smiled Gary. 'He must have slipped out and come back while you were dozing. That's happened to us a couple of times lately, I think he does it on purpose to make you feel like you're losing your mind.'

We ate and chatted and reminisced about life in Las Palmas. Eventually Gary reminded me there was still a pudding to devour.

'So what's the plan for tomorrow?' asked Miranda, as she served us with generous dollops of carrot halwa.

'Touristy stuff,' said Gary, yawning. 'Ramparts and a river, so I'm told.'

'That sounds great,' said Ron.

'I wouldn't get your hopes up, Ron. It's probably just an old ruin, but Liza's determined we should go.'

'Doesn't he just *ooze* enthusiasm?' I groaned. 'It'd be different if we were going to see Lugo playing at home.'

'So it's a castle?' asked Miranda.

'Yes,' I said. 'Castillo de Pambre. It was built at the end of the fourteenth century. Apparently, it's of great significance in Galicia's feudal history. According to the guidebook it's the one of the few fortresses to survive the peasant revolts.'

'Wow,' said Miranda. 'It sounds exciting. And a river as well?'

'Yes,' I grinned. 'The castle overlooks the Río Pambre. That might not be *quite* so exciting. Unlike the Río Ulla, the Río Pambre isn't even on the map.'

Gary wasn't *exactly* sure where we were going, but he vaguely remembered seeing a turn-off for the castle on a previous visit to Palas de Rei. Sure enough, as we approached the outskirts of Palas a signpost for Pambre came into view. We followed the winding road through dense countryside, passing through countless *aldeas* along the way. After twenty minutes I was convinced we'd taken a wrong turn.

'If it's only eight kilometres from Palas, that's about fifteen minutes – shouldn't we be there by now? I'm wondering if we've missed a turn-off somewhere, don't you think we'd be better to retrace out steps?'

Gary ignored me and drove on regardless. There was an awkward silence for a moment; wary of incurring the wrath of the driver, the passengers all seemed reluctant to speak. Just as I was about to repeat that it might be better to do a U-turn, Miranda spotted a sign.

'Look, Gary, "Pambre three kilometres". You need to take a left about here.'

I said nothing; we'd almost gone round in a circle. Not that it mattered; our guests had enjoyed their impromptu detour and, against all odds, the driver had managed to keep his cool.

We parked up at the bottom of a steep slope, with Castillo de Pambre looming above. As we stepped out onto the shingle, we could hear the rushing current of the Río Pambre beyond the trees. When we finally reached the top of the slope there were no smiling guides to greet us; a strip of red and white tape across the arched entrance suggested we might not be welcome today. To the right of the entrance a small but official-looking notice bearing the Xunta de Galicia logo confirmed our suspicions.

'Building work in progress, Sorry for the inconvenience. Do not pass beyond the tape.'

Our collective 'Oh, *no*!' must have echoed across the valley. We all looked at one another in dismay.

'Well, how bloody stupid,' I moaned. 'Why didn't they put the sign at the bottom? It would've saved us hiking all the way up.'

'Perhaps they thought people might like to see the castle anyway,' reasoned Miranda. 'If they've come some distance, they can at least get to see it from the outside.'

'It doesn't *look* particularly dangerous,' said Gary, who'd moved forward to get a better look through the huge open archway into the space beyond the thick stone wall.

We all shuffled forward and peered through. At the far end of the courtyard the mouth of a concrete mixer gaped redundantly, and a length of blue hosepipe snaked across the ground.

'You're right.' agreed Ron. 'There doesn't seem to be any scaffolding, and look, it's an open courtyard, it's not as if the roof will cave in.'

'I don't think it'd do any harm to have a quick look,' said Gary. 'It's Sunday, nobody's working. it's not as if we're going to get caught.'

'On your heads be it,' I grinned. 'They're probably all sat in deckchairs round the corner; I bet they've only stopped for a fag and a brew.'

'Come on,' smiled Miranda. 'We can duck under the tape and walk through the courtyard. If we get so far and it starts to look dangerous, we can come straight back the way we came.'

'You go,' I said, opening my rucksack and reaching for my drum of tobacco. 'I'll stay here and keep lookout. If anyone appears at the bottom, I'll yell a warning. You'll have plenty of time to nip out before they get to the top.'

'Are you *sure* you don't want to come with us?' asked Ron.

'No, honestly. They say walls have ears, and have you seen the size of the mouth on that concrete mixer? I'm perfectly happy to stay here, I'm ready for a fag.'

The intrepid trio were back before I'd even docked my ciggie. So much for my itinerary of exciting things to do.

'It's not a *total* ruin,' explained Miranda. 'The walls form a square and there's a tower in each corner. There's a bigger tower in the middle – it looks like they've been working in there.'

'I'm ever so sorry,' I said. 'I honestly thought it would be worth our while.'

'Don't worry,' smiled Ron. 'It isn't *your* fault. Anyway, it gives us an excuse to come back next year.'

'The river then?' suggested Gary.

We followed a steep shingly pathway down to the young river, where the waters tumbled forcefully behind veils of foliage, and shafts of sunlight made intermittent rainbows in the spray.

'*Wow*,' breathed Miranda. 'I *must* take some photos! The journey's been worth it for this view alone.'

I smiled to myself. What an ironic conclusion to our outing: the important chunk of Galician history had been a non-starter, but the river that wasn't worth putting in the map book had saved the day.

'It'll only be a whistle-stop tour,' I explained, as I washed up the plates and eggcups. 'If we set off shortly we'll be in Lugo around eleven, but by the time we've parked up, walked into the centre and stopped for a coffee it'll be nearer mid-day. We need to be back around five for Anxo. He's not used to being left on his own for too long.'

'I read something about Lugo,' said Miranda, 'Do you remember, Ron? It was in one of your *History* magazines?'

'Yes,' Ron nodded. 'There was an article about the best-preserved examples of Roman architecture. Isn't it Lugo that's famous for its wall?'

'That's right,' I said. 'Apparently it's the only complete Roman city wall remaining in the whole world. Hold, on, let me read you what it says in the guidebook.'

I dried my hands on the tea towel and reached into my rucksack, pleased with myself for being well-prepared. 'Here we go. "The most ancient city in Galicia is enclosed by two kilometres of thick wall. In the first century the emperor Augustus was committed to conquering the Celtic resistance and in order to ensure victory and later expansion he created Lucus Augusti, a populated city which is still conserved today, along with an aqueduct and hot spas."[9]

'Wow, so it's almost two thousand years old.'

---

[9] Ignacio Velázquez and Flor Tilve, *Galicia III: El Viajero*, (Madrid: El País, 2005) p.119

'Not quite. The *city* is, but the wall was built around it later. Hold on, let's see... "In the year 260 a wall was constructed to protect the Lucus Augusti populous from possible barbarian attacks. Its six metres of thickness guaranteed its defence, along with eighty-five towers, many of them circular and with a window from which one could keep watch and hide."'

'You do realise,' said Gary, 'we could have been halfway to Lugo by the time Liza's finished showing off with her history lessons.'

'Bugger off,' I grinned. 'Right then, before we get going, who needs the loo?'

'I'm sorry it's only pizza and salad,' I said as I plonked a hot 'n' spicy down at one end of the table and a Neapolitan at the other. Gary was bringing up the rear with the salad bowl.

'There you go,' I nodded. 'Stick it in the middle.'

'They're the size of dustbin lids!' exclaimed Miranda. 'I wish I hadn't eaten so many *tapas* this afternoon.'

'Very fitting,' said Ron as he opened the bottle of Albariño we'd bought at the *vinoteca*.

We looked at him quizzically.

'Romans... Italians... pizza...?'

'Aww!' Miranda groaned.

'Very good,' I smiled. 'I can assure you it's a complete coincidence.'

'Wait 'til they see the pudding,' grinned Gary. 'That's even more appropriate.'

I frowned to myself. Tonight's dessert had nothing to do with Italy or the Romans. Gary's memory was definitely getting worse.

'Sorry folks, The pudding's *not* Italian. Gary's got it wrong.'

'I didn't say it was *Italian*. I said it was *appropriate*. You'll love it when I tell you.' He paused for effect.

'Go on then,' urged Miranda.

'It's *WALL*-nut tart.'

It was late on Tuesday morning when we set off along the main road for Santa Mariña. Miranda and I strode away purposefully but Gary and Ron ambled, weighed down with rucksacks of butties, cold pizza, water and pop. The sun was warm, and the sky was cloudless, but where the road bordered the woodlands, it was chilly in the shade of the trees. As we passed the tiny village of Penela, three German shepherds leapt up from their doorstep and ran towards us barking. When we sauntered on and ignored them, they settled back down to doze,

'So, you've never been as far as the River Ulla?' asked Miranda, as we paced along the verge.

'No,' I said. 'We've walked to Santa Mariña. It takes roughly an hour at a leisurely stroll. The river beach is a bit further, but I'm sure it won't be too far.'

At Gradoi we picked up the first blue sign for the Río Ulla and turned onto a narrower, windier stretch of road. It was less than two months since Gary and I had made our first trek to the Black Eagle; it was amazing how the landscape had taken on a lush opulence in such a short space of time. The canopies of the oaks seemed heavier and greener, and, on the chestnut trees, catkins dangled beneath fans of shiny leaves. The grassy verges were studded with a profusion of colour from the camomile, calendula, mallow and celandines, and clusters of delicate pink alpines and sturdy mauve foxgloves leaned out from the fissures in tumbledown walls. Eventually I spotted a scattering of houses in the distance, and ten minutes later the sombre Pazo de Santa Mariña came into view.

Miranda and I were admiring a coat of arms carved above the entrance when Gary and Ron finally arrived.

'Another castle!' exclaimed Ron.

'Not *quite* a castle,' said Gary. 'It's a *pazo*. I'm not sure how you'd say it in English. What do think, Liza? Is it a stately home?'

'I reckon it's as good a description as any. You could say it's a small-scale fortified palace, I suppose. Either way, there are thousands of them all over the region. They were home to the *hidalgos* – the idle rich, basically – who owned the surrounding land.'

As we began the short walk through the village, Gary was ready to eat.

'I'm starving,' he announced. 'I wonder how far it is to the beach.'

'Tom didn't say,' I answered. 'It could be ten minutes, it could be half an hour. We could always eat first then carry on walking. We could sit on the benches, over there on the green.'

'That's a brilliant idea,' Miranda nodded. 'It'd lighten the load in the rucksacks and the men might keep up.'

Having made short work of the picnic, we left Santa Mariña, passing a trio of stone crosses by the side of the road. After twenty minutes, there was still no sign of the Río Ulla. Gary was the first to suggest that it might be better to turn back.

'We've come this far,' said Miranda. 'Let's keep going a bit longer, it might be just round the next bend.'

Three 'next bends' later I was inclined to agree with Gary. There was Anxo to consider, and we'd still have a long walk back. It was all down to Ron now; poor devil, he had the casting vote. It was the prospect of a cold beer that swung it.

'I think Gary's right, Miranda. Let's head back to the village. We can stop at the Black Eagle on the way back.'

That evening the trout was cooked to perfection, served on a bed of baked fennel and topped with a rich almond sauce. Gary, ever the joker, couldn't resist a quip.

'There you go, Miranda, why do all that walking when you can have a bit of the Río Ulla served up on a plate?'

On Wednesday morning Ron, Miranda and I were looking forward to our final excursion. We were off to a Galician ethnographic museum, promising exhibits spanning three centuries of rural life and rustic crafts. Gary was less enthusiastic; it was an unknown destination, and he was dreading the drive.

Thankfully, the Muséo Casa do Patrón was well signposted. We parked at the edge of the village of Doade only ten minutes after leaving Lalín. Much to our surprise, Doade was an authentic, inhabited *aldea* with hens pecking about in a farmyard and a pack of *podenco* hunting dogs barking excitedly in a pen.

The visitor's centre was situated in one of the first houses in the village, but there was no-one at the reception desk when we walked in. We hovered for a moment, expecting someone to appear through one of the doors at the back, but it soon became clear there was nobody home. As we stood contemplating our options, a woman came in through the door.

'I'm sorry to have kept you waiting, I was in the *huerta.* Have you come for the tour?'

We all nodded

'Do you understand Castilian?'

We nodded again.

'Good. Come on then, follow me.'

We walked a short distance to the next cluster of stone houses, along a recently tarmacked road. I thought of the potholes and stones that littered the way through our own *aldea*. Perhaps if we had enough visitors, we could call it tourism; it might persuade our council to resurface the lane.

Our guide unlocked the door of the first house we came to. She explained that the museum was based in three different buildings within the *aldea*, and ushered us in. The ground floor was set out like a workshop, showing an intriguing variety of rural crafts. There was a potter's wheel, a wood-turning lathe, a spinning wheel and a loom where a dummy in traditional costume was weaving a thick woollen rug.

The second building housed reconstructed rooms of typical rural dwellings from the late 1700s to the early 1900s. The biggest space by far was a kitchen, complete with a traditional open fireplace at one end.

'Look!' I exclaimed. 'A *lareira*! Isn't it gorgeous?' I turned to Ron and Miranda: 'I'd love one of these!'

'Thank God the house hasn't got one,' said Gary. 'Look at the size of the logs they needed to keep it going. We can barely find enough branches to burn in the range.'

Along the opposite wall was a long, oak table. I was surprised to see that the chairs around it were strikingly similar to those in our dining room.

The eighteenth-century bedroom was quite an eye-opener. If *my* only option was to sleep on a mattress stuffed with corn husks I don't think I'd ever bother going to bed again.

The second bedroom looked a sight more civilised. By the turn of the twentieth century the notion of comfort had finally hit home. The fluffed-up feather bed looked decidedly inviting; I thought of Rufo and wondered if we could make one of our own.

'There's one of your trunks,' gasped Miranda. 'That's amazing!'

'Look here, then,' smiled Gary. 'Here's one of our treasure chests as well.'

The trunk was much the same as those beneath the windows in our living room. It was the chest that intrigued me the most. When Gary had discovered ours a year ago, they were dilapidated boxes of rust. I'd been determined to restore them but hadn't much of a clue about their original appearance. I'd done my best with varnish and Hammerite and was satisfied with the result. As I gave the exhibit the once-over it was gratifying to see that I hadn't been too far off the mark.

For the final stage of our tour, we returned to the visitors' centre. The exhibition room behind the reception area was given over entirely to food production. It was, without a doubt, the highlight of the day. Fishing, hunting, baking, cheesemaking, brewing, farming... the list seemed endless. Tagged on to the end of the dairy section, we spotted our hives.

'We still don't know what tree they come from,' said Gary. 'Let's ask the guide.'

I smiled when she gave us the answer; no wonder they'd soaked up so much varnish. They were made of cork.

'I'm glad we saved the museum 'til last,' said Miranda, as we pulled out of Doade. 'After spending time in your house so many of the artefacts seemed familiar. It's helped to put them in context, seeing how they were used all those years ago.'

'Yes,' agreed Ron. 'Like filling in the last pieces of the jigsaw. It's fascinating how you've recycled things like the trunks and the beehives; it's as if you've created a real-life museum of your own.'

'Do you mind if Ron and I go for a wander this morning?' asked Miranda, as she passed me a bundle of bedsheets and towels. 'We wanted to take some more photos before we leave for the airport, and I'd like to have a better look at the church and the tombs.'

'Not the jolliest way to end your holiday,' quipped Gary.

'Ignore him,' I grinned. 'You'll enjoy it. The church dates right back to the late seventeen-hundreds. A couple of the original gravestones are still standing, but if you look closely, you'll see that some more have been used to make the pathway up to the church.'

'That'll make a good photo,' said Ron. 'And we must get the bell and the cross on the green.'

'Ooh,' I remembered, 'you'll be able to see the tomb of José Val, whose house we live in. He's in there, buried with his wife. It's one of the flat ones, a bit like a coffin. It's the third on the right as you go in.'

'I'll have a look,' said Miranda. 'It'd be nice to…'

'Put names to faces?' laughed Gary.

'Ignore him,' I frowned.

'I was going to say, "pay our respects".'

'Carmen's a widow, isn't she?' asked Ron. 'Is her husband in there as well?'

'Yes,' I nodded. 'He's on the left. It's about the fifth one in after the corner…'

'You don't need to sound so eager,' said Gary. 'You sound like a tour guide. Perhaps you could start up a business: "Daytrip to the Dearly Departed" – it's got a ring to it. You could even sell plastic flowers as souvenirs.'

On Friday morning I had a text message from Miranda:

Thanks for a marvellous time. Could you email me the nachos recipe please? x

I was flummoxed for a moment. There *was* no recipe. I'd been making the nachos for years, yet I hadn't a clue about the quantities or cooking times. It was pretty much guesswork really, but they always worked out. I'd have to see what I could do.

Liza's Chilli Nachos

Put flour in a bowl
(Eight ounces will do),
Add chilli and salt
(The amount's up to you).

Now add some cold water
To bind to a dough
(About half a cupful,
But see how you go).

Divide into lumps
(About ping-pong ball size),
And roll each one thinly,
Then put to one side.

Now warm up a skillet
And dry cook each one –
(The surface puffs slightly
To show you it's done.)

Next, cut up each disc
In triangular shards
(Like cutting a pizza –
It's really not hard).

Now heat up some oil
and fry them like chips
(But do smaller batches)
'Til golden and crisp.

These nachos are truly
Too good to embellish,
But if you insist
Use a hot chilli relish!

Chapter 9

Mountains and Molehills

For the whole of Friday I'd been in a state of mixed emotions. I was sad about saying goodbye to our visitors but being a creature of habit, I was glad to get back to my daily routine. When I rose on Saturday morning, I was feeling refreshed, recharged and ready to face whatever the weekend had in store. It was over a week since I'd sat out on the bench with my cigarette and coffee, and it struck me how much I enjoyed this unhurried start to the day. For a while I listened to the cockerels and the birdsong, and of course, the shouts and the whistling down at number fifteen.

Twenty minutes later, I put Anxo back in the kitchen; I couldn't sit daydreaming for ever, it was time to let out the hens. As I opened the gate, I stopped dead in amazement. What on earth were those little brown mountains? The lawn looked like the surface of the moon.

'We've got moles,' I told Gary, as I passed him his cuppa.

'What, in the garden?'

I gave an exasperated frown. 'Obviously.'

'There's no need to get tetchy. I meant as opposed to the *huerta*.'

'The *huerta*? Oh, crikey! I didn't think to check in there!'

'Don't worry about it now, I'll have a look when you take Anxo. Sit down for a minute and finish your fag and your brew.'

When I unpacked the shopping on Monday there was something in the bag I wasn't expecting. I rolled my eyes skywards; Gary was forever buying things that weren't on the list. I pulled it out and waved it at him.

'What's this?'

'It's a mole trap.'

'A *mole* trap?' I stared at it for a moment. It looked like a bit of plastic drainpipe to me. It was roughly six inches long and slightly wider than the inside of a toilet roll. There was a detachable rubber cap at one end. The mole was obviously supposed to crawl into the pipe and get stuck, but somehow I couldn't see it working. I was sure there was enough wriggle room for the hapless creature to push its way backwards and escape. I pulled a face.

'You don't seem impressed.'

'I'm not. I can't see the point of it. The mole comes up against the lid, realises he can't get any further and wriggles back out again. What use is that?'

'There's a hinged bit inside, have a look.'

I tipped it up to examine it. I nodded. 'Yes, I see.'

'The mole runs into the tunnel and pushes the flap forwards. Once he's in, it springs back and he's trapped.

'Ah, *now* I get it. It's the same principle as the chicken killer we saw that day in Lugo. You lift the plastic lid off and when he starts to push forward you chop his head off.'

'Of *course* you don't chop his head off! It's nothing *like* the chicken killer. It's a humane trap, silly. The mole gets trapped in the tunnel and then you take it over the field and let him go.'

'Right.'

'You don't sound convinced.'

'I'm not. Moles aren't renowned for running up drainpipes. Think about it. There's Mr Mole tunnelling his merry way through the garden when he comes across a plastic subway. Does he think "oh, whoopy-do, that'll save a bit of elbow grease, I'll take the tube"? Does he heck as like! He senses danger and dashes off the other way.'

'Sometimes you're such a cynic. It'll work, you wait and see.'

My usual walk with Anxo took us along the track at the side of the garden, over the stepping-stones, through the forest and across Javier's five fields. Apart from the seasonal changes in the landscape, the occasional hunt or a tractor, our surroundings remained the same.

On Tuesday morning, Anxo bounded ahead as I weaved my way through the gaps in the bracken at the edge of Field One. When I stepped out into Field Two, half of it wasn't there! A massive expanse of grass had been torn away, exposing a huge brown patch of damp, crumbly soil. I thought of the mountains in our garden; either a much larger animal had jumped on the excavation bandwagon or a heck of a lot of people had been releasing their moles.

'It must be the cows,' said Gary when I told him over coffee. 'If the ground's wet it probably gets churned up when they eat.'

'I don't think it's that,' I frowned. 'It *can't* be. 'This is Galicia. The ground's often wet but I've never noticed *that* before. Perhaps a bird of prey's done it. If there are moles about perhaps the birds have been trying to catch them, clawing away at the earth.'

'Could be,' he nodded. 'Or what about the roe deer, they graze don't they?'

'They graze, yes, but they don't *dig*. My money's still on a bird.'

'I'm going to check the phone when I've finished my coffee. If Maruja's about I'll ask her, she's bound to know.'

While Gary went up to the church I wandered out into the garden to check on the mole trap. I squatted down and eased off the lid. It was empty – surprise, surprise. As I replaced the lid, I became aware of a strong pungent odour. It was familiar, but at first I couldn't quite place it. Suddenly it dawned on me: it was the smell of a tom cat, and it was still fresh in the air. For a while now I'd had my suspicions, but this latest evidence left no doubt in my mind. There was another cat in the village; a cat who bore an uncanny resemblance to Scholes. As I cast my eyes over the garden to see if the culprit was lurking, I was distracted by footsteps. Tom was coming past with Maud and The Ox. It was the first time I'd seen him since Ron and Miranda's visit. It was time to test out the lay of the land.

'Morning,' I called. 'Did you have a good holiday?'

'Lovely,' he smiled. 'Just what the doctor ordered. I'd been feeling stressed out if I'm honest and I was missing Isabel. It's done me the world of good.'

'I'm glad,' I said, wondering whether or not to mention Anxo. I decided against it, there was nothing to be gained by opening up old wounds.

'How did it go with your visitors?'

'Great,' I said. 'They loved the village. They loved the landscape. They loved Galicia full stop.'

'*I'm* having a visitor next week. I bet you can't guess who?'

I thought for a moment. It wouldn't be Isabel: she had a comfortable apartment, so Tom always went to hers. He'd mentioned having a couple of brothers, friends from college, that sort of thing, but if he was asking me to guess it had to be someone I knew. That only left one possibility...

'Is it Paul?'

'It is.'

'I thought he wasn't coming 'til August, I thought he was flying out to work on the roof?'

'He was. But he's decided he's out of condition. He's going to have a month of the outdoor life to get fit.'

I thought of Paul's overgrown land that began at the side of Carmen's and turned to make an L-shape running behind our chooks. It was a massive area. There was a wilderness of bracken, bramble and gorse to clear and a myriad of trees with precariously dangling limbs. He'd be up close and personal with the natural environment and working like a navvy to boot.

'It's a good idea,' I nodded. 'Clearing the garden will be a decent daily work-out. He'll be in great shape by the time he starts on the roof.'

Tom started laughing. 'This is *Paul* we're talking about. His training won't be out there in the garden. He's talking about running over the fields and walking up the mountain. He wants to be at one with nature, out in the wilds.'

'That seems like a waste of time to me,' I frowned. 'He'll need to build strength as well as stamina, why not kill two birds with one stone?'

'Talking of killing birds,' said Tom. 'Maruja told me it wasn't Anxo that killed the duck and the chicken. I'm sorry I jumped to the wrong conclusion. He was just in the wrong place at the wrong time.'

When Gary came in at lunchtime, I was looking forward to telling him the latest news.

'I've got *loads* to tell you,' I announced excitedly. 'But first things first, what did Maruja say about the field?'

'I didn't see her. Perhaps you'll catch her when you take the rubbish. Until then it's still a mystery I'm afraid.'

'There's another one.'

'What? Another excavation?'

'No. Another mystery. I think we've had a tom cat in the garden. It's been spraying, I could smell it near the broom.'

'*I* haven't smelt anything unusual.'

'You wouldn't, you're olfactorily challenged, I've been telling you that for years.'

'I hate it when you sound like a dictionary, I wish you'd just say what you mean.'

'You've got a terrible sense of smell. I've told you what it means a thousand times. You've got a terrible memory as well.'

'So how do you know it isn't Scholes that's been weeing?'

'*Spraying*,' I corrected him. 'Scholes is neutered. He doesn't need to leave messages to tell other males to keep away.'

'If there was another cat about we'd have seen it.'

'I think we already have. If you ask me there's an imposter at large.'

'I think you've got an overactive imagination. Anyway, what was the other news?'

'We haven't caught any moles yet.'

'Is that *all*?'

'No, I'm just being annoying, I wanted to keep you in suspense.'

'So what's the real news?'

'We're back in Tom's good books. He's apologised for getting the wrong end of the stick.'

'That *is* good news. In fact, it's brilliant. When did you see him? What else did he say?'

'He was walking the dogs. He said Paul's coming back in about a week.'

'For the roof?'

'No, to run up the mountain.'

'Let's hope he wears some clothes.'

Maruja was out on the doorstep when Anxo and I took the rubbish.

'*Hola*, Maruja,' I said, as Anxo ran up to her wagging his tail.

'*Hola.* Elisa. *Hace calor.*'

It was, indeed, hot, though not unpleasant. The oppressive keep-you-indoors heat would come in July.

'Has something been digging over the fields?' I asked her. 'I noticed the grass has been disturbed.'

'It'll be the *jabalí*,' she sighed.

'Really?' I said, surprised. I hadn't thought of wild boar.

'Oh, yes,' Maruja continued. 'They're a nuisance. They can be very destructive. We've been lucky really; there's an article in yesterday's paper. Somewhere in Ourense they've ruined an entire field.'

She went into the kitchen and came back with *El Progreso*. There was a photograph of a farmer standing in a field that was almost bare. Thanks to the wild boar the land was now useless and there was absolutely nothing he could do.

While we were talking, Pastora appeared on the corner. It was obvious by the shape of her abdomen her pups could arrive at any time.

'She's hungry again,' frowned Maruja. 'She only has to hear us and she's at the back door.'

'She'll need double once she's feeding the puppies,' I sighed. 'I'm worried about whether she'll cope.'

'She might not have to,' said Maruja. 'It depends on whether Tonito wants to keep them I suppose.'

I understood what Maruja was saying. Old habits die hard in the Galician *aldeas*; it was still common practice to kill puppies and kittens at birth. Of course, the whole business was needless and barbaric, but as I looked again at Pastora I couldn't help thinking it might be a blessing in disguise.

Over the next couple of days I worried myself senseless over Pastora. I took to setting the alarm clock early and pacing about by the doorstep in case she came by.

'I don't see why you're getting up at such a ridiculous hour,' said Gary. 'It's as though you're expecting her to have her puppies round here.'

'It's a possibility,' I insisted. 'She knows she'd be looked after. Look how she came everyday over summer. She spent all her time here and hardly ever went home.'

'That was a year ago: she was only a puppy. She's a cow dog now. She's used to a different routine.'

By Friday I was feeling despondent. I'd still seen neither hide nor hair of Pastora and was convinced that something was wrong.

I was filling the kettle for our morning coffees when I heard Gary calling me from the barn. Even before I opened the door, I could guess the reason. Pastora was waiting outside in the lane.

'Pastora!' I cried. 'Oh, Pastora! Thank goodness you've come to no harm.'

Pastora jumped up me, her tail wagging madly. When Anxo ran up she gave a low growl.

'She's hungry,' said Gary. 'I'll fetch her some food.'

He went inside and I stared down at Pastora. Her hips and ribs were visible, and her long, swollen teats left me in no doubt that she was feeding a litter of pups. When Gary returned she bolted down the kibble like there was no tomorrow.

'She was more than hungry,' I seethed. 'She was ravenous, poor girl.'

It wasn't until Saturday that I finally received news of the puppies.

'She's had six,' Solina told me. 'Maruja saw Tonito when she went to the bin.'

The news wasn't ideal, but at least I knew what was happening. We'd be able to make sure Pastora didn't go hungry, but I had to accept that there was nothing we could do about her pups.

Over the next three days Pastora came by every morning and evening. As soon as she'd eaten, she'd hurry back up the lane.

On Wednesday Tonito was walking up from the *río* with his bucket. Pastora was with him, which I found rather strange.

'How are the puppies?' I smiled, disguising my true feelings.

'They're dead,' he replied, matter-of-factly. 'Pastora was bored with them. She killed them all.'

'Paul arrived last night,' announced Gary, on Friday morning. 'I saw him while you were walking Anxo. He was coming back from his morning run.'

'He's started running *already*? Crikey, he must be keen.'

'Keen's not the word I'd have used; crackers would be nearer the mark. Apparently he used to run marathons. He reckons he'll be running all the way to the mountain and back by the end of the month.'

'I'll believe it when I see it. What else did he have to say?'

'He's cycling to Lidl tomorrow.'

'*Lidl*? Are you winding me up?'

Lidl discounter stores began to spring up in England during the 1990s. A decade later it had become a popular supermarket chain.

'No. I'm serious. Apparently, there's a Lidl in Lalín.'

It was nothing short of amazing. In the four years that Paul had owned number ten he'd learned next to nothing about the way of life in the *aldea* and barely understood a word of Castilian, yet he'd manage to find a supermarket half an hour's drive away where he could buy English food. Talk about getting your priorities right.

'He's cycling to Lalín on a pushbike? You're right, he *is* crackers. It'd take him well over an hour to get there.'

'An hour and three quarters, he reckons. He's done it before.'

I was incredulous. 'But what have they got at Lidl that makes it worth all that time and effort?'

'Cheddar. "I've got to have my cheddar. I like to stock up." They were his exact words.'

'But the Galician cheeses are scrumptious…'

'That's what I told him. Apparently, they're not strong enough and they're too soft.'

'Not all of them,' I frowned. 'That's rubbish. *We've* had some super zingy ones, and those made from ewe's milk are lovely and hard.'

'I told him all that, but he wouldn't have it. He's a cheese butty short of a picnic if you ask me.'

Having no regular income meant having no internet, but Maribel allowed me to use the estate agency's computer whenever I wanted to go online. It was over two months since I'd last checked my emails; our family and friends were aware of our basic existence and usually sent letters by post. On Monday I drove into Monterroso with Gary; I could spend half an hour in the office while he did the weekly shop. I was expecting to find nothing but junk in my inbox so the message from friends in Las Palmas came as a lovely surprise.

From: Jan Rogers
To: Liza Grantham
Subject: Greetings from Las Palmas!
Date: Wed 25 June 2012

Hi Liza and Gary

Hope you're both well and getting used to wearing wellies and thermals. Graham has some holiday due in July and we want to spend most of it getting some DIY done on the house. It would still be nice to have a few days away though and we wondered if we could fly over for a long weekend. We'd be arriving on the evening of Thursday 17th July and leaving on the Sunday afternoon. Let me know asap if it's ok and if so, is there anything you'd like us to bring.

Love, Jan and Graham

As I walked along the main street, I noticed posters on some of the lamp posts. A *Feira de Artesanía* was to be held at Os Pendellos marketplace in Agolada over the coming weekend.

When I met Gary back at the carpark, he could see that I was excited.

'Don't tell me you've had a message? By the look on your face, I'd say it's good news.'

'We've had an email from Jan and Graham. They want to come over for a long weekend in July.'

'Crikey, our second round of visitors. We're certainly doing our bit for local industry; we're keeping tourism alive.'

'Did you see the posters for the *artesano* market?'

'I did. I thought it might be interesting, and Agolada's not that far.'

'Agolada. We've never been there, so why does the name ring a bell?'

'It's on the route to the airport, not far from Melide. It sounds familiar because we've driven through it a few times. So, shall we go?'

'Not half. I bet we'll see lots of the crafts we saw at the museum. There might be local breads and cheeses to try as well.'

'Ah, yes, a bit of sampling.'

'Exactly. We missed out at the cheese festival, after all.'

That evening I sat poring through my guidebooks. 'Are you sure you don't want to have a look?' I asked Gary. 'It'd be nice if you joined in.'

'I'll let you do the organising,' he said. 'You enjoy it. You know I'm happy with anything as long as it doesn't involve a long drive.'

'Okay then, let me tell you what I've got in mind. They're coming from Thursday to Sunday, so that only gives us two full days. If we kept the trips short and fairly local, we could manage a couple of outings each day. What do you think?'

'I think it's a great idea, it rules out Lugo and Lalín.'

'Right. What about Santa Mariña? I know we've been twice now but…'

'That doesn't matter. Graham would love the Black Eagle; you know how he likes his beer.'

'Perfect. We could go in the car instead of walking. We'll head straight for the river beach and have a picnic lunch at the side of the Río Ulla then we'll stop off at the pub and have a look at the *pazo* on the way back.'

'Brilliant. What about Pambre? Is it worth checking if the building work's finished?'

'I shouldn't think so. It looked like they'd only just started a month ago and don't forget, lots of people have the whole month off in July.'

I carried on thumbing through, but I was struggling. Some of the places to visit looked truly amazing, but most of them would mean a good two hours' drive. Eventually I found something practically on our doorstep. 'This looks interesting. There's a church with fourteenth century frescos near Palas de Rei. That sounds ideal.'

'Ideal for *us* maybe, but Graham would hate it. He'd be bored out of his mind.'

'It's a pity there's nothing to show them in Monterroso.'

'Wait a minute, maybe there is. Didn't Maribel mention some outdoor leisure thingy when we came to look at the house?'

'Oh, yes, I remember. It's called A Peneda. But I don't see what's interesting about tennis courts and an outdoor pool.'

Gary sighed. 'Go on then, pass me a guidebook. You never know, I might see something you've missed.'

I stood up and walked over to the window. The sun was low in the sky, and it was almost dark outside.

'I'm going to shut the chooks away. Keep searching, you never know your luck.'

Even though it was twilight, it was a lovely warm evening; Jan and Graham were definitely coming at the right time of year.

When I came back into the kitchen Gary was looking pleased with himself.

'Don't tell me you found something suitable?'

'I might have. There's a couple of pages on Agolada. it mentions Os Pendellos. Here, see what you think.'

He passed me the book.

'Right then. "Os Pendellos de Agolada is a marketplace built in the 18th century. The precarious roads meant that the merchants had to spend the night where the market was held – the reason for the unusual design of this construction, where the roofs of the stalls meet to form a very well-preserved stone colonnade."[10] Ooh, that's thoughtful. If you sold stuff at the market at least you could be sure of a roof over your head for the night.'

'Look at the photo.'

'Oh, wow! It's so full of character. The stalls are like little houses, they look really quaint.'

'I think it'd be an interesting place to take visitors. We could have a wander around Os Pendellos then drinks and *tapas* at a bar... maybe a stroll through Agolada as well. The beauty of it is, we can check it out when we go to the fair next weekend. What do you think?'

'I think you're a genius. Perhaps *you* should be Chief Organiser from now on,'

On Saturday morning Agolada was heaving with people. We didn't know where we were going but followed the hoards until we found ourselves in the main square. A row of hardware stalls filled the centre, and a collection of vintage cars were parked down one side. At the far

---

[10] Ignacio Velázquez and Flor Tilve, *Galicia III: El Viajero*, (Madrid: El País, 2005) p.33

end was an ornate granite fountain, and a couple of café-bars with tables set out in the sun.

'This isn't it,' frowned Gary. 'You saw the photo, it's rows of little shelters, all made of stone,'

He was right, this wasn't Os Pendellos, but I was certain it was somewhere close by. I scanned the crowds for a moment and soon came up with the answer; people laden with leaflets and bags were coming out of a narrow alley in the corner of the square.

At the end of the alley was the quaint, cobbled marketplace. It was bigger than I'd expected, with four rows of stalls arranged in two tiers. The construction was simple, yet no less impressive. Each stall had a stone-built wall at the back, and low stone counters on the remaining three sides. The roofs extended outwards some distance beyond the counter tops, supported by enormous pillars, each of which was a single column of solid stone.

We wandered from stall to stall, watching as potters, carpenters, cobblers, lacemakers, weavers and silversmiths all performed their crafts. I marvelled as a man added the finest, most intricate details to colourful trout-fishing flies, while Gary was especially impressed with the range of chestnut pieces crafted with the old-fashioned lathe.

'They're fantastic,' he enthused, 'Look at the plates, they're perfect circles. They'd look really good on a wall.'

He was right, the edges were flawlessly smooth, and the grain of the wood made every single piece unique.

'We should buy something,' I suggested.

'The plates are expensive. We can't justify twenty euros for something to hang on the wall.'

'That's true,' I agreed. 'Not if we're going to choose cheese and stuff for the visitors. The trouble is there don't seem to be any stalls selling food.'

'I think there are. Follow me.'

We made our way to the second tier and carried on until we came to a gap in the stalls. On the other side there were steps leading up to a third level lined with wooden stalls selling locally produced food and drink.

'Fantastic! But how did you know where to come?'

'I kept seeing people come past with bags full of jars and boxes. I guessed there must be another tier.'

'Right then,' I said, 'let's get sampling. I skipped breakfast 'specially, where shall we start?'

The first 'stall' was a van, and we did quite nicely, with chunks of cheese and *chorizo* and a slice each of *empanada* filled with tuna and veg.

'Better than the cheese fest, then?' grinned Gary.

I beamed at him. 'Not half.'

For the next hour we ambled along the rows, nibbling the bite-sized samples that tempted us at every stall. There were cheeses in abundance, and we finally plumped for an extra mature ewes' milk and a creamy cows' and goats' milk mixed.

After all the cheese I'd eaten I fancied something sweeter. Fate was on my side this morning; the jam stall was next. The samples were blobbed onto little wooden spatulas laid out on trays.

'Chip forks,' laughed Gary.

'Trust you,' I grinned. 'They've got no prongs, they'd be useless. Shut up and eat your jam.'

I cast my eyes over the selection. There were at least a dozen flavours; I couldn't try all of them, I'd look such a pig. In the end I opted for a couple of the more unusual choices.

'Ooh, this one's good,' I said, as I tried the cherry and orange. 'Sweet, with a hint of a zing.'

'The peach is nice. And the strawberry…'

'Ooh, crikey, Gary, try the spiced fig!'

The *higos especiados* was to die for. It should have come with a health warning; it would be easy to eat a whole jar. I passed Gary a spatula.

'You're right,' he agreed. 'It's gorgeous. Should we buy a jar?'

'You're joking. Have you *seen* the prices? It might be divine but it's also extortionate. It's five euros for a three hundred and forty gramme jar. The going rate for organic *honey*'s only six euros a kilo. I think that's better value by far.'

'Haven't we still got some of the honey we bought at the cheese fair?'

'Only a smidgeon. We should get some more.'

Two stalls down we located our honey and were surprised to see different varieties on sale.

'Surely honey's just honey?' frowned Gary.

'Apparently not,' I grinned. 'Meadow flowers, apple blossom, chestnut, eucalyptus... I s'pose we'll have to try them all.'

The meadow flower and apple blossom were lovely, but there was no discernible difference between them or any other honey I'd eaten before.

'There you go,' said Gary. 'What did I tell you? They just taste like normal honey to me.'

The chestnut honey soon altered his conviction. It had a richer, almost earthy taste.

'It's good,' nodded Gary. 'There's something nutty about it. Should we have one of those?'

'Definitely. Well, *almost* definitely. We ought to try the eucalyptus, just to be sure...'

The eucalyptus honey was much darker than the other varieties; it was the colour of the horrible cough stuff I'd had as a kid. This time the flavour really *was* distinctive; there was a noticeably herbal quality about it which left an aftertaste of sharp, but sweet.

'Well?' asked Gary.

'I know we're on a budget....'

He nodded at the stall holder, who'd been watching. 'We'll take one of each.'

As we made our way back across the *plaza* I noticed an artist painting beside the fountain. There was a selection of her work displayed on easels nearby.

'Look,' I said. 'There's an artist working, let's go and see.'

The paintings were oils, all linked to the theme of water. There were rivers, waterfalls and mist over mountains, all typical of the landscape surrounding our home.

'They're very good,' said Gary admiringly, 'Look how she's captured the movement, and the shadows and the light.'

'I wish you'd paint again,' I told him. 'You're good, and the landscape out here is so lovely...'

'You're right,' he nodded. 'Today's inspired me. I think I might give it a try.'

On Sunday morning I could hear Paul sneezing in the garden.

'I'm going to pop round and tell Paul and Tom about the *artesano* fair.' I told Gary. 'After all that Lidl nonsense it sounds like he could do with a bit of educating. He might actually learn something about Galician culture, and he'd get to try some decent cheeses for free.'

'It sounds fantastic,' said Paul when I'd finished giving him a detailed report of our visit. 'The trouble is we're having company later. Tom's invited a woman for lunch.'

'A *woman*?' I frowned. 'But what about Isabel?'

'Oh it's nothing like *that*. It's someone called Rose who we met at the ex-pats' thing on market day. She's married, but her husband's still working in England. She rides a big motorbike. Tom invited her on a whim after he'd been on the wine.'

'So what are you cooking?'

'*I'm* not cooking anything. It's Tom who's invited her, the dinner's up to him. We've not got much in to be honest. There's a small chicken and plenty of potatoes. I think he's doing us a roast.'

At that moment the gate clanged open and Tom walked onto the threshing floor. I recognised the bleary-eyed look of a man with a very big hangover. I hoped that poor Rose wasn't travelling far.

'Morning, Tom. I hear you're donning your chef's hat later. Will you be up to it? You don't look so grand.'

'I'm not, I've got a blinding headache. I'd forgotten all about it until yesterday when what's her name, Rose, sent me a text.'

'Act in haste, repent at leisure,' Paul chuckled.

Tom didn't look amused.

'So what's Rose like then?' I asked.

'She's fun,' said Paul. 'I think you'd like her. Why don't you and Gary come round for a drink with us later on?'

'I'd like to.' I nodded. 'I'll have word with Gary. What time are you eating? We could nip round when you've done.'

At ten past three Gary took a six-pack of beers out of the fridge and looked at me expectantly. 'Are we set?'

'They were eating at two, but with Tom not feeling so grand I reckon it might be later. We don't want to turn up while they're still having their lunch.'

'We can stick our heads over the gate and see what the score is. We can always come back if they haven't quite done.'

With Anxo in tow, we sauntered up the lane and said '*hola*' to Carmen who was hovering by her back door.

'I bet she's spying,' whispered Gary, as he opened Paul's gate.

At that moment I heard a distinctive high-pitched crowing.

'That's Neurotic Cockerel,' I said, catching hold of Anxo's collar. 'Carmen's not spying, she's bringing her birds into the garden. We'll have to keep a close eye on Anxo and make sure Paul's gate stays closed.'

Out on the threshing floor Paul was lying on a sun-lounger wearing only his boxer shorts. Beneath the shade of the *hórreo* sat a short, chubby woman in jeans and a tee-shirt. I assumed she was Rose.

'We thought you were never coming,' grinned Paul. 'Gary and Liza, this is Rose.

'Pleased to meet you,' I smiled. 'We'd have come sooner, but I thought you were eating at two.'

'So did I,' grinned Rose.

'It's Tom's fault,' laughed Paul. 'I warned him the butane's low, so the oven takes much longer. I said, "get the chicken in early," but he wouldn't have it. At this rate it'll be nearer four o'clock.'

'By which time we'll all be pissed,' laughed Rose.

I chuckled and noticed the empty bottle of *cava*. It was clear that Rose was already well on the way.

Gary handed me a beer and we settled ourselves into patio chairs. Rose was friendly and witty. I could see why Paul found her good fun.

Half an hour later the gate clanged open. I called Anxo to me as Tom appeared with a rather diminutive chicken and a huge amount of roast potatoes piled on a tray.

'Where's the gravy?' asked Paul. 'Got to have gravy.'

Tom glared at him. 'I've only got one pair of hands.'

When Tom reappeared with a saucepan of carrots and a mug of gravy I thought it was time we made tracks.

'We'll be off then,' I said tactfully, 'We'll leave you to enjoy your dinner in peace.'

'Don't be silly,' Paul protested. 'The more the merrier. I'm only sorry there's not enough to offer you some.'

'Well…' I hesitated, looking at Gary.

'If you're sure you don't mind…' he began.

'Have another beer,' giggled Rose. 'I'd offer you a *cava*, but the bottle's empty.' She turned to Paul. 'Is there any more wine?'

I'd expected Tom to rally once the pressure of making the dinner was over; alas, I couldn't have been more wrong. He'd started the day in a mood and two hours of cooking and boozing had done nothing to raise his spirits. As soon as he'd finished eating he retired to a sun-lounger where, oblivious to his visitor, he fell asleep in the shade.

While Paul took the plates back to the house Gary and I listened with interest as Rose told us she was living in a tent because the house she'd bought recently was in such a ruinous state.

'I'd ask you over to dinner, but I don't have a kitchen. You'd be welcome to come over for bread and cheese, but I have to warn you, there's no bathroom. I'm peeing in a bucket.'

'I don't mind camping,' said Gary, 'but I couldn't cope with sleeping on the floor night after night.'

'I don't' she laughed. 'There are some things a girl *can't* do without. I brought a double bed over. It takes up almost the whole of the tent.'

I tried to picture her struggling to squeeze past a double bed for a pee in a bucket in pitch darkness. It all sounded rather calamitous to me.

I was about to ask if the house had a water supply when I was interrupted by a cacophony of clucking and squawking coming from over the wall.

'Anxo!' I called, glancing over to Carmen's garden.

'Don't worry,' said Gary. 'He's been lying behind your chair.'

At that moment we heard an ear-splitting shriek from Carmen, followed by quacking and barking. Within seconds the quacking and barking stopped dead, but the shrieking continued. Suddenly The Ox charged in through the gate with a duck in her jaws.

Gary and I leapt up from our chairs.

'Grab her!' I shouted.

Gary lunged for The Ox, who loosened her grip on the duck. Anxo shot forward, barking loudly as the duck took flight past Paul's *hórreo*, over the stone wall and into the garden of the uninhabited house beyond. By now, Maud, who'd been dozing in the barn was wide awake. She dashed over to join Anxo who was barking and scratching at the wall. Gary was holding onto The Ox for all he was worth, while Carmen now came storming over the threshing floor still shrieking and waving her arms.

'What the *fuck* is going on?' bawled Tom, raising himself from his lounger. When he saw Gary restraining The Ox he was beside himself. 'Let go of my dog!' he roared.

Paul and Rose stared at one another, speechless, as Gary released his hold on The Ox. Meanwhile, I was halfway up the crumbling wall, determined to retrieve the poor duck. As I stepped over the top onto the long grass, I turned to see Carmen scrambling up behind me, while Tom continued raging in the garden below. I began to part the weeds and bracken around me, but it was hard to focus while I was listening anxiously to the raised voices next door. Eventually I left Carmen to carry on searching and dropped back down into Paul's.

Tom was now standing face to face with Gary. 'Get Anxo out of here. Now.'

Gary was furious. 'What's he supposed to have done?'

'*He* brought the duck in. He started the trouble in the first place.'

Gary stuck his hands on his hips. 'He most *certainly* did not. The Ox was…'

'Leave it, Gary,' I said, as I walked over. I eased myself into the space between them and, with my back to Tom, murmured, 'You're wasting your breath, Gary. He's way too pissed to see reason. Come on. I think it's time we went home.'

The next day I went round to see Carmen; I hoped against hope that she'd rescued the duck.

'I found it this morning, Elisa. It was dead by the *río*. There were feathers everywhere… *everywhere*… feathers and blood.'

Paint Me Galicia

Paint me a mountain, a valley, a hill,
Paint me a river, a stream and a rill,
Paint me a farmhouse, a barn and a mill,
Paint me Galicia.

Paint me a forest of chestnuts and pines,
Paint me a trellis of roses and vines,
Paint me a cellar stocked up with good wines,
Paint me Galicia.

Pain me an hórreo *filled up with corn,*
Paint me the kisses of dew on the lawn,
Paint me the birds as they herald the dawn,
Paint me Galicia.

Paint me the seasons that Nature decrees,
Paint me the dryads that hide in the trees,
Paint me their secrets blown in on the breeze,
Paint me Galicia.

Paint me the huerta *close-planted in rows*
Paint me the fruit as it ripens and grows
Paint me the harvest at summertime's close
Paint me Galicia.

Paint me the rhythm of pitter-pat rain,
Paint me the drone of the gaita*'s refrain,*
Paint me the clanking of bells down the lane,
Paint me Galicia.

Paint me a landscape where I'm free to roam,
Paint me the woodlands and hedgerows I comb,
Paint me the place that I now call my home –
Paint me Galicia.

Chapter 10

Under A Cloud

A week after the flare-up, relationships still hadn't returned to normal. Tension hovered like a dark cloud over the village and a war of attrition lingered along a certain stretch of lane. Carmen was ignoring Tom. She'd turn away whenever she saw him and now kept a stick by the doorstep which she'd grab if his dogs walked by. Tom was ignoring us *and* Carmen. He'd taken to walking Maud and The Ox down the back lane and had given us the cold shoulder when our paths had happened to cross. He'd hung an old tyre across the gap in the wall that led into the woodland. A sign saying '*PRIVADO*' left no doubts as to why it was there. Paul was ignoring the fact that everyone was at loggerheads. With his typical childlike naivety, he believed peace would prevail again soon.

'I'm sure Tom'll come round,' he told us. 'He's had a lot on his mind lately. He's pissed off about having to spend August helping with the roof, and all the house hunting's been getting him down. He's found a place he likes though, and he's put in an offer…'

'Let's hope it's accepted,' said Gary. 'He's outstayed his welcome around here.'

I was saddened by the turn of events, but with only a week and a half to go before our guests descended I didn't have time to brood. There were preparations to attend to and I was grateful for the distraction; Jan and Graham couldn't have chosen a better time.

Gary, meanwhile, had been working flat-out on the pointing; he was determined to have the front of the house *and* the annexe finished before the visitors arrived. With the weather on his side, he achieved his objective with two days to spare. The difference was remarkable; the buildings seemed to have merged together into a house of impressively large proportions. The overall effect was really quite grand.

'It's fantastic!' I enthused. 'The house looks enormous! It's the Pazo de Cutián!'

'I'm glad it's to your liking,' he said, affectedly. 'On Wednesday I shall attend to the grounds.'

'The *grounds*?'

'The grounds of your *pazo*, milady; I'm going to give the lawn a good strim.'

'You should have a day off tomorrow, then. Relax, do some weeding, pick a few beans.'

'Actually, I thought I might attempt a painting.'

I was absolutely delighted; it would be his first in two years.

On Tuesday evening he brought a small canvas in from the barn. The image was a stone archway spanning a fast-flowing river cascading over rocks. He'd done a thoroughly good job.

'I think it's brilliant,' I said, 'See, the muse hasn't left you. The setting looks stunning; is it anywhere we know?'

'I haven't a clue, actually. I copied it from a photo in one of the guidebooks. Do you *really* like it or are you being kind?'

'I like it enough to suggest you go into Antas and buy a frame for it tomorrow. I'd like it on the wall of the guestroom when Graham and Jan arrive.'

By lunchtime on Thursday a mass of black cloud had gathered over the mountain. It crept closer and closer to the village throughout the afternoon. Trust the Galician weather to live up to its reputation when our guests were arriving; there was no doubt about it, we were heading for a storm.

'I'm not sure this is such a good idea,' I frowned, as I spread a cloth over the barn table.

'You worry too much,' said Gary. 'The roof doesn't drip where the table is, and anyway, it'll be more fun for Jan and Graham than sitting indoors.'

It was almost half past six when we drove out of the village. The heavens opened within minutes of us hitting the road.

'Graham might *have* to put up with the frescos at this rate,' I muttered.

'Rubbish,' said Gary. 'It'll be over in no time. I forecast a thoroughly pleasant weekend.'

When our visitors came through the arrivals door, we greeted one another with hugs and smiles. As we made our way out of the door and across to the carpark Jan was brimming with excitement, but Graham seemed unusually subdued.

'Is Graham okay?' I asked Jan, while the men were loading the cases into the boot.

'He's just tired,' she assured me. 'He came off a twelve-hour shift and drove straight to the airport. He'll soon be laughing and joking once we've plied him with beer.'

It was dark when we pulled out of the carpark, and the drizzle had turned into a downpour just as I'd feared. Even with the wipers swishing full tilt across the windscreen, Gary was struggling to get a clear view of the road ahead. Through the passenger windows we could see absolutely nothing; our visitors wouldn't be enthusing about the landscape today.

Once we'd turned off the main road the conditions were decidedly dangerous; now and again Gary slowed to a crawl, for fear of driving the car off the road. We were almost at Antas when the first flash of lightning lit up the landscape around us. By the time we reached the *aldea* we were smack, bang in the middle of an electrical storm.

Despite my reservations the barn was an excellent venue for supper. We were warm and dry and had a ringside view of the lightning as it forked across the sky. Jan warmed instantly to her somewhat irregular dining experience, but Graham's dark mood, like the storm, lingered long into the night.

There wasn't a cloud in the sky when I threw back the kitchen curtains on Friday morning. Gary had been right with his forecast; this weekend we were going to be blessed with some sun. Despite the good weather, Graham *still* didn't look cheerful when he surfaced. I had the distinct impression that a minibreak in a muddy *aldea* wasn't really his idea of fun.

'I think we should keep the village tour brief,' I said to Gary, while our guests were upstairs fetching anoraks. 'I don't think Graham's enjoying himself, do you think you could jolly him along?'

'I'll do my best,' he nodded. 'If I mention a pint at the Black Eagle, that's *bound* to cheer him. He'll be as right as rain once he's sat with a beer in the pub.'

'So you've never been as far as the river beach?' Jan asked, as I stuffed serviettes and beakers into the bulging picnic bag.

'No,' I laughed. 'We *almost* got there with Ron and Miranda, but we'd misjudged the distance and had to turn round.'

I was determined there wouldn't be any hiccups this time. Come what may we *would* see the Río Ulla and we were definitely going in the car.

'It's so pretty,' said Jan as we drove through Santa Mariña. 'It looks almost English, the way the houses are scattered around the village green.'

Graham was quick to spot the sign outside the Black Eagle. 'Now *that* looks English,' he grinned. It was only half past eleven, but suddenly he was in holiday mode. 'Shall we stop?'

'Later,' I said firmly. 'There's a river to visit and then there's a picnic. There's plenty of beer in the bag.'

Once out of Santa Mariña we drove for another three kilometres until we could see the houses of Frádegas up ahead.

'Here we are then,' said Gary, as he pulled the car to a halt at the side of the road.

Ahead of us was a tiny hump-backed bridge. The Río Ulla flowed fast and noisily underneath.

'So where's the beach?' asked Graham, as we scanned the stretch of riverbank.

Gary pointed to a clearing in the trees. 'There it is.'

The beach was much smaller than I'd expected. If the truth be told it was little more than a stretch of fine shingle leading down to the river's edge. The water was crystal clear but the fast-flowing current and the rocky riverbed made me question whether it was a suitable spot for bathing. Perhaps people lay on the beach and let their feet dangle over the edge.

'Not exactly a beach,' laughed Graham.

'The river's beautiful though,' I said.

When Jan had finished taking photos we wandered back round to the foot of the bridge. As the others began to cross over, I lingered, my attention drawn to a tumbling stone building set on the very edge of the bank.

'Wait!' I called, waving them back towards me. 'I've found something! Come and see!'

'I think it's an abandoned mill,' said Gary, staring across at the ruin.

'I think you're right.' I nodded. 'Shall we go down and have a look?'

'We can certainly try. Jan, Graham, are you coming too?'

The four of us picked our way gingerly down the steep slope and into a muddy courtyard scattered with weeds. The two-storey building was in a state of dilapidation, but it was clear that it had once been quite grand. We entered an open doorway to the right and were immediately hit by an awful, nauseating smell. This was an odour even the olfactorily challenged Gary couldn't miss.

'Good *God*!' he gasped. 'Has something died?'

'Rotten eggs,' frowned Jan, wrinkling her nose up. 'The water must have turned stagnant over time.'

'Here,' said Gary, moving further into the building. 'This is what's causing it. There's water pouring into two holes in the floor.'

We walked over and looked to where Gary was pointing. Sure enough, water was pouring from two pipes in a low wall into two small wells in the floor. The surrounding rock was covered in thick white precipitation, spotted with lurid orange fungus and streaked with green slime.

'The smell must be sulphur,' said Graham, touching the white crusty residue. 'Perhaps it's rich in other minerals as well.'

'I've got it!' Jan exclaimed, suddenly. 'It's a spa!'

'*That's* it,' nodded Graham. 'The water must have had beneficial properties at one time. I wonder if it still does?'

I lowered my hand slowly into the water. 'Urgh!' I exclaimed. 'It's really greasy to the touch.'

'I wonder if it's still drinkable,' mused Graham.

Strangely enough, not one of us was prepared to find out.

Satisfied that we'd seen enough of the festering fountains we trod carefully through the middle section of the U-shaped building, where the ceiling had collapsed in places and some tarnished pipework ran overhead. In the far wing, foliage filled most of the arched window recesses and visibility was poor.

'Careful,' said Gary, taking out his cigarette lighter. 'It might be dangerous. Don't move until we've got some more light.'

'I've got a little torch,' said Jan, surprising us. 'I didn't realise you'd have streetlamps in the village. I brought it in case we needed to go out at night.'

She rummaged in her handbag and pulled out a small plastic torch. The second she flicked on the light there was movement above us and, without warning, something flitted over our heads.

Instinctively I gasped, and Jan gave a surprised shriek.

'Don't worry,' laughed Graham. 'It's only a bird.'

As Jan directed the torch upwards a startled bat whizzed past the beam.

'My God!' I breathed, as Jan brought the light to rest on the rafters. There were bats in abundance, suspended from the rafters, tightly cocooned by their wings.

'Awesome,' said Graham.

'Fantastic,' said Gary.

'Gorgeous,' said Jan.

I was speechless. It was one of the most fascinating sights I'd ever seen.

'Right,' said Gary once Jan had taken more photos. 'Let's see if we can find a picnic spot over the bridge.'

At the end of the bridge, stood a single-storey, windowless stone building. There was a carved wooden sign above the door.

'Refugio de Pescadores,' read Graham.

'It's a fishermen's refuge!' exclaimed Jan.

We followed a track to the left, tracing the course of the river until we came to a stretch of bank where enormous flat stones were raised up above the water's edge.

'This is perfect,' smiled Jan. 'Nature's own picnic area. There's plenty of room to sit and to spread out the food.'

We ate and chatted and soaked up our surroundings, soothed by the sound of the river tumbling by.

'The local trout's excellent,' said Gary. 'It would have been nice to see someone fishing today.'

'It's incredibly fast-flowing,' said Graham. 'It looks as if the current's quite strong.'

'Yes,' I nodded. 'The river here is still in its young stages. According to the map it reaches the sea somewhere close to Padrón.'

'Not *the* Padrón?' asked Graham, 'Where the peppers come from?'

'Yes,' I nodded. 'The very same.'

Padrón peppers are eaten throughout the whole of Spain. They're used in many meat and fish dishes but are most frequently served as a *tapa* or aperitif, fried in oil and tossed in coarse salt. This was how Gary and I enjoyed them most and we'd often eaten them this way when we lived on the island.

'I remember reading about them in our Galician food and drink book,' I added. 'They were brought to Galicia from Mexico in the fifteenth century by the Franciscan monks.'[11]

'Well fancy that,' said Jan. 'I never realised Padrón was in Galicia. From now on I'll think of this visit every time we have *pimientos de Padrón*.'

Before long I felt the call of nature. To the side of us the forest extended for some distance and around a bend. The fisherman's refuge was closer and there was always the chance that it might have an outside loo.

'I could do with a wee,' I announced. 'I'm going to walk back to the refuge, there might be a toilet round the back.'

Behind the refuge I found no outbuildings, but the dense bracken and bramble afforded me ample privacy and I was pleased with my choice. Before returning to our picnic spot, I walked up to the front to get a closer look at the fascia with its expertly carved sign and the studded wooden door with its heavy iron loop handle. Instinctively I turned it and the latch lifted. Sunlight flooded in as I pushed the door open. I cast my eyes quickly round the room, and then behind me. Deeming it safe to enter, I called to the others.

'The refuge is open! It's open! Come and see!'

The spacious single room reminded me of a medieval tavern. Heavy wooden tables and long solid benches were set out in two lines. In the corner was a magnificent *lareira*, still full of ashes, and above them a blackened grille bore the charred, sticky remnants of cooked fish.

Back in Santa Mariña we sat outside the Black Eagle. From our table we could see over the wall of the house next door.

'Now *that's* something you'd never see in England,' said Jan.

---

[11] Gabriel Pollarés, Juan, *Guía de Productos de la Tierra: Galicia* (Madrid: EDAF, 1998) p. 30

'What's that?' asked Gary.

'A front garden planted with vegetables, from the gate all the way up to the door.'

I pictured the street where we'd lived in Burton. At this time of year the front gardens would be a profusion of colour, with flowers abundant in baskets and borders and pots.

'It'd get nicked in England,' said Graham. 'There's no sense of community. People don't look out for one another the way they did before.'

'I'll tell you what *I* think,' began Gary.

We didn't find out what he thought because at that moment we heard a low moaning coming from over the wall.

'Whatever was *that*?' frowned Jan. 'It sounded like a person.'

'It did,' nodded Graham. 'Do you think someone's fallen?'

Whoever it was moaned a second time.

'Come on,' said Gary. 'Let's have a look.'

We leaned over the wall and scanned for signs of life between the densely planted rows of kale.

'Over there, look,' cried Jan, pointing to the furthest corner. 'Can you see? There's somebody moving.'

'I see it,' said Gary, 'behind the last row of kale. 'There, look, right at the back.'

I peered along the tall leafy column and finally saw the cause of the commotion.

'Aah!' gasped Jan and I in unison, as a tiny, rust-coloured calf rose shakily to its feet.

Graham had rallied during the visit to Santa Mariña. On Saturday morning he was bright and chipper and keen to set off on the countryside walk. We paused at the fence of number fifteen while Jan took a photo of Másimo's *hórreo*, and we all breathed in the floral fragrance of Solina's laundry blowing on the line.

The *río* met with an enthusiastic response from our visitors and its role of the village launderette was verified when Carmen turned up with a bucket of clothes.

'The best's yet to come,' said Gary, 'In a few minutes you'll have the view over the valley. You can see all the way across so it's a great spot for watching the birds of prey.'

We followed the track down past Masi's *huerta*, but Thursday night's storm had left it thick with sludge. I noticed that Jan was picking her way gingerly. Eventually she stopped.

'I really can't go any further,' she sighed. 'I'm wearing the wrong sort of shoes.'

I looked down at her feet and managed to suppress my exasperation; canvas pumps weren't the best choice of footwear for plodding through mud.

'Oh, *no*,' groaned Graham. 'I wanted to see the place where they used to kill the village virgins…'

'*What*?' I exclaimed. 'Whatever has Gary been telling you?'

'That's not *quite* how I put it,' grinned Gary. 'I was explaining the story of Sacrificial Stone.'

'There's no reason for us *all* to turn back,' said Graham sensibly. 'Why don't I go with Gary?'

'That's a brilliant idea,' nodded Gary. 'We'd only be gone an hour. If Jan gives Graham her camera, he can take photos of the things she's missed.'

Jan looked put out but couldn't really argue; we *had* advised her to bring some sturdy shoes.

'Come on,' I smiled. 'We can potter about in the garden. We've got a few beans that want picking, and how do you fancy collecting the eggs?'

As we walked back past the *río* I told Jan the saga of Rufo and how the waterproof trousers had spared him an early death.

Jan stared at her shoes again.

'Oh, he's fine now,' I assured her.

When I ushered her into the chicken run twenty minutes later, Rufo behaved like a perfect gent.

'The chestnut tree's enormous,' said Jan, as I led her across to the henhouse. 'And look at your damsons as well!'

'*Damsons*?' I frowned. I looked up to where she was pointing. Above us the trees were laden with golden fruit.

'Wow,' said Jan. 'They're dropping even as we speak.'

'I didn't know,' I stammered, aware that I was gaping like a goldfish. 'I always thought they were... well... just trees.'

As another damson dropped to the ground two of the hens dashed over. One squawked in protest as the other ran away with her prize in her beak.

'*That's* why you haven't noticed them,' laughed Jan. 'The chooks have been getting there first.'

'We need to collect them,' I said, coming to my senses. 'If we shake the trees I bet they'll come raining down. I'll fetch us a couple of buckets, we've got ages before the men come home.'

'Bring a brush, as well,' Jan called after me. 'If we bash about in the branches we'll be sure to get them all.'

The kettle was almost boiling when the men came back from their ramble. Jan and I had done wonders and we were ready for a brew.

'Oh, good, you've picked the beans,' said Gary, peering into our buckets. 'But how come there're damsons as well?'

'Because we collected them,' laughed Jan, 'before your chickens could eat them all.'

'You mean those tall skinny trees in the chooks' pen are *damsons*?'

'Incredible, isn't it?' I grinned. 'All this time and we hadn't noticed. We'd have missed them completely if it hadn't been for Jan's shoes.'

We strolled into Agolada's main *plaza* at two-thirty. By now most Galicians were lunching so the terraces of the café-bars were only half full. We chose a table bathed in sunlight and while we waited for a beer and three coffees, we told Jan and Graham about our plans for the coming year.

We hadn't been seated long when a small black and tan dog trotted up wagging its tail.

'It's thin,' said Jan. 'Do you think it's been abandoned?'

'No,' said Gary, as he leaned over to stroke it. 'Look, there's not a tick in sight, that's a sure sign it's owned.'

'You're right,' I nodded, surveying our gate crasher. 'It's not skinny, it's lean. It seems to be familiar with its surroundings. It probably lives nearby.'

'I've been watching the fountain,' said Graham. 'People have been coming up with saucepans and filling them with water. It must be to do with the healthy mineral thing again.'

As we looked across, an elderly woman in a checked pinafore was lowering an enormous pot into the water. Suddenly, as if from nowhere, a huge brown rat shot across the square. The dog saw it in an instant and moved like lightning. Within seconds it grabbed the rat between its jaws and shook it violently, before dropping it, stone dead, at the entrance of the bar.

'I wouldn't mind one last stroll round the village before we leave for the airport,' said Graham, on Sunday morning. 'I wasn't feeling so great on Friday, I didn't have chance to take it all in.'

As we passed number ten, Paul was leaning out of his stable door.

'Morning,' we chorused.

'*Hola*,' he grinned.

'This is Jan and Graham, our friends from Las Palmas,' said Gary. 'They're having a last look round the village before they go home.'

'Would you like to see my house?' Paul asked them. 'It's very basic, but you won't have seen anything like it before.'

I winked at Gary and he grinned.

'And you *must* see my *hórreo*. Best *hórreo* in the village, you know.'

Graham looked at Gary and me. 'Would you mind?'

'Not at all,' said Gary. 'You've still got an hour before we leave for the airport. I'm sure Liza won't mind.'

'Go ahead,' I added. 'But you'll forgive me if I don't join you? I can get the sheets in soak ready for Monday. The laundry's always on a rolling programme, it's the only way to manage when it's all done by hand.'

'I'll join you,' said Gary a tad too hastily. 'I could do with checking the oil before we set off on the drive.'

As Graham and Jan were whisked into the bowels of number ten, we walked away chuckling.

'Poor devils,' grinned Gary. 'I bet he'll be telling them his plans for the tennis court and the sunken bath…'

'Not to mention the flying pig. Come on, let's get our jobs done, it'll only take ten minutes. We'll have time for a natter with a fag and a brew.'

Almost an hour had passed and there was still no sign of our visitors.

'They must be enjoying themselves,' I giggled. 'They obviously can't bear to tear themselves away.'

'I bet they're bored shitless,' Gary grinned.

'You're wicked. Ooh, listen… that sounds like them now.'

'Good time?' asked Gary wryly, as Graham and Jan came into the kitchen.

'You *could* have warned us,' frowned Graham. 'The house isn't fit to live in. It's damp, it's dirty, the floorboards are rotten, and the ceilings are coming down in nearly every room.'

'Even so, it was interesting,' said Jan. 'The *hórreo* was nice, and I *loved* the big trunks in the attic. And the little *bodega* in the courtyard, and that *huge* wooden cart. I have to say, though, we had a shock when we went into the kitchen…'

'Talk about unhygienic,' began Graham.

'I didn't mean *that*, Graham. I'm talking about that *rude* little man.'

'Rude little man?' smirked Gary. 'Let me guess what his name was.'

'That's just it,' said Jan. 'we didn't get to find out. When Paul took us into the kitchen he said, "I'm giving Gary and Liza's friends a quick house tour", and that ill-mannered devil picked up his mug and walked straight out of the room.'

'We hadn't a *clue* what we'd done to offend him,' Graham frowned.

'It's a long story,' said Gary. 'We'll tell it you on the way to the airport. It's called "The Old Woman, the Duck and the Ox".'

Hórreo

I am the silent sentinel on stilts of stone.
Two centuries of wakeful watch have passed,
yet still I stand.
I have my cross to bear:
Age-old amulet and reverent reminder
of sanctity and superstition,
faith and fallacy,
devotion and dread.
Give us this day our daily bread.

I am the guardian of the grain.
By man's artistry
and by God's hand,
I am both stronghold and sanctum.
No vermin shall penetrate,
no weather shall permeate,
no evil shall infiltrate,
and every mouth shall be fed.
Give us this day our daily bread.

I am the faithful fortress
of fortune and fate.
Year upon year, men toil
with plough, scythe, flail and mill.
With fortitude and fervour,
I hold the harvest
of those who have laboured,
whose hearts and hands have bled.
Give us this day our daily bread.

I am the silent sentinel.
I am the faithful fortress.
I am the guardian of the grain.

Chapter 11

The Cowboys

'*Jam*min'… *Jam*min'… Jammin' until the break of dawn,' sang Gary, as he came into the kitchen on Monday morning.

'What on earth's got into *you*?' I frowned. 'You don't usually make such a racket first thing.'

'You *are* slow,' he chuckled. 'Jammin'. Isn't that what you're s'posed to be doing today?'

'Daft bugger,' I grinned. 'Trust you.'

When Gary came back with the shopping, a row of sterilised jars adorned the windowsill, and the damsons were simmering gently in the pan.

'I don't know how you can stand it,' he said, tossing *El Progreso* onto the marble surface. 'It's like a sauna in here. Why don't you open the window? You'd at least get rid of the steam.'

'The flies,' I answered. 'If I open the window the kitchen will be full of them. It's the devil and the deep blue sea.'

'I'll leave you to it,' he muttered. 'There's your paper. I'll go and read *Marca* in the barn.'

The damsons had to simmer for another fifteen minutes before I added the sugar. The heat and humidity were already unbearable; how much worse would it be once the jam was off to a rolling boil? I let out a sigh and unlatched the window. Pushing both sides wide open, I watched as the steam drifted into the lane. Satisfied that the damsons could tick over for a while, I sat down to flip through the paper. *El Progreso* wasn't the most inspiring of reads, but if you had a passion for politics, football or car crashes you were in for a treat. I was reading about the alarming increase in Galician forest fires when I heard the clanking of cow bells. It seemed a good time to check on the damsons; concentration would be out of the question when the herd came thundering by.

The damsons had softened down, and it was time to stir in the sugar. Two full bags seemed rather a dangerous amount to me. I was groping about at the back of the cupboard when the clamour outside was punctuated with the most *almighty* crash.

'Shit!' I wailed, 'The cows! The *jars*!'

Cursing my own stupidity, I withdrew myself from the cupboard and glanced over to the windowsill. Sure enough, two of my jars were missing; if the noise I'd heard was anything to go by they'd be nothing but shards by now. I cast my eyes over the floor until I spotted them. It was incredible; each jar was still in one piece.

Half an hour later, with five jars of jam sitting safely on the dresser, I stood on the doorstep to call Gary in for a makeshift ploughman's lunch. Along the lane flies buzzed eagerly over the fresh cowpats. I groaned and glanced instinctively at the window; the window where *something* was now *very* wrong. At that moment the barn door opened. Gary stopped dead in his tracks and stared straight ahead.

'What the *fuck* is our window frame doing in the lane?'

Since Sunday I'd been wanting to thank Paul for his spur-of-the-moment house tour; the place wasn't exactly a *pazo* but it had been thoughtful of him all the same. On Tuesday he was out on the doorstep when Anxo and I set off for the bin.

'Morning, Paul,' I smiled. 'Thanks ever so much for Sunday. Jan and Graham really enjoyed the house tour, though I gather Tom wasn't too sociable by all accounts?'

'I'm sorry about that. Perhaps I should have said something, but he's so short-tempered at the moment. He's been stressed since he heard the news on Friday – his offer's been accepted on the house.'

'But surely that should have cheered him? He's been searching for almost a year.'

'The sale's been agreed in principle but now there's a problem with the paperwork. It's to do with the boundaries or something. Everything's got to be remeasured and well, it could take at least a month.'

'That's nothing in Galicia,' I laughed. 'He should think himself lucky. Some people wait six months to a year.'

'A month will *seem* like a year the way things are at the moment. There's no chance of him building bridges with Carmen, they're both being stubborn. I've taken the tyre and the sign down. I like Carmen and I don't want to upset her, but Tom's taken it as a snub.'

'Sod him,' I glared. 'It's *your* house. It's not fair to involve you in all the unpleasantries. And as for poor Carmen... she doesn't deserve any of this.'

'I agree,' Paul nodded. 'I hope I can find a way to make it up to her eventually...' His eyes suddenly drifted to the side of me, and his face broke into a smile. 'Here comes another of Tom's bugbears…'

I turned to see what he was looking at. Scholes was sauntering towards us up the lane.

'But Tom *likes* Scholes,' I protested. 'He loves that he can retrieve and stuff. He thinks it's really cool.'

'He might like him, but he doesn't want him in the house. Cats jump up on things, you see, and Tom always has food lying around.'

'So Scholes has been coming in then?'

'Only as far as the courtyard, but that isn't the problem. It became an issue for Tom when I started putting scraps down, even though it was usually just pasta or bread.'

I frowned to myself. Scholes didn't like bread and, as far as I could remember. he wasn't keen on pasta…

'But when I gave him *chorizo*,' Paul continued, 'he turned his nose up and walked away.'

'It's not Scholes.' I said.

'Not Scholes? I thought that was his name?'

'It *is*. I didn't mean that. I meant whoever you're feeding, it's not Scholes. He won't touch bread, but he'd take your arm off for a lump of *chorizo*; it's his favourite titbit, apart from cheese.

'So there's another cat in the village that looks like him?'

'Yes,' I nodded. 'There is. I haven't actually *seen* him yet, but I've been weighing up the evidence. Gary doesn't believe me, of course. He thinks it's all in my imagination. I don't have to have seen the cat to know he's there.'

When I told Gary later he was sceptical.

'It doesn't prove *anything*. Scholes doesn't eat bread at *our* house because there's food in his bowl. He might eat it at Paul's because there's nothing else on offer. You don't know *how* his mind works.'

I wasn't prepared to argue, but something told me that my doubting Thomas would soon be eating humble pie.

A week passed and there were no further sightings of the Imposter. Gary continued to pooh-pooh my theory and I was beginning to think I might have been wrong after all. The breakthrough finally came on Tuesday morning when I went down to let out the hens.

As I neared the enclosure, I heard a spine-chilling keening. There was no doubt about it, somewhere close by an animal was in distress. For a moment Carmen's words came back to haunt me: 'Feathers everywhere…' I ran the last few metres up the garden and stared through the wire; the door of the hen house was fastened and there was no sign of feathers or blood. At that moment the sound came again, and it was then that I realised: it *wasn't* coming from the hen house, but from the wilderness over the wall.

'Waaah… waaah…'

It was a cat fight. The sound was unmistakeable; I chided myself for not recognising it before.

Somewhere out there in the bracken Scholes had come face to face with the Imposter. This bloodcurdling yowling marked the ominous stand-off stage when the opponents would eyeball each other in a white-knuckle battle of nerve. There was no telling how long it would last, but eventually one of the rivals would make the first move, all hell would break loose, and fur would fly. There was nothing to be gained by intervening; these cats had a score to settle and all I could do was hope that Scholes would have the upper hand. I moved closer to the wall and waited with my heart in my mouth until the noise came again.

'Waaah… Waaah…'

'WAAAH!'

There was a shuffling in the bracken, and I could make out intermittent glimpses of ginger shifting through the stems. Suddenly a giant two-cat furball exploded out from the undergrowth, prised itself apart and flung itself back together again. I'd seen as much as I could cope with; it was time for a fag.

'I've seen the Imposter,' I announced when Gary came into the kitchen. 'And before you say anything, it *definitely* wasn't Scholes because *he* was there as well.'

'Good God! You were right then. I s'pose I'll have to eat my words. So they were together, were they? That's nice.'

'Nice isn't quite the word I'd have chosen. They were having a full-blown fight.'

'A fight? You do surprise me. Scholes has never been aggressive. I hope he's alright.'

'I'm sure he is. If anything it's the Imposter we should be worried about. Scholes was relentless, it was his opponent that threw in the towel.'

'Good old Scholes. He copes with everything, doesn't he? So what's he like then, the Imposter? Does he *really* look like Scholes?'

'Oh, yes. And it's not just a vague resemblance, he's an absolute ringer for him. You'll be amazed, I swear.'

'It's unbelievable. What are the chances of that? Scholes is quite an unusual colour. He's not a *true* ginger, he's much paler, he's more like…'

'A cup of tea.'

He frowned into his mug. 'Similar, I s'pose. Where was it, this cat fight?'

'On Paul's overgrown bit, just behind the hen house. I heard this horrible wailing and…' I leapt up suddenly. 'Shit!'

'What is it? Liza, what's wrong?'

'I haven't let the chickens out! In all the pandemonium I forgot to open the door!'

On Wednesday morning, there was no sign of the Imposter. It was hardly surprising after the trouncing he'd been given by Scholes. I wondered if he'd moved on to greener pastures or whether he was simply lying low and licking his wounds.

I thought I might be about to find out when Gary came in for coffee. I could tell by the grin on his face he had news.

'Have you seen him?'

'Yes, about half an hour ago. He's had a delivery from the builder's yard and....'

We clearly had our wires crossed. 'I meant the Imposter. Never mind, go on.'

'You'll never guess where they've left it?'

'I'm sure I won't, enlighten me.'

'In front of the church, by the cross on the green.'

'Never! That's *miles* away. Well, it *isn't*, but it'll seem like it if he's got to cart it all the way down to number ten. Is there much?'

'Tons, literally. Even if he uses the wheelbarrow it'll take a week.'

'I need to see it,' I grinned as I stubbed out my ciggie. 'I'm going to nip up to the church to have a look.'

As I stepped outside I saw Paul walking across the lane in his boxer shorts. Judging by the wine box and the glass he was holding the barrowing wasn't going to be happening any time soon.

'Morning,' he called. 'Is that Scholes down there, on the bench?'

I glanced round. Sure enough, Scholes was stretched out in the sun. 'That's him,' I nodded.

'In that case, it's his lookalike that's joined me for lunch.'

'The Imposter? Crikey, is he still there?'

'I should think so. He was in the courtyard eating pasta a minute ago.'

'Brilliant,' I grinned. 'I'll fetch Gary. This is something he *has* to see.'

By the time Gary appeared on the doorstep the Imposter had left the courtyard. In an act of blatant effrontery he stood, bold as brass, staring down the lane.

Scholes sat bolt upright and stared back at him… hard.

'Oops,' I whispered. 'This means war.'

The rivals locked gazes like two cowboys in a western, sizing each other up before a shoot-out along a deserted, sun-baked road. We watched and waited in silence. After what seemed an eternity, the Imposter began to yowl. Scholes gave a low growl and slunk down into a crouching position. Seconds later he wiggled his bum and sprang forwards as the Imposter turned tail and took off up the lane.

'Entertainment on your doorstep,' grinned Gary. 'You could sell tickets – Cat Fight at the Cutián Corral.'

On Thursday morning Paul sprang into action. By lunchtime it was clear he'd bitten off more than he could chew.

'Struggling?' I asked, when Anxo and I passed him on our way to the wheelie bin.

'It's a nightmare,' he groaned. 'But I've got to get it shifted by Monday. There won't be any time to do it once Kev arrives. Apparently we'll be starting at eight.'

'Crikey, that's early.'

'Tell me about it. He wants us to keep to a strict timetable. Eight 'til eight, Monday to Friday. At least we get Saturday and Sunday off, but Tom's not happy about it at all.'

Thanks to the cat fight I hadn't actually made it up to the green to see Paul's delivery. Now seemed like a good time to ask.

'How much stuff have you got to move?'

'Two hundred square metres of uralite, a ton of sand, a ton of gravel and ten bags of *mortero*.'

'How on earth are you going to shift all that?'

'I'm persevering with the barrow for the meantime, but Tom's busy making a trolley out of a metal bedframe and some pushchair wheels. We'll be able to get much more on it and if we push it between us we should do it in half the time.'

'The trolley's not been much help,' said Gary at teatime. 'A wheel fell off outside the farmhouse. Tom flew into a tantrum and Paul was almost in tears. Javier saw it all from the doorstep. When he'd finally stopped laughing he told Paul he'd bring the rest of it down with the tractor some time over the weekend.'

'I don't know why they didn't ask Javier in the first place. It would've saved them a heck of a lot of work.'

'It would also have involved speaking Spanish,' grinned Gary.

'Ah,' I nodded. 'Good point.'

'White rabbits,' I smiled when Gary emerged on Friday morning. As I passed him his cuppa I noticed he was frowning. 'Whatever's the matter? Had you forgotten that today's the first?'

'I could hardly forget,' he grimaced. 'We're off to the bloody market. Monterroso will be heaving; it'll be a nightmare finding somewhere to park.'

I'd been quite excited about this morning; we were finally going to the ex-pats' get-together at the Hotel Río Ulla. Determined that Gary's Irritable Driver Syndrome wouldn't put a dampener on the occasion, I put forward a clever idea.

'Why don't we miss out the market completely? It'll be a lot less stressful if we drive straight through Monterroso and park up outside the hotel.'

As it turned out, it was a stroke of genius; parking was a doddle and Gary was in high spirits as we strolled up to the hotel. A dozen or so people were gathered on the terrace, sitting or standing around tables, enjoying the late morning sun. Paul and Tom were chaining their bikes to a railing, chatting to a stocky man leaning on the window ledge nearby. Paul grinned when he saw us:

'Well, I never! This *is* a surprise.'

Heads turned in an act of collective surveillance as Paul introduced us:

'This is Gary and Liza. They're my neighbours from Cutián.'

Everyone smiled, bid us good morning, and introduced themselves before returning to their conversations. I had the vague sensation that I was intruding on the ex-pats' inscrutable clique.

As we walked over to the entrance I spotted a familiar, friendly face. Rose was sitting at a table, in front of a laptop.

'Hiya!' she called as we made our way over. 'I was hoping I'd see you here. What with the duck and everything I didn't have chance to say goodbye.'

'Never mind,' I smiled. 'I wondered if you'd get home in one piece, you'd had a fair bit to drink.'

'You're so polite – I was arseholed. I ended up staying over. I had the hangover from hell next day.'

'So how's the house coming on?' asked Gary.

'It isn't,' she laughed. 'It's a complete ruin. I've got some photos on my laptop; sit down and I'll show you if you like.'

The first few photos showed a house in ruins. A vine had grown rampant over what remained of the fascia, and bracken and bramble crept uninvitingly over a massive expanse of land.

'Crikey,' I breathed.

'My first priority is to get a roof on. I'm waiting for Kev, the builder, to give me a start date, but he can't do that yet; he's got another job on when he's finished at Paul's. I've had the wood delivery for the rafters though…' she scrolled through the album. 'Ah, here we are.'

I was beginning to wonder how many photos of planks I could feign interest in, when Rose's phone rang.

'I'll have to take it,' she frowned. 'It's Pete, my husband. He'll be ringing to moan about what I've spent on the wood.'

'Let's go and grab a coffee,' said Gary, ushering me away from the table.

'See you later,' I mouthed to Rose.

In contrast to the terrace, the hotel's café-bar was almost empty. We walked over to the bar where another couple stood waiting to be served. Unlike the crowd outside they greeted us warmly. Their names were Russell and Jenny, and they'd been living in Galicia for almost five years. After the inevitable introductions and small talk our conversation soon came round to self-sufficiency. They were enthusiastic organic vegetable gardeners and were keen to hear how we were getting along.

'We've not done too badly with beans and courgettes,' I began. 'The peas were doing well until something ate them. We ended up with a portion each in the end.'

'The onions were tiny,' said Gary. 'So we ended up pickling them. We'll have beetroot as well, eventually, but I don't think we'll fill more than two jars.'

'The carrots didn't come up,' I continued. 'Nor the sweetcorn.'

'Nor the cabbages,' added Gary. Nor the cauli, nor the swede…'

'Hark at us,' I giggled. 'You must be thinking how hopeless we are.'

'Not at all,' smiled Jenny. 'It sounds a lot like *our* first harvest. We had an absolutely disastrous first year.'

'I don't understand it,' I frowned. 'Gary's done nothing but dig since January and the weather's been a perfect balance of rain and sun.'

'The soil's weird, though,' added Gary. 'Even when it's drenched on top, it's like dust a few inches further down. There aren't any earthworms either; I swear I haven't seen a single one.'

'It'll get better every year,' said Russell, 'as long as you keep turning the soil and barrowing on the compost… and I can't emphasise enough the value of poo.'

'I collect what the cows have left,' nodded Gary. 'And what bit we get from the chickens goes in as well.'

'Where did your seeds come from?' asked Jenny. 'It might sound an odd question, but it can make a difference, you know.'

'I doubt it's the seeds,' I said. 'Most of them were from a friend in England; they were from her own veg. She keeps the seeds from the best of each crop every harvest. She's been growing off the same veg for years.'

Jenny and Russell looked at each other knowingly.

'That's probably what the problem is,' said Russell. 'Your seeds.'

'But surely each generation should get bigger and better…'

'They will,' nodded Jenny. 'But only if the veg was grown here.'

'It's to do with acclimatisation,' explained Russell. 'Seeds that would have thrived back in England might not cope so well here.'

'We did exactly the same,' said Jenny. 'We brought seeds over from veg that we'd grown in England. We were already experienced gardeners but hardly anything came up.'

'The beans were fine,' said Russell. 'In fact so were all the legumes. The bigger seeds are more robust, of course. Like you, our carrots and beetroots struggled. It was a very disappointing year.'

'We've got fruit trees,' I said, in an effort to make things look brighter. 'We've had damsons already, and in autumn we'll have apples and chestnuts and figs.'

'We get plenty of eggs from the chickens,' added Gary. 'The trouble is we've accidentally got them on someone else's land.'

Jenny and Russell exchanged a knowing look again.

'*That's* happened to us as well,' laughed Jenny. 'It's a good story actually. Go on, Russell, I'll let you explain.'

'Okay,' began Russell. 'To the side of our house there's a small grassy triangle with an apple tree on it. Given that our nearest neighbours are about fifty metres away on either side we assumed it was ours.'

'Sounds reasonable,' nodded Gary.

'Well,' Russell continued. 'We were so busy working on the house and the *huerta*, it wasn't a priority; after a year it was terribly overgrown. Eventually I took the strimmer to it and gave the apple tree a really ruthless pruning...'

'It looked lovely,' added Jenny. 'I was so pleased with what he'd done.'

'Anyway,' said Russell. 'We were having our dinner that evening and there was a knock at the door, and there was our neighbour, Manolo standing on the doorstep...'

'Oh no!' I gasped.

'Shh,' said Gary,

'He handed me a big bag of cheese and *chorizo* and told me what a good neighbour I was for tending his land.'

'The builder's arrived,' I told Gary when he surfaced on Monday morning.

'Already?' he yawned. 'What's he like?'

'I've no idea. I've not seen him. There's been a lot of shouting and laughter and a voice I didn't recognise. Beyond that I know nothing; your guess is as good as mine.'

Over the next two days the trio worked relentlessly, Paul and Kev up on the rooftop and Tom with his feet firmly on the ground. I watched him from the chooks' pen sagging behind the wheelbarrow, as he shifted load after load of old tiles to the far end of Paul's land. Kev, in a bid to motivate his flagging team-mate, hollered his inspirational mantra: 'That's the spirit, Jedi warrior! Keep it up!'

It came as no surprise that Carmen spent most of the week in the garden instead of the *finca*. It was a pity that neither she nor Tom had offered the olive branch; she'd have enjoyed the spectacle immensely, had she not been too stubborn to watch from the lane.

On Wednesday morning, all was quiet when Anxo and I came back from our walk.

'They've had to go to Lugo,' explained Gary. 'There's been a problem with the wood.'

'Oh dear,' I said. 'What's happened?'

'The yard in Antas doesn't have deliveries in August. They've driven off to Lugo to try their luck.'

At lunchtime, the prospectors returned. Kev was unloading the wood when I set off up to the wheelie bin.

There was no mistaking the smell of cannabis as we passed in the lane.

For the rest of the week, Paul and Kev heaved and hammered at the crossbeams and uralite, while Tom barrowed away the old rafters and roofboards, decidedly lacking in the Jedi spirit enjoyed by his mates.

By the time they downed tools on Friday, Gary had made his mind up about Kev:

'He's completely bonkers and he's permanently stoned.'

'I'm sure you're right, though I hadn't given much thought to his mental state. It's his proficiency as a tradesman that concerns *me*.'

I wasn't the only one having doubts. I watched Maruja and Javier pausing to inspect the job on their way to fetching the cows.

'*Hola*,' I called, as I made my way up to join them.

'*Hola*, Elisa,' said Maruja. 'Does the builder know what he's doing? That wood's no good, it's too thin.'

Javier pointed towards the chimney. 'I can hear someone talking up there.'

Maruja and I looked over. Something was glinting in the sun.

We edged further up the lane for a better view. Paul, was standing on the furthermost slope with a wine glass in his hand, singing into a mobile phone.

'He's drunk!' laughed Javier. 'Look he's swaying!'

'*Dios*!' exclaimed Maruja. 'He's not drunk – he's swaying because of the *uralita*. What if he loses his footing? He'll break his neck if he falls.'

'He won't fall,' laughed Javier. 'He's been working up there all week.'

Suddenly the singing stopped and Paul turned round. He looked surprised to see he'd attracted an audience.

'Are you okay?' I called.

'I'm fine,' he nodded. 'I've not gone crackers. I can get a mobile signal up here.'

On Saturday morning Paul was picking blackberries when I went to let the chooks out.

'Morning,' I called.

'Morning,' he grinned sheepishly. 'Sorry if I had you all worried last night.'

'You didn't,' I smiled. 'Javier found it highly amusing. It was only Maruja that was scared. I'm surprised to see you out so early on your rest day. I thought you'd be enjoying a lie-in.'

'I intended to,' he sighed. 'But I think my body clock's altered. By quarter past seven I was wide awake. Tom's lucky, though – he's still fast off. He'll be glad when he finishes on Thursday, he's had a bad back all week.'

Paul's words surprised me. Neither he nor Tom paid any heed to Galician customs; next Friday was a big religious holiday, surely they weren't having the day off to celebrate the *Asunción*?

'You're having Friday off for Bank Holiday then, are you?'

'*I'm* not. Kev and I will still be working; Tom's off to do a week's house-sit, it couldn't have come at a worse time.'

'But didn't you have an agreement? I thought Tom had committed himself to helping you with the roof?'

'He had, but Luc asked him at the ex-pats' meeting – he's the Belgian chap you saw us talking to.
He's a lovely man, and it was him that put me in touch with Kev in the first place. I could hardly complain.'

When I told Gary he was incredulous.

'The crafty sod,' he frowned. 'I *knew* he'd find some excuse to get out of it. He wasn't happy about doing it all along.'

The 15th of August marks the Catholic festival of the Assumption of the Virgin Mary; it's an important national holiday throughout the whole of Spain. When we'd flown out to Galicia the previous summer we'd been surprised to see our peaceful *aldea* transformed into a hive of activity during the countdown to the *Asunción*.

While the rest of Spain was busy getting into the spirit of feasting and *fiestas*, life in the village had ticked along peacefully and I'd been expecting the season of festivities to pass us by. At the start of the second week in August, however, a poster had appeared on the telegraph pole opposite the farmhouse: on the 15th of August three masses and a procession of the Virgin Mary would take place in the parish church of San Xoán. Másimo and his son Javi had assured me that the event was well worth attending; people would flock to the village from far and wide. I was convinced that they were exaggerating, but as it turned out, I couldn't have been more wrong.

'I'm getting excited.,' I grinned, when Gary came into the kitchen. 'It's the *fiesta* on Friday. I bet the poster will be up by the time you get back from the shops.'

'What poster?' he yawned. 'Oh, you're talking about the advert for the masses and the procession. It'll be the same one they used last summer. Másimo and Javi said it's the same every year.'

'I know,' I nodded. 'But it's more than an advert, isn't it? It's sort of symbolic in a way. Last year it seemed to trigger all the preparations. I reckon once it's on the telegraph pole, the build-up will really begin.'

'You don't half exaggerate. Preparations? I remember them strimming the grass in the churchyard, that's all.'

'Actually, they strimmed just about *everything* between the farmhouse and the bus stop – the green, the field they used for parking, the hedgerows…'

'Okay, then, *apart* from the strimming. what else did they do?'

'Some women – don't ask me who they were – turned up with mops and buckets to clean the church, and people were coming back and forth all week arranging flowers on graves. José Manuel scraped up all the mud and cow poo in front of the farmhouse and Maruja shifted all the clutter except for the brollies and the cow sticks, *and* she rearranged all her plants.'

'Crikey, yes, I'd forgotten how clean the lane looked. I'm surprised you've remembered so much.'

'I *also* remember…' I grinned mischievously, '…how an uninitiated bloke from Las Palmas tried his hand at herding a cow.'

'Good God, *now* you're talking. I was a natural as I recall.'

I giggled as I pictured him in charge of the bovine maverick. The panicked expression, the perspiring brow… 'Natural isn't *quite* the word I'd have used.'

'I don't know why *you're* laughing – *you* ended up having nightmares because of that bloody icon. You said she was evil and swore you'd been cursed.'

I shivered at the memory. When we'd arrived for the final mass the church was packed to capacity, with people crammed like sardines in the aisles and spilling out into the churchyard beyond. We'd stood on the grass in the scorching heat listening to the priest through a speaker, swotting at flies and desperate for some shade. When the service had finished, we'd watched as a hideous porcelain icon enshrined in a glass case had been paraded around the churchyard. The evil-eyed effigy was *Nuestra Señora de Las Necesidades*, the sacred benefactor of the parish who would comfort the faithful in times of need. I'd found the menacing image profoundly disconcerting; that night I'd slept fitfully, and the memory of the Virgin in the Vivarium had haunted me for days.

This year I was determined we'd slip away before the terrible avatar made her appearance; even twelve months later I still shuddered at the thought of those sinister eyes.

'It won't happen this year, I can assure you.'

'Does that mean we haven't got to go?'

'Of *course* we've got to go. The difference is we'll leg it as soon as we hear the blessing through the speaker. I never want to see that monstrosity again.'

On the morning of the fifteenth it was drizzling. It was typical of Galician weather and it couldn't have come at a worse time.

'We've got two choices,' I said, as I handed Gary his cuppa. 'We can get there half an hour early in the hope of getting a seat, or we can turn up late and not have to stand for so long in the rain.'

'There *is* a third option,' he yawned.

'Don't even think it,' I glared. '*Everyone* turns up for the village *fiesta*. To cry off would be *very* poor form.'

'I bet Paul and the hippy builder won't be attending.'

'That's different, Paul doesn't even *try* to fit in.'

'*En el nombre del Padre y del Hijo y del Espíritu Santo…*'

'Right,' I whispered. 'Now!'

As the crowd outside the church moved sideways to clear the exit, I grabbed Gary's hand and made a dash for the gate. Once we were safely out on the green I relaxed my grip on him and delved into my handbag.

'Fag!' I grinned, as the bell began to toll.

'Here she comes,' said Gary. 'Are you sure you don't want a quick peek before we head back to the village?'

'Gary,' I smiled. 'Piss off.'

As we strolled back down the lane Másimo wasn't far behind us.

'Elisa, Gary,' he called.

We hovered at the corner, waiting for him to catch up.

'What do you think about your neighbour's roof?' he grinned.

'Well,' I began cagily, 'I think it's going to be a long job.'

'It's a disaster,' declared Masi. 'Come, on let's go and have a look.'

While the rest of the village was respecting the *fiesta*, the outlaws, predictably, had continued to work on the roof. As we reached number ten Kev was singing cheerfully as he hammered another skinny strut onto the beam. With no attempt to disguise his disapproval, Másimo pointed upwards and shook his head.

'It's a disaster,' he repeated, loudly. 'The job's rubbish. The builder doesn't know what he's doing – look at the thickness of the wood.'

I cringed inwardly. Kev was only six feet above us; there was no doubt he must have heard. Sure enough, at that moment he turned round and looked down at us. I braced myself for whatever was coming next.

'*Hola*,' he called cheerily. The smile on his face said he hadn't understood a word of what Masi was saying. Either that, or he was just too stoned to care.

Liza Grantham

Man on the Roof

The sun's going down
And I've finished my labours.
I walk down the lane
And bump into the neighbours.

They seem most surprised
As they look to the sky,
I follow their gaze
'Cos I want to know why.

The reason's absurd,
I exclaim: 'I'll be damned!'
On top of the roof,
Sure enough there's a man!

He's making a phone call
In spite of the danger,
And drinking red wine –
Well, it couldn't be stranger!

The three of us stand there,
All giggling and staring,
'Cos boxers and flip-flops
Are all that he's wearing.

He's stumbling about
On the tiles that aren't finished,
Like someone who's crackers,
All reason diminished.

'Dios!' says Maruja,
'The Englishman's manic!'
'Don't worry,' I say,
'Cos she's starting to panic.

How Now, Mad Cow?

The scene's getting weirder,
He's just started singing,
It looks like he's drunk
'Cos he's swaying and swinging.

At last he rings off
'Cos the signal is waning,
I want to applaud –
It's been so entertaining.

He spots us all staring
And comes to the gutter:
'I'm here for the signal,
Don't think I'm a nutter.'

Chapter 12

Bangers and Beans

On Saturday morning Paul was up early again. This time he wasn't picking blackberries, he was sporting a huge rucksack and getting on his bike.

'Morning,' he called.

'Morning,' I smiled. 'Are you doing a runner like Tom?'

'Not likely. The work's got to stay on schedule. I'm going back to England at the end of the month and Kev's off to his next job. Right now I'm off to Lalín for some shopping. With Tom gone it's down to me to cook.'

'Can't you go into Antas and save yourself the hassle?'

'Sausages,' he grinned, by way of explanation. 'Proper ones just like in England. On Monday I'm doing bangers and mash.'

'The *chorizo criollo*'s very like English sausage, you know.'

'I'm not *only* going for sausage. You can get all sorts in Lidl. I'm going to stock up.'

'You're bonkers,' I laughed. 'Good luck.'

'What time did you see Paul?' asked Gary when he came in for coffee.

'I don't know,' I frowned, thinking. 'I'd just let the chooks out so... about eight o'clock, I should think. Why d'you ask?'

'He won't be back for at least another hour then. That's a shame. Carmen's snooping about in his outbuilding, I wanted him to catch her in the act.'

'That's wicked,' I grinned. 'I doubt he'd challenge her anyway, he's far too soft. I wonder what she's after?'

'Well, it's where they've stashed all the old roofboards. I'm betting she's half-inching some wood.'

'Did she see you?'

'I don't think so.'

I smiled slyly. 'She might still be there then. I'm going to have a look.'

I nipped up the lane and crept round the corner. Carmen was standing in the doorway of the outbuilding, furtively scanning the lane. She looked a little taken aback when she saw me approaching, so I assumed a cheery air.

'*Hola*, Carmen,' I smiled.

'*Hola*, Elisa,' she half-whispered, before scurrying back down the lane.

At tea-time there was a lot of bashing and thudding coming from Carmen's garden. I crept over to the herb bed to look. Tucked away safely behind her *hórreo*, Carmen was bringing an axe down hard on a long, flat piece of wood.

'She's a crafty devil,' said Gary when I told him. 'I wonder if that's why she sneaks into Másimo's garden. Crikey, I hope she hasn't nicked any of ours.'

'I don't think she would. You think about it; the second Anxo hears footsteps he barks. Even if we'd gone out she wouldn't risk drawing attention to herself. No, I think we're safe on that score.'

'Do you think we should mention it to Paul?'

'Definitely not. There's been so much tension since the duck business; we don't want to go fanning the fire. Tom and Carmen have still got it in for one another; the last thing she needs is *two* overgrown schoolkids taking the hump with her. I think we should keep schtum.'

Monday morning signalled week three of the roof job and so far only half of the crossbeams and uralite were in place. Neither Paul nor Kev would be here after August. With only a fortnight left I couldn't see how they were going to meet the deadline; when the uralite was secured there were still the tiles to go on. I wondered what would happen if the job wasn't finished on time. As luck would have it an opportunity to find out came later that day.

'We've had an invite,' announced Gary, as he brought in the last of the shopping. 'Paul's asked if we want to pop round for a drink on the patio tonight.'

'The patio?'

'That's what he calls the threshing floor.'

'Right.'

'He'd like us to meet Kev properly. He didn't feel comfortable about asking until Tom had gone.'

I was about to jump at the chance to be nosy when the memory of our previous visit caused me to think again.

'I'm not sure I want to go. I'm wary after the duck fiasco. What do you think?'

'I don't think the duck business has anything to do with this, to be honest. Look at it this way, what was the cause of the problem?'

'Well, there were two things really. Tom being pissed and grumpy, and the fracas with The Ox and the duck.'

'There you go then. Tom won't be there, he's house-sitting. The Ox won't be there, she's gone with Tom. The duck won't be there, it's dead.'

'*Gary*!'

'Well it *is*. So there's nothing to be wary about is there? I think we should do our bit for what's left of neighbourly relations and go round for a drink.'

'What time does he want us?'

'They knock off at eight and then they'll have dinner; he said anytime around nine.'

When we walked through the gate Paul was lighting a fire on the threshing floor. It was a welcome surprise, there was already a chill in the air.

'Change of plan,' he grinned, when he saw us. 'I'm not doing mash. I found Heinz baked beans in Carrefour. I'm doing us bangers and beans outside.'

They hadn't eaten yet. This didn't bode well. It was shades of the duck incident all over again.
Paul must have read my mind.

'Déjà vu, eh, Liza? Don't worry. It won't be a repeat of last time you were round here. I've got everything under control.'

Once the fire was going, Paul went inside to fetch the baked beans and sausages. As Kev began to roll himself a joint I seized the opportunity to probe.

'Paul says you've only got two more weeks, Kev; do you think you'll have it finished by then?'

'No problem. We're about halfway there already, and Tom's back on Friday.'

'But that's only the uralite, surely?' said Gary. 'Aren't you putting tiles on the top?'

'Paul's doing the tiles himself,' replied Kev, as Paul reappeared with the sausages and a saucepan.

You could have knocked me down with a feather. Was this another of Paul's pie-in-the-sky delusions, or had the last fortnight given him the motivation to get stuck in? As if reading my mind for a second time, he explained the plan.

'I'm coming back in January to put the tiles on. Kev's going to show me what to do before he goes.'

'He'll have no problem,' said Kev confidently. 'It's really straightforward. He's a Jedi warrior, he'll cope.' He leaned over to offer me the spliff.

I shook my head. 'I don't anymore. Not since my student days.'

'Nor me,' added Gary. 'I'm fine with a beer.'

Paul spread the sausages over an oven shelf raised on bricks above the fire. He stuck the saucepan of beans on top of the outermost pieces of wood.

'The secret,' he explained earnestly, 'is to let the fire die down before you put the meat on. You need hardly any flame, but you mustn't let the fire go out.'

For a while we all fell silent, staring into the fire and enjoying the warmth of its glow. The sweet, heady scents of cannabis and wood smoke made a pleasing combination. I sipped on by beer contentedly, lulled by the sizzling of the sausages and the crackling of the wood.

'This is the life,' sighed Kev, dreamily. 'Sitting round a campfire cooking bangers and beans. I feel just like a cowboy.'

I grinned inwardly. I couldn't have put it better myself.

Next morning Paul didn't look happy. He'd been in high spirits last night when we'd left him. I asked him what was wrong.

'I've had a text message off Tom,' he frowned. 'Luc's extending his stay in Belgium. Tom won't be back 'til next week.'

'That's a bugger,' I said. 'You'll still be wearing the chef's hat. It's a good job you've stocked up.'

By the following Wednesday the crossbeams and *uralita* stage were finished. Even with one man short, the unflinching Jedi warriors had cracked it with two days to spare. Whether out of benevolence or a penchant for cowboy suppers, Kev said he'd stay until Friday lunchtime to give Paul a head start with the tiles.

When I went out to shut the chooks away on Friday evening, Paul was out in the lane looking up at the roof.

'Good work,' I called, 'You're doing a great job with the tiling.'

'Thanks,' he smiled. 'It's not going badly so far. Tom's back, by the way. He's a lot happier, he's finally signed for the house.'

'That's great news. When's he moving in?'

'Not 'til October. There's a lot that needs doing so he'll be backwards and forwards for a while.'

'And you're off on Sunday, aren't you?'

'Tomorrow, I'm afraid. My flight's early Sunday morning, so I'll be leaving tomorrow lunchtime. I'll walk it to Palas de Rei and catch the bus from there. It makes me depressed just to think about it. I really don't want to go back.'

On the 1st of September we were off to another ex-pats' gathering in Monterroso. We'd umm-ed and ah-ed about whether to go a second time, but in the end, we'd decided it would be nice to see Jenny and Russell, and there was always the chance we'd bump into Rose.

This morning only the smokers were milling outside the Hotel Río Ulla; the intermittent cloud cover and nippy wind were keeping most of the regulars in the warm. A bike chained to the railing looked vaguely familiar. You could have knocked me down with a feather when Paul came out through the door.

'Good God!' exclaimed Gary. 'I thought you were setting off early so you could walk to Palas? Is Tom taking you in the van instead?'

'I'm not going,' Paul sighed. 'I can't do it. By the time I'd made a cup of tea this morning I'd made my mind up. I'm going to stay 'til October and finish the roof.'

Inside the café-bar the throng of stalwarts were sitting at a cluster of tables near the window. It didn't look as though there was room for two more. I tried to recall the names of the people I recognised from the August meeting. Gemma, Tracey, Andrew, Jez, Angela... they hadn't been very forthcoming in the way of introductions; I couldn't remember any more.

'Hi,' I ventured, hopefully. 'Will Rose be here today?'

'No,' said Tracey. 'She was supposed to be. She texted me this morning to say she couldn't make it after all.' She turned to the rest of the company. 'She wanted some redcurrant bushes. I was out at half past seven digging them up. She might have saved me the trouble; she didn't send the message 'til ten.'

Crikey, I thought. Remind me never to be late or cancel unless I'm on my death bed. Poor Rose. She must have had a good reason not to turn up.

'Did she say why?' I asked, cautiously.

'Something to do with taking the help-ex back to the airport.'

'Honestly,' sighed Angela. 'Couldn't she have dropped them off earlier and got here late?'

I looked at Gary. 'Shall we grab a coffee?'

His relief was obvious. 'Yes, lets.'

As we stood at the bar sipping coffee, Jenny and Russell arrived carrying cardboard trays loaded with stuff.

'Hi!' Jenny called to the collective onlookers. 'We're going to put these at the back on a table. Help yourself to anything you like in this tray. The jams...' she nodded to the tray that Russell was carrying. '...are three euros a jar.'

'We should buy some jam,' I said, looking over.

'You've just made some, haven't you? Do we need any more?'

'It's good to support cottage industry. Once we're having better luck with our harvests I'd like to think people will do the same for us.'

'Come on, then, Let's have a look.'

There was a pile of freshly picked cucumbers and a selection of dried beans in labelled plastic tubs. There were also a couple of dozen calendula plants.

'Look, Gary. I could put some of those in the raised bed where the tomatoes and peppers were supposed to grow.'

'You could try them, I s'pose.'

'They're pretty hardy. I've seen them growing on waste ground and along the roadside.' I turned to Jenny. 'How much do you want for the plants?'

'Nothing,' she laughed. 'Please take the lot. We put a few in the *huerta* last year to stave off carrot fly; now we've got them growing all over the place, they love to spread.'

'They sound exactly what I'm looking for. Thanks very much.'

'Help yourself to cucumbers, won't you? And some beans for next year.'

'It's really good of you,' said Gary. 'I'll nip to the car and fetch a bag.'

By the time Gary came back I'd chosen a fascinating assortment of beans. Borlotti, haricot, flageolet... the names alone would take some recalling; I'd no chance of remembering which ones were which.

'Look,' I pointed, as we pored over the collection. 'Those are like Cadbury's mini-eggs, don't you think? The pink ones with spots?'

'And the beans they yield are purple,' said Jenny.

'Really?' said Gary. 'Imagine *them* on your plate.'

'Don't worry,' laughed Jenny. 'They go green when you cook them…' she paused to wave to a woman who was approaching the table. 'Hi, Vicky! This is Gary and Liza, have you met?'

'We haven't,' Vicky smiled. 'Hi.'

'Vicky makes amazing cheese,' began Jenny.

'Wow!' I exclaimed. 'You're Tom's goat woman! You don't know me from Adam, but I'm a big fan of your cheese.'

'Thank you,' laughed Vicky. 'That's what I came to tell you, Jenny. The nanny's pregnant. I won't have any more cheese 'til next year.'

At that moment Russell came over and handed Jenny a coffee. 'Hello, again,' he beamed. 'Has Jenny had chance to ask you yet?'

'Ask us?' I looked at him quizzically.

'Our neighbour's given us an apple press,' explained Jenny, 'but we've only got a couple of apple trees…'

'…And one of them isn't yours,' quipped Gary.

Russell grinned.

'Anyway.' Jenny continued, 'you mentioned having apple trees and we wondered if you'd like us to bring it over one day and we could make apple juice and cider.'

Gary grinned at me. 'I think that's a marvellous idea.'

'Me too,' I nodded. 'Let's set a date.'

'I would've suggested mid-October,' said Jenny, 'But I'm doing a house-sit from the fourth to the eighteenth.'

'What about the last weekend in September?' said Russell. 'The apple harvest wouldn't be at its peak, but I'm sure we'd have enough.'

'Fine by me,' I nodded.

'Me too,' said Gary. 'How about an afternoon's pressing followed by supper in our barn?'

While Jenny and I exchanged phone numbers, Gary jotted down the directions for Russell.

It was only as we were leaving that I remembered there was something we'd been intending to buy.

'Jam!' I exclaimed. 'We were going to buy some. Look, Jenny's still talking to Vicky on the terrace. Let's catch her before she goes.'

I dashed through the door just as Jenny and Vicky were parting.

'Jam!' I gasped. 'We meant to buy some earlier, but somehow…'

'Strawberry or raspberry?' laughed Jenny, reaching into the box.

'Raspberry, please. I'm ever so sorry.' I held out three euros.

'Don't worry,' she smiled. 'Just take it. It's my welcome-to-Galicia gift.'

When I came back with Anxo on Tuesday morning Paul was walking towards us down the lane.

'Good timing,' he smiled. 'I was on my way to see you. Is Gary in? There's something I wanted to ask you both.'

'Come on,' I smiled. 'I bet it he's still having his breakfast. He's under orders to eat eggs.'

The eggs were still coming as regular as clockwork and Gary had stopped grouching about the hens not earning their keep. Over summer I'd been expecting one or more of them to go broody; it was then I'd planned to announce my intention to rear chicks for meat. Alas, September was upon us and I was still waiting, resigned to the fact that I'd have to patient until next year.

'I'll buy half a dozen, if you can spare them,' said Paul. 'I know Tom's had some off you. He said they were great.'

While I played shopkeeper Paul explained the reason for his visit.

'I've booked another flight for the second week in October. Even allowing for bad weather six weeks should give me enough time to finish tiling the roof. That's what I've come to see you about. There's a favour I need to ask.'

I froze as I closed the lid on the eggbox. Surely he wasn't going to ask Gary to help with the tiles?

I thought of last summer when Gary had been up on our own roof. He'd looked like an accident waiting to happen. It had scared me so much I'd been willing to fork out twelve grand just to keep him alive.

'Gary doesn't do roofs,' I said firmly.

'No worries,' smiled Paul. 'I wouldn't dream of asking. I just wondered if I could bring the ladder and have a proper look at yours.'

''Course you can,' said Gary.

'But don't go making any phone calls,' I giggled. 'We don't want you stumbling about and cracking the tiles.'

Halfway through September we began to collect the first windfall apples. After a week we still had a long way to go.

'I don't think we'll have enough for next Saturday,' frowned Gary.

'Not if we rely on our own trees,' I agreed. 'Which is why we should invite Paul.'

Gary looked at me curiously. 'Go on.'

'Paul's got loads of apple trees.'

'He's got six, actually.'

'Okay, six. But they're far bigger than ours and he's already gathered buckets full of apples…'

'Ah, I'm with you – "bring us your apples and you'll get a share of the cider". He'll be up for that.'

'Exactly. I doubt he'll want to join us for the pressing because of the tiling, but he could come for the supper when we've done.'

Paul thought it was a splendid idea. 'I'd like to be involved in the pressing as well, but what with the tiling, and Tom moving out on Sunday…'

'On *Sunday*?' I exclaimed. 'That was quick work.'

'Apparently the house is just about habitable. He's cleaned the kitchen up and the range is working. And he's sorted out a bedroom as well. He says it'll be luxury compared to the time he was living in the camper van. To be honest I think he's just desperate to get out.'

For the next six days I collected our windfalls while Gary worked hard on preparing the barn.

On the last Saturday in September Jenny and Russell arrived at eleven.

'We've parked outside the farmhouse,' said Russell, 'so we won't have as far to carry the press. I'll move the van up to the church when we've done.'

As we helped to unload the equipment from the van, Tom was barrowing his belongings up towards the church. He wandered over to look at the press. I thought for the umpteenth time what a pity it was that things had turned sour. I was sure that cidermaking would have been right up his street. He said good morning to Jenny and Russell and had no option but to do the same with us.

'Are you joining us as well, Tom?' asked Russell.

There was a pregnant pause. Gary and I looked at one another, wondering how Tom would respond.

'No, unfortunately. I would've loved to, but I already have other plans.'

As we sat in the barn drinking coffee and chopping apples, we told Jenny and Russell about the many adventures we'd had during our first year in Cutián. Eventually the conversation came round to the problems I'd had with Rufo. They were in stitches when Gary regaled them with the saga of my cardboard cylinder and how I'd looked like a human toilet roll as I waddled about in the lane.

'Our first cockerel was aggressive,' said Jenny. 'He soon ended up in the pot. The second one was fine, but we ate him eventually. We decided we weren't going to have chicks, we'd more than enough work with the house and the garden. We don't bother now; we only have hens.'

'I was hoping to hatch some chicks this year, but so far no-one's been broody. It's surprised me really; the weather's been great and they're coming up for a year old.'

'Are they Galician reds?' asked Jenny. 'The sort that everybody keeps?'

'Yes,' I nodded.

'You'll be waiting forever then. They don't sit.'

'Seriously?'

''Fraid so. The broodiness has been bred out of them for commercial purposes – once a hen's broody it stops laying even if you don't let it sit.'

'And they're not profitable if you're feeding them for nothing,' added Russell. 'Nature pays a heavy price for man's greed.'

'Too true,' I nodded. 'Look at the effect of the eucalyptus plantations. It's criminal. I read in the paper about Galicia's forest fires. I had no idea that eucalyptus was such a big threat.'

'It's not just the fires either,' said Russell. 'Eucalyptus affects the whole ecosystem. So many animals and plants lose their natural habitat. And of course, there's also the impact on the water table – they take up massive amounts of water, you know.'

'But going back to your hens,' said Jenny. 'You could buy an incubator from the market.'

'That'll be expensive, won't it?' Gary frowned.

'I'm not talking about a *machine*,' smiled Jenny. 'I mean an incubating hen.'

'You might as well buy a new cockerel while you're about it,' laughed Russell.

'Why?' I asked. 'I've told you; he's grown out of it. He's fine.'

'He might be fine *now*,' said Jenny, 'but don't be surprised if he starts up again next spring. It might sound a bit of a cliché but when the saps starts rising…'

'It won't,' I said confidently. 'He's turned into a steady, reliable bird.'

'Don't say we didn't warn you.' Russell grinned.

We'd been chopping for over an hour when Paul appeared.

'Mind if I join you for a while? I could do with a break from the tiles.'

'Better get yourself a knife and a chopping board,' laughed Jenny. 'It's all hands on deck.'

Once we'd filled two builder's buckets Russell announced that we'd chopped enough apples to press the first load.

We carried our buckets down to the ground floor and tipped them into the slotted wooden cylinder. Russell tightened the wingnuts on the lid and turned the handle, while the rest of us took it in turns to collect the golden juice in buckets held under the reservoir below.

When Russell was satisfied he'd squeezed every last drop from the apples, he and Gary began to syphon the juice into bottles while Jenny and I carried builder's buckets of apple pulp down to the composter.

'So you didn't enjoy living in the Canaries?' Jenny asked.

'I *loved* it at first, it was such a contrast. When we left England it was October; the nights were drawing in, it was turning colder and constantly drizzling. Next thing we were on Paradise Island with nothing but sunshine every day and a beach at the end of the street.'

'So what changed?'

'After a couple of years the beach lost its appeal, so did the weather... the bottom line is I was bored. I missed having a garden, I missed the seasons, I missed the colour green.'

Jenny laughed. 'You've certainly come to the right place for all of those. This *aldea*'s in a beautiful setting. It's in a sort of basin, isn't it? You can see out to wooded mountains on every side.'

'It's the woodlands I love most,' I smiled. 'It might sound daft, but they're like an enchanted fairyland. It's like being inside the storybooks I read as a child.'

'I know what you mean,' nodded Jenny. 'And they're at their most beautiful in the autumn, it's such a magical time of year.'

Where the Wood Nymphs Weep

Now autumn's dwindling sunlight swathes the wooded valleys,
The pallid rays seep idly through the dells
Where oaks, once proud, have lost their robes of emerald.
Their erstwhile majesty barely remembered
In a carpet of russet and gold,
Where the wood nymphs creep.

Then comes the first chill of winter on the wind,
Stealing softly down the hillside, carrying a whispered warning.
The forest, hushed and weary, yields to the spell of Morpheus,
Cast through the deepest darkness,
Where the wood nymphs sleep.

The cuckoo's ostinato heralds spring's arrival
And a rousing chorus in crescendo fills the air.
The wakening forest rings with vibrant harmony
And the mighty oaks rejoice in the promise of renaissance
Stirring in their budding branches,
Where the wood nymphs peep.

The sun burns fiercely into summer, oppressive and relentless,
Wielding Vulcan's curse. A glint! A spark! A flame!
A merciless inferno rages though the choking woodlands,
Where the valiant oaks fall helplessly to their cruel fate,
Their remains charred and smould'ring,
Where the wood nymphs weep.

Chapter 13

Point of No Return

On Sunday morning I was closing the door of the chooks' pen when I spotted Paul mooching about in his wilderness on the other side of the wall. He was holding a mug of tea in one hand and rubbing his head with the other. His gloomy expression told me something was wrong. He'd been chatty yesterday when he'd joined us all for supper, and decidedly chipper when he'd left around seven to spend the last evening with Tom.

'Morning,' I called.

'Morning.'

'Are you okay?'

'*I* am. It's Tom. He's had a terrible bust-up with Carmen; this time it's gone too far.'

'What do you mean?'

'It happened last night, about nine o'clock. We were sitting outside on the patio. Tom went inside to fetch another bottle of wine and Maud followed him. While he was in the house, Carmen started herding the chickens and cockerel out of her gate and in through the back door. The cockerel was still on the bit of path between the gate and the back door when Maud came back. Tom was bringing up the rear, but Carmen didn't see him. She must have been worried for the cockerel because she threw a big stone at Maud.'

'Oh, my God.'

'Tom saw red. He grabbed her by the cardigan and yelled at her. Then he let her go and came back in.'

'And he's leaving today?'

'Yes. He's not up yet but I doubt his plans will have changed.'

'That's good then. I don't mean it nastily. It'll be better for him *and* for Carmen; there won't be any more flak once he's gone.'

Paul nodded. 'He'd been in a bad mood all day because he'd missed out on making the cider. He used to make alcohol out of potatoes when he lived in Poland. Cidermaking's something he's always wanted to do.'

'He'd have been invited if things had been different. I felt sorry for him, to be honest Paul. I feel sorry about the whole wretched business. If he'd seen fit to apologise for flying off the handle we could have let bygones be bygones; as it is, he'll be leaving under a cloud.'

When I came back into the kitchen Gary was making his cuppa. He was wearing a pained expression and winced when he sat down.

'Morning,' I said. 'You're another one who doesn't look happy. Are you in pain?'

'It's my back,' he grimaced. 'It's twinging. It must be from all the bending and lifting yesterday. I'm sure it'll pass.' He winced again as he reached for his bacca. 'Anyway, who else doesn't look happy? I'm surprised there's anyone up and about.'

'I saw Paul when I was letting the chooks out. It's all kicked off between Carmen and Tom.' 'Crikey, what's happened?'

As I recounted the saga to Gary I stuck the kettle on the cooker and rolled myself a fag.

'That's disgraceful. Attacking an old lady…'

'He didn't *attack* her.'

'Okay, he grabbed her.'

'He grabbed her *cardi*. I wouldn't want *you* in the witness box; innocent people could hang.'

He grinned at me. 'Better safe than sorry.'

I giggled in spite of myself. 'Trust you.'

I drew on my cigarette and looked down at Anxo. I wasn't an aggressive person but if anyone should ever raise a hand to *my* dog…

'I can understand it. Don't look at me like I'm a monster, Gary. I'd be the same with Anxo. Protecting a loved one doesn't make you a thug.'

When Gary came in for coffee he was frowning. 'There's been a development. I'm glad I'm not Tom.'

'*Now* what's happened?'

'When I went up to the church I saw Carmen on her way back from Maruja's. She told me about the set to with Tom. She said, "I was frightened. He grabbed me here – like this." And she scrunched her collar up under her chin. She told me she'd been to the farmhouse to ring her son in Bilbao and tell him what had happened. He told her to ask Javier to call the *Guardia Civil*.'

'Bloody hell, Gary – it sounds like he's in the shit.'

Maruja's door opened when I passed the farmhouse on my way to the wheelie bin.

'Elisa,' she called.

'Yes, Maruja?'

'Is it true that Tom grabbed Carmen by the collar? She's been round here to phone her son. He wants Javier to ring the *Guardia*. We're not sure what to do.'

'I wasn't there, Maruja, but Paul saw it. She threw a stone at Tom's dog and he overreacted. It won't happen again though; he's leaving later, for good.'

'Leaving the village? Are you sure about that?'

'I'm certain. It's not because of what's happened. It's been planned for a while now. He's bought a house.'

'That's good news. We don't want trouble in the *aldea*. When Javier knows that Tom's going, he won't call the *Guardia*. I'll explain things to Carmen and we'll leave it at that.'

On Monday morning there was a spring in my step as I went down to the chooks' pen. The air was tinged with the chill of autumn, yet my world felt charged with a newfound dynamism reminiscent of spring. There hadn't been any *tangible* changes to our lives since the summer, but I'd been weighed down by a sense of apprehension all the same. I knew I wasn't the only one who'd been sapped by the hostilities; it was time for us all to bounce back and dust ourselves down.

Over the next few days Carmen began to look less strained and anxious and went back to using Paul's garden as a shortcut to the woods. Paul himself became more purposeful, applying himself to the tiling instead of lounging about in the sun. Unlike the rest of us Gary didn't seem to have been affected one way or the other by Tom's departure; or so I believed until Friday, when I called him in for his lunch.

'What do you say to a drive out on Sunday?' he beamed. 'We can take in a bit of scenery, see life from the open road.'

I couldn't believe what I was hearing. This was the man who *hated* driving; these couldn't be the words of the irritable driver *I'd* come to know.

'Whatever's got into you? What's all this guff about the open road?'

'We've had a message from Rose,' he chuckled. 'She's invited us over to visit while the weather's still decent. She says to ring her for directions if we'd like to go.'

'I'd love to, the house sounds intriguing. We could take her a bottle of cider for a house-warming gift.'

'We don't know if it'll be any good yet. It won't be ready to try 'til spring.'

'It doesn't matter. If it goes wrong she's got a bottle of cider vinegar. *I'd* be happy with that.'

'Okay then, I'll ring her later for the directions. We'll have a well-earned, leisurely Sunday afternoon.'

Rose had spent a good ten minutes giving Gary directions over the phone on Friday. When he handed me his jottings on Sunday morning I knew we were in for some fun. The journey went smoothly for the first forty minutes; before I knew it, we'd made it all the way to Chantada and not a single expletive had defiled the blessed Sunday air.

Five minutes later the road wound its way around the mountainside, with a breath-taking view of the Río Miño meandering far below. With its steeply terraced banks lined with tier upon tier of vineyards and *bodegas*, this was the famous Ribeira Sacra valley, origin of the highly acclaimed Galician wines.

As I gasped and exclaimed and pointed, Gary's Irritable Driver Syndrome kicked in.

'Liza! For God's sake sit *still*! I'm trying to drive!'

Resisting the temptation to point out that it was Gary's idea to "take in a bit of scenery" I applied myself to the directions.

'You want the turn off to Ferreira de Pantón,' I sighed.

As our route took us away from the valley, we drove in silence; Gary focused on the road ahead, while I sulked as I tried to make sense of his scribble, making sure that I spotted the landmarks in time.

Eventually we passed a small farmyard.

'I think it's the next turning,' I said. 'Look, "Vilabeira" – we need to turn left here.'

We followed a winding track down through a section of woodland which opened out into outbuildings and barns.

'I think this is it, I can't see a tent though. Pull up here, we'll have to get out and have a look.'

We got out of the car, lit cigarettes and surveyed our surroundings.

'This must be wrong,' frowned Gary. 'She told me it's a lovely stone ruin with a beautiful bread oven and it's all overgrown with vines.'

'Look,' I said. 'Over to the right. There's a stone ruin but it's got an ugly brick-built house attached.'

Gary looked across to where I was pointing. 'That *can't* be right – it's s'posed to be quaint and pretty with a wonderful view.'

'Hiya,' called a voice, as Rose appeared from round the corner. 'I'm surprised you could follow my directions I'm glad you found it okay.'

'It's Gary's forte,' I chuckled. 'He loves finding his way to unknown destinations, seeing life from the open road.'

'House tour first?' asked Rose.

I glanced over at the ruin and nodded. Something told me the house tour wouldn't take long.

Rose led us through a doorway into a small courtyard then through a second doorway into the 'house' itself.

'Look,' said Rose, pointing. 'This outer wall has a fault running through it and over there…' she pointed again, '…the inner wall's on the verge of collapse.'

Gary and I stared at the precarious shell that surrounded us. With only the skeleton of a roof remaining much of the upstairs had succumbed to the elements and none of the floors were intact.

'It doesn't look very safe to me,' frowned Gary, stating the obvious. 'You don't want to go poking around until it's been straightened up.'

'That's exactly what the architect said,' Rose giggled. 'When she came to do the survey she made me wear a hard hat. The great news is Kev's starting tomorrow. It won't take him long to sort the walls out, and then he'll get going with the roof.'

I cast my mind back to our own roof job. We'd had a *falta* in the wall of the annexe and Pepe had taken down the entire corner and rebuilt it before he dared risk banging about on the beams. Gary must have been having similar recollections:

'Wouldn't it be better to take the whole wall out and rebuild it?'

'*What*?' laughed Rose, as though the idea was preposterous. 'It'll be fine with a bit of *mortero*. Once the wall's been pointed it'll hold it together like glue.'

'So whereabouts is the bread oven?' I asked.

'That's out in the courtyard, come on.'

I could see at once that the bread oven would have been magnificent in its heyday. It was a typical, circular construction with the traditional domed ceiling. Alas, it too had fallen prey to the ravages of neglect and harsh winters; like the house it was in need of a complete overhaul.

'What are your plans for the house once the structure's sound?' asked Gary.

'The architect's drawn up the plans for the doors and windows and a balcony. She's applied for the *permisos* from the council, so we just have to wait. On top of that I'm still waiting for the electric board to come out and connect me. I've been without power now for over two months.'

'So, you'll be heading back to England when the weather changes?' I asked her.

'Not if I can help it. Pete's coming over at the end of November and I know he'll want me to go back with him, but at least *part* of the house will be functional by then.'

I glanced at Gary and he raised his eyebrows; there was no doubt about it, Rose was even more of a dreamer than Paul.

The Imposter had become a permanent fixture in the village and now turned up at number ten every day to be fed. With Tom gone, Paul was happy to oblige him, and occasional scraps quickly waxed into regular meals. There had been no further battles with Scholes and the pair had settled for studiously ignoring one another. Even so, it was clear they'd never be buddies, Scholes always growled a reminder if their paths crossed in the lane.

When Gary was unloading the shopping on Monday morning, The Imposter was weaving round him and yowling like a cat possessed.

'I don't know what's got into him,' frowned Gary, as he dumped the last of the bags onto the floor of the passage.

'I think *I* do,' I grinned. 'He's determined to get at whatever's in that bag.'

The Imposter was trying to push his head into a large carrier with the handles tied together.

'Posster, no!' I laughed, grabbing the bag from under him.

'Posster?' said Gary, curiously.

'It's what I've been calling him. We can't keep saying "The Imposter" – it's too much of a mouthful. Apart from that, the poor lad deserves a name.'

'Right,' he nodded. 'It suits him.' He turned to Posster. 'Okay, Posster, bugger off out and play.'

Once Posster was safely out in the lane with the back door closed firmly behind him I began to undo the handles of the bag.

'Ah, yes,' said Gary. 'I think you'll be pleased with that. Have a look.'

I pulled the handles open and peered in.

Three large bones sat proudly on a bundle of blubbery pig fat. It was like staring at the unwanted gift from Masi all over again.

'I take it the bones are for Anxo, but whatever possessed you to buy all this fat?'

'I didn't buy any of it. It was free.'

'Free? Ah, that's okay then. How did you manage that?'

'Last week when I was at the butcher's counter the woman next to me was asking for dog bones. The assistant went over to the table where they chop the meat up. There was a blue bucket underneath and she emptied the lot into a carrier bag, just like that. I made up my mind that next time I was in I'd try my luck. Are you pleased?'

'I'm delighted. He can have a bone now and I'll put the rest in the freezer.'

God alone knew what I'd do with all that fat.

The week passed peacefully and there were no further surprises until Friday morning; I'd not long come back from walking Anxo when there was a knock at the back door.

'It's either Masi or Carmen,' said Gary.

'I can tell you for certain it isn't. It's not one of the neighbours. Let's find out.'

When I opened the door Maribel was on the doorstep.

'*Buenos días*,' she beamed.

'Maribel! *Buenos días*. Come in.'

'I won't,' she said. 'I'm not stopping. I'm showing a Dutch couple some houses – I mustn't be late. I've a message for you from Hermitas. She wants to know if you're interested in buying the land.'

'The land where our hens are?' I stepped out into the lane and pulled the door shut behind me. Gary had made a cock-up negotiating a price for the land that was Hilda's; I didn't want him leaping in with his size eights again.

'Yes.'

'Has she given you a price?'

'A thousand euros.'

It was exactly the price I'd been hoping for, but this was Galicia and things weren't *always* quite as they seemed. I'd learned a lot in the last eighteen months, and I wasn't prepared to take any chances; I had to know that the chestnut tree was included in the deal.

'Does that include the *castañeiro*?'

'Yes.'

'In that case, we have a deal.'

'Perfect. I'll fix it up with the *notario*. It'll be sometime next week.'

'No, not next week. I'll need to move some money from England.'

'But it's only a thousand euros…'

I'd also learned to stand my ground.

'The Spanish account is for day to day living. I'll make the transfer next week and we'll arrange the date when the money's in the bank.'

'*Muy bien*. I'll let Hermitas know.'

On Saturday Paul turned up before lunchtime, weighed down by his rucksack and wearing a smile.

'Can I leave the key with you?' he asked. 'I wondered if you'd mind keeping an eye on the ceilings if turns rainy. The water will still come in above the kitchen window, but as long as there are no leaks upstairs I'll be happy with that.'

'That's no problem,' said Gary. 'And in case you come back when we're not expecting you, I'll keep it on a hook just inside the barn door. Do you want us to put buckets under the draining board like Tom did when it was torrential?'

'If it's not too much trouble, that'd be brilliant, Gary. And I don't want to tempt fate but here's Kev's mobile number in case.'

'You seem happier about leaving this time,' I said.

'I am,' Paul nodded. 'I'll miss the village and if I'm honest I'll miss The Imposter. I don't know what'll happen to him when I've gone.'

'I've been thinking about that,' I frowned. 'I'm worried that he might start coming in through Schole's flap.'

'There is a solution,' ventured Paul, tentatively.

'Go on.'

'If I were to leave you some money to buy a bag of cat food…'

'…We could go round and feed him? I think it's a brilliant idea.'

'It'd be doing us a favour,' added Gary. 'I could go round in the mornings while Liza's walking Anxo.'

'And I could top him up when I put the chooks away at night.'

'What's "posster"?' frowned Gary, as he cast his hungry, critical eye over the shopping list. 'Should it say *postre*? I'm not sure what you mean.'

'Don't panic. It's not like icing sugar, it won't break the bank.'

'There's no need to be sarcastic, I just wanted to know what to buy.'

'It's means the food for Posster. Had you forgotten Paul's left us the money to buy him some grub?'

''Course I'd not forgotten. It was the spelling that confused me. I didn't realise it was spelt with a double "s". I'd assumed it was "imposter" without the "im".'

'It was. Or rather, it *should* have been. The trouble is, that gives you "poster" – if you don't stick the extra "s" in it doesn't work.'

'Got you. You're right, it doesn't. English is weird.'

Once I'd transferred a thousand euros into the Spanish account, I sent Maribel a message. I told her it was fine to book the *notario* for the following week.

When Gary came in for coffee, something had amused him. 'We've had a message off Maribel,' he grinned.

'Whatever it is, it's tickled you. Go on then, what does it say?'

'You'll love it, I swear.'

'*Gary…*'

'Okay. Where is it…' He fumbled annoyingly with the phone.

'Can't you just tell me?'

'Be patient, you'll understand when I read it. Ah, here we go.' He paused and cleared his throat. 'Ready?'

I nodded.

'"The deed cannot be done. We must warn Hermits."'

I giggled delightedly. 'That's priceless! It sounds so menacing. Hold on, though, does it *really* say that or are you winding me up?'

'On my life. Here, see for yourself.'

He passed me the phone.

'My God, so it does. I suppose she's saying: "We can't do the signing yet, we've got to let Hermitas know."'

'I prefer the other version.'

'So do I. It needs to be read in a dark, mysterious voice, though, like this: "The deed cannot be done. We must warn Hermits."'

'Ah, yes, that's really sinister. It sounds medieval. What could it mean?'

'I think there's a conspiracy and dark powers are at work. Someone must warn the Hermit. His life is in danger, and they can't do the deed that might have saved him.'

'So they end up chopping his head off at Sacrificial Stone.'

I giggled. 'Trust you to lower the tone.'

'It was good, *I* liked it. Either way, there's definitely a story in there. Or maybe…'

'Maybe what?'

'Nothing. I've had an idea, that's all.'

It was only a week since Paul had left, but we were already becoming fond of Posster. I'd begun to look forward to putting the chooks away; it was a pleasure to give him his evening feed. He hadn't been shy for long; within days he was weaving round my legs and buffeting his head against my hand when I put down his bowl. He ate hungrily and noisily and showed his gratitude afterwards by purring as I gave him a fuss.

On Saturday evening it began to drizzle. By the look of the garden next morning it had turned into a heck of a downpour during the night.

'Paul's ceilings are fine,' said Gary, when I came back with Anxo. 'There's no sign of any water coming in upstairs.'

'That's great news. Perhaps we were too critical about the roof then. It sounds like it's doing its job.'

For the next two days the rain hammered down relentlessly. Round at number ten there was a row of buckets under the draining board, but so far the roof had prevailed. On Tuesday evening I wasn't expecting to find any problems but up in the living room water was now dripping intermittently from the beam.

'It's not as bad as last time,' I told Gary. 'The drips are only occasional, and I've put some saucepans down to catch them. I'm not really sure it's worth phoning Kev.'

'I think we ought to. It wasn't dripping at all this morning – who knows, by tomorrow it could be pouring in.'

'I could go now if you like, while I'm still in my waterproofs. It's torrential out there, there's no point in you getting drenched.'

As I passed the farmhouse, Maruja and Javier were standing outside under brollies. They were staring down intently at something under the bench.

'*Hola*,' I called, walking over to see what had caught their attention.

'*Hola*, Elisa,' said Maruja. 'Look, here.'

A huge salamander was plodding purposefully between a pair of wellies and a ball of blue twine. Despite its striking black and gold markings it wasn't the most attractive of creatures; there was something hideously primordial about its oversized head.

'It's a *salamanca*,' said Javier. 'The rain brings them out of their holes.'

'It's enormous,' I marvelled. 'I thought it was a *salamandra*?'

'That's Castilian,' explained Maruja. 'We say *salamanca* in *galego*. Some people call them *pinchorra*s as well.'

Up at the church I was glad of the waterproofs. The wind was gusting in across the valley and driving the rain hard against my side. I turned my back to the elements and tapped rapidly on the keypad before shifting my hood to one side and shoving the phone against my ear.

'Hello?'

'Hi, Kev. It's Liza, Paul's neighbour. He's finished the tiling and gone back to England. I'm sorry to bother you but the rain's still getting in.'

'Do you mean in the kitchen above the sink?'

'No, it's coming in there but that was expected. It's upstairs in the living room I'm ringing about, it's dripping in through the beam.'

'Hmm. That shouldn't be happening if the tiles are on properly and the ridge tiles overlap.'

'He hasn't done the ridge tiles yet.'

Kev sighed. 'Well that's why, then. It's no wonder the water's getting in.'

'You wouldn't be able to get over and have a look at it for him?'

'I'm sorry, there's no chance. I'm committed to finishing Rose's job at the moment. I did tell Paul the ridge tiles were essential. Couldn't Gary have a go?'

'He bloody well couldn't. I'll let Paul know. The rest's up to him.'

'Okay. Sorry about that. Hold on, I think Rose wants a word.'

There was a pause, a giggle and Rose's breathless voice said: 'Hiya!'

'Hi Rose. How's the work going?'

'Frantic. There's no way I can spare Kev at the moment. We're no nearer to getting the roof on. Remember the interior wall I showed you? It's fallen down.'

'Oh dear.'

'Yes, and Pete's coming over at the weekend for a fleeting visit. I wasn't expecting to see him 'til November. He won't be pleased.'

'Oh dear.'

'Not to worry. Hopefully things will have moved forward by then. And it'll be lovely to see him, it's been three months.'

'Crikey.' I thought of the tent and the weather and the bread and cheese. 'Would you like to bring him over for dinner one evening?'

'It's kind of you, but we just won't have time. He'll be coming back out for Christmas – we could do something then.'

'That'd be lovely. Okay, Rose, I won't keep you. I hope all goes well.'

'So do I,' she giggled. 'Speak soon.'

When I told Gary what Kev had suggested I could tell he wasn't impressed.

'What a bloody nerve! We've already gone above and beyond the call of duty. I'm not prepared to do any more.'

'You're right,' I nodded. 'We'll empty the buckets each time we feed Posster and I'll send Paul a message in the morning, so he knows the score.'

On Wednesday morning Gary looked like a drowned rat when he came in for coffee.

'More fool you,' I sighed when he told me what he'd been up to; he'd spent the last hour laying polythene over the ridges on Paul's roof.

On the 31st of October we were off to a meeting. It wasn't in a deep, dark forest as might befit a Hallowe'en assignation, but at the *notario*'s office in Monterroso; we were finally meeting Hermitas to buy the chooks' land.

From past experience we knew there was no point in turning up early; appointments in Spain rarely started on time. At two minutes to mid-day, we walked up to the reception desk and were shown straight into a small conference room, where Hermitas was waiting with Maribel's assistant, Cruz. No sooner had we finished our greetings when the *notario* came in.

After introducing himself, he established the purpose of the meeting, collected our identification cards and said, 'Okay, let's begin.' He read aloud from the deed of sale, pausing at the end of each section to make sure we all agreed. When the price of the land came up, I was taken aback.

'Eight hundred euros?' I frowned.

'Yes,' said the *notario*. 'Is that not correct?'

'That's correct,' nodded Hermitas.

'I'm sorry,' I smiled. 'Maribel told us a thousand euros. This *is* a pleasant surprise.'

Cruz looked at me. 'It *is* a thousand,' she explained. 'Eight hundred is for Hermitas, two hundred is Maribel's fee.'

'Two hundred?' exclaimed Hermitas, clearly shocked by the revelation.

The *notario* moved swiftly on. "The land is an arable plot with no buildings or residents..."'

Hermitas and I grinned at one another. 'No!' we shouted in unison.

The *notario* looked from one to the other, surprised. 'There *are* buildings?'

'No,' said Hermitas earnestly. 'There are residents.'

The *notario* and Cruz looked confused.

'The *gallinas*!' shrieked Hermitas, dissolving into laughter.

We giggled like a pair of errant schoolgirls until the exasperated *notario* tapped his pen on the table.

'Shall we proceed?' he sighed.

Ten minutes later he left the room discreetly and Gary doled out the *dinero negro*. When Cruz had counted Maribel's hard-earned share, she mumbled something about a lunch appointment and was off through the door.

'I'm so sorry,' said Hermitas. 'Two hundred euros! It's criminal. I really had no idea.' She reached into her handbag and took out twenty euros. 'Here,' she smiled, stuffing it into Gary's hand. 'Treat yourselves to lunch.'

As soon as we arrived home, I ran down to the chooks' pen.

'You're not squatters anymore!' I announced triumphantly.

Not one of the hens looked up from their scratching and pecking. Undeterred by their lack of enthusiasm I tried again.

'Nobody will be evicted! Nobody will be sent to the freezer!'

Rufo beat his wings, threw back his head and crowed.

At teatime Gary came in from the barn with a canvas.

'There you go. A spooky Hallowe'en picture. Don't touch it, it might still be wet.'

I looked at the canvas. It was a night-time scene, with two hooded figures coming face to face in the moonlight while forbidding mountains loomed behind.

'Crikey, Gary, that's creepy. It's so sinister, so

eery… hold on a minute – it's Maribel's text, isn't it?'

'It's The Hermit's Warning,' he grinned.

The Hermit's Warning

A sorcerer, in times of old,
penned cyphers on an ancient scroll,
which one poor hermit's fate foretold.

The gentle hermit, good as gold,
had read the words upon the scroll
and shuddered 'til his blood ran cold.

It said that there would come a day
when with his life he'd have to pay
and just one deed would grant him stay.

The key to freedom from the spell
did nothing for his fear to quell:
he'd have to sell his soul to Hell.

Each day he prayed beside his bed
with darkest visions in his head,
'I will not sell my soul,' he said.

His faith and fortitude held fast,
he knew that soon he'd breathe his last
because the ancient runes were cast,

One day through swirling mists at dawn,
masked men on horseback come to warn
the hermit, pious and forlorn.

He listened as he came awake:
such dark and dismal words they spake
that caused his very soul to quake.

He kept a vigil 'til the night
and wrapped his sack cloth round him tight
and shuddered, pondering his plight.

Liza Grantham

Before the dawning of the day,
unseen, the Devil passed that way
and stole both life and *soul away.*

Hell's fires raged hotter than the sun:
the evil sorcerer had won
because the deed could not be done,

Chapter 14

The Living and the Dead

On the 1st of November the mist hung like a muslin veil over the garden. From the doorstep I could see no further than the threshing floor; there could have been anything lurking in the ethereal world beyond. The drips from the trees and the intermittent thud of falling chestnuts now replaced the once familiar twitter of birdsong; many of our avian visitors had moved on to warmer climes. A damp patina of flattened leaves lined my well-trodden path down to the chooks' pen, but inside the enclosure the leaves still scrunched underfoot. Here and there soft brown apples lay rotting amongst the myriad shiny chestnuts and their prickly cases that littered the ground.

My finger ends were numb by the time I came back into the kitchen. I scrabbled about in the cubby hole for kindling. I wasn't willing to play the martyr this morning; it was high time I was lighting the range.

Once the fire was off to a good blaze, I tossed a slice of bread onto the hotplate. I loved that the range had so many different uses; I couldn't imagine a nicer breakfast than thick golden toast and Jenny's home-made raspberry jam.

'White rabbits!' shouted Gary as he came into the kitchen.

'Da chea'in!' I waved my arms in protest.

'Come again?'

l stopped chewing and swallowed. 'That's cheating! You had an unfair advantage. I had a mouthful of toast.'

'Toast? You only have toast when the fire's lit. You've always said it takes too long under the grill.'

'It does.'

He stared at the range where a scattering of crumbs was now turning to carbon. Finally, it clicked. 'Aha, we have *fuego*! I must say, it's about bloody time!'

'I've been wanting to light it for days, to be honest – I've been holding off to save wood. Even with the beams from last year and the stuff that we've gathered, I don't think we'll last until spring.'

'If the worst comes to the worst we can have a delivery. There's no point worrying about it, you never know, something might turn up.'

'I expect the fire'll go out anyway while we're in Monterroso. It never stays in for more than a couple of hours at a time.'

'Hmm. I'm glad you mentioned that, actually.'

'What, the fire going out?'

'No, Monterroso. Do we *have* to go to the market *and* the hotel?'

I paused and reached for my bacca. Today wasn't just *any* market day, it was All Saints Day. Like the festival of *Asunción*, it was another important bank holiday in Spain. Once more, people would be descending from all over the mainland, this time to pay their respects to loved ones now at rest in their family tombs. On top of that there was the big cattle market close by on the showground – if parking was normally a nightmare, this morning it would be a living hell.

'Maybe not, now I think about it. Today's *Todos los Santos* – hundreds of families will be out in their droves. On top of that, there'll be extra traffic for the *feira do gando*... no, sod the market, let's drive straight to the hotel.'

Two hours later we were driving through Monterroso. I'd never seen the town so busy and thanked my lucky stars we'd skipped the market after all. As the line of traffic crawled further out of the centre and closer to the Hotel Río Ulla, hordes of people were strolling in both directions along the pavements, and cars were parked nose-to-tail on both sides of the road. As I steeled myself for the backlash of the driver's frustration, I caught sight of a sign on a lamppost up ahead:

PARKING
HOTEL RÍO ULLA
(SOLAMENTE CLIENTES)

'Turn right here,' I said 'There's a driveway. It looks like we can park round the back.'

Outside on the terrace I spotted a few familiar faces. Rose and the man I recognised as Luc were leaning on the railing having a fag.

'Hiya!' called Rose. 'Have you been round the market?'

'I thought better of it,' I grinned, and looked at Gary. 'The husband goes doolally when it's crowded, he starts to slobber and grows hair on the palm of his hands.'

Rose giggled. 'Poor Gary. So, how's life in Cutián?'

'Stress-free, peaceful, idyllic. And no-one absconded from the cemetery last night. What about you, though? How's Kev getting on with the roof?'

'He isn't. He *has* absconded. Pete's upset him bigtime. Let's go inside and I'll tell you the news.'

While Rose bagged us a table, Gary and I went to order the coffees. I gulped when I spotted Tom at the far end of the bar. To my surprise he smiled when he saw us. Life outside the *aldea* must have been treating him well. Leaving Gary to do the honours, I plucked up the courage to nip over; perhaps it wasn't too late to build bridges after all.

'Hi Tom,' I said. 'How's it going?'

'It's great,' he beamed. 'I've already bought some chickens and believe it or not, I'm getting a couple of goats.'

'I *am* pleased. How does Isabel like it? Is she tempted to join you?'

'Definitely not,' he chuckled. 'She hates the house, she says it's too cold, too dark, too dirty. She's a city girl, remember; she loves her apartment 'cos it's clean and it's warm.'

I moved to one side to make way for a girl carrying a huge tray of pastries. '*Tarta de castañas*!' she called. 'Who'd like some chestnut tart?'

Tom and I took a piece. The pastry was soggy, but the sweet chestnut filling was to die for. I wondered if Gary had any plans for later; it really was about time we collected ours. I looked across to where he was now waiting with the coffees. Tom and I might be ready to bury the hatchet, but Gary wouldn't be making the peace any time soon.

'Listen, Tom, you take care of yourself, won't you? And if you start making goat's cheese, do let me know.'

We made our way over to where Rose was waiting.

'So,' said Gary, as we settled ourselves down at the table. 'What did Pete do that caused Kev to leave you in the lurch?'

'Well,' she began. 'Remember I said the inside wall had collapsed? Kev was worried that the wall with the fault would do the same. He cemented in a column of breeze blocks to stop it caving inwards. When Pete saw the pillar, he went mad: "*I'm* not forking for something that's built out of bloody Lego!" he said, and he ripped it out.'

'Never,' said Gary.

'Yep. He took a lump hammer to it. Thwack! And down it came.'

'So what's going to happen now?' asked Gary.

'We've been in touch with a Spanish builder. He'll give us a quote when Pete comes back at the end of the month. Oh, by the way, did you know that Tom's my new neighbour? His place is only a ten-minute drive from my house.'

'Ooh,' I said. 'Have you been round?'

She nodded.

'Go on, then,' grinned Gary. 'What's it like?'

'It's big and it's creepy,' she shuddered. 'It gives me the willies to be honest. I wouldn't want to be in there at night.'

'Talking of nights,' I said. 'You must be freezing in the tent?'

'Oh, I'm not in the tent anymore. I've got a little caravan that a chap in Escairón was scrapping. It's very old and it smells kind of mouldy, but it keeps out the rain and the wind. Once the electric's on I'll be able to feed a cable through the window and have a radiator running day and night. It'll make my plans to stay over winter perfectly feasible. I might even get Pete to come out and join me for Christmas after all.'

'How about we collect the chestnuts after lunch?' I asked Gary, as he squirted ketchup over his cheese and chive omelette. I sometimes wondered why I bothered with subtle seasonings and flavours; his penchant for Día's scarlet slop was an affront to my carefully prepared cuisine.

'We can do, I s'pose,' he said between mouthfuls. 'I wouldn't get your hopes up, the ones that have fallen so far look a bit scrawny. I thought the later ones might be bigger, but I think that's as good as we'll get.'

'It doesn't matter if they're small, just as long as we've got plenty. I could do with three or four bucketfuls. I'm looking forward to experimenting with different recipes. And I want to make chestnut flour for the freezer – I can't wait to see what it's like in cakes and pastries and breads.'

'You could make a chestnut tart like the ones at the hotel this morning. Did you get to try some, by the way?'

'I did. The girl came past while I was talking to Tom.'

'So do you think you could make one?'

'I can have a go. It wouldn't be exactly the same but I'm sure I could come up with something similar.' My efforts might even be worth it, I reasoned – he wouldn't go daubing ketchup on sweet chestnut tart.

After an hour we'd barely filled two buckets between us. I was ready for a fag and tired of pulling spikes out of my skin.

'I tell you what,' I said airily, 'you keep up the good work and I'll go and stick the kettle on. I don't know about you but I'm ready for a brew.'

As I made my way back up the garden I pondered on the pitiful fruits of our labours. It looked like I wouldn't be tweaking chestnut recipes after all.

'*Hola*!' called a voice I didn't recognise.

I was taken aback to see a man with a huge bucket looking over the gate.

'*Hola*,' I said. '*Buenos días.*'

'*Buenos días*,' he nodded. 'I'm Manolo, I'm the uncle of Mónica who sold you the house.'

'*Encantada*,' I smiled. 'What brings you to Cutián?'

'I've got a *finca* down there, past the *río*. I've come to collect the chestnuts. Is your husband about?'

'He's collecting chestnuts too,' I grinned. 'Hold on, I'll call him. Gary!'

As Gary came across threshing floor, Manolo peered over the gate to look into his bucket.

'They're not very big, are they? It's the same all over – thanks to the weather and the *bichos* it's been a bad year.'

'Gary,' I said, in English. 'This is Manolo, he's Mónica's uncle. He's come to collect chestnuts from his *finca* and he's been asking for you. I'll leave you to it, shall I? I'll go and see to the brew.'

Gary's coffee had gone cold by the time he came into the kitchen. He didn't seem at all bothered. The grin on his face told me he had some good news.

'Well, what did Manolo want you for? You're looking like the cat that got the cream.'

'He took me up to his *finca* to show me the chestnut tree. He's got parcels of land all over the place, so he's only making this one-off visit to Cutián. He said we can help ourselves to the rest of his chestnuts for as long as they fall.'

'Crikey, that's generous. Good old Manolo. It'll save us having to go scrumping up in the woods.'

'It gets better. You know the row of elder trees growing between the track and the entrance to the corner field?'

'The ones opposite Carmen's magical bramble bush?'

'Yes. Well, that little strip – it's actually a triangle but you can't tell 'cos it's so overgrown – that's Manolo's as well. He said I can cut all those trees down and keep the wood.'

'Bloody hell! That's fantastic! That'll give us a heck of a lot of wood. If you stack it in the top of the barn it might be dry enough to burn in a couple of months. If we get desperate, we could always put some in the oven now we're lighting the range.'

'I've been thinking about that. After your dry-wood-quickly disaster last year when the branches caught fire in the oven, I wondered if I might be able to do a patch up job on the corroded bits inside.'

'You mean fill the holes in with something?'

'No, don't be daft. I was thinking of buying some metal sheeting from the *ferretería*. If I bolt it to the oven walls it'll create a flame-proof lining. That way we *could* use your strategy without the risk of setting the house alight.'

'That's a brilliant idea. What made you think of it?'

'It was something Manolo told me. You know the metal sheeting along the bottom of our back door?'

I nodded. Although it was there to protect the door from the elements and the splatter of cow poo it was really rather an eyesore. I'd made my mind up I'd paint over it when I glossed the door in spring.

'Manolo told me he nailed it on years ago when he lived here.'

'Manolo lived *here*?'

'Yes. When he and his wife were newlyweds, apparently. There was José Val and his wife, Mónica's parents, Manolo and his wife and two other couples as well.'

'Ah, yes. I remember Mónica saying that five couples lived here. That's a heck of a lot of people under the same roof.'

'Manolo said it was common in those days. Tonito's Mum and Dad lived with Hilda – that's why Tonito's still living in her house now.'

'Fancy that. So where exactly *is* Manolo's *finca*? Surely there's only the Dry-Your-Laundry Field between the *río* and the woods?'

'Not quite. There's a pathway that runs along the side of that field, remember? We followed it once and it came to a dead end at a gate. That's where his *finca* is. There's an enormous chestnut tree smack in the middle of a small circle of land. Despite what Manolo said about the weather and the *bichos* I couldn't *believe* the size of the chestnuts; there were so many I could hardly see the ground.'

Since October the nights had been drawing in quickly. It would have been no fun stumbling across the fields in darkness, so Anxo's 'evening' walk now fell just before tea. After all the talk of chestnuts I fancied a stroll through the woodlands; if now was the time to collect them I wondered who else I might see. Half-way along the track I spotted a hunched figure scrabbling about amongst the leaves. As we drew closer Anxo barked. The figure looked up; it was Carmen. She began to trudge towards us, and it was then that I realised she was hiding something clutched up in the folds of her skirt.

'*Hola*, Elisa,' she half-whispered. 'I've been looking for chestnuts. I didn't find many, they haven't done well this year.'

'Happy birthday, gorgeous,' I smiled, as I stepped into the passage on Sunday morning. Anxo, with his great, gangly frame and overly large ears, rushed to greet me; it was hard to believe that my one-time little black bundle was now a year old.

'Shall we sing to Anxo now, or when you've had a fag and a cuppa?' I asked when Gary came into the kitchen.

'Sing to Anxo? Oh heck, I'd forgotten! Happy birthday Anxo! You might want to go into the passage, your Mum says we're doing a song.'

'Come on then, the Spanish one, after three.'

Gary groaned.

'One, two three… *Cumpleaños Feliz, Cumpleaños Feliz*… Gary, join in! *Te deseamos todos, Cumpleaños Feliz.*'

'Hooray,' said Gary, as he reached for his bacca. 'I'm glad we don't have birthdays every day.'

'Miserable bugger,' I grinned. 'If you've nothing better to do while I'm walking Anxo, you could start peeling the chestnuts. I'll use some tomorrow; I'll make chestnut soup for lunch.'

'As it happens, I'll be busy. My first port of call's Manolo's *finca*. If I find us some whoppers we'll have them roasted tonight with our beers.'

'Three more casualties,' proclaimed Gary, when he came in for coffee.

I looked at him blankly. 'Whatever do you mean?'

'The chestnut bug, it's spreading like wildfire – us, Manolo, Carmen… The family have gone down with it now. I've just seen Masi, Solina and Begoña all carrying buckets. I bet they've got a chestnut tree somewhere up in the woods.'

'Ooh, that's exciting. I think I'll nip down after coffee and see how they're getting on.'

Half-way down the track the family were tramping about in wellies along the embankment.

'*Buenos días*,' I called.

'*Buenos días*, Elisa.' beamed Masi. 'We're collecting chestnuts for the *magostos*. This big *castañeiro* here is our tree.'

'It might be big, but it's not given us many chestnuts this year,' frowned Solina. 'I'd have expected more to have fallen by now.'

I glanced around me. This was the spot where Carmen had been foraging yesterday; no wonder the family's harvest was thin on the ground.

'What *is* the *magostos*?' I asked them. 'I've not heard of it before.'

'It's the chestnut festival,' explained Masi. 'In Galicia it's a very big event. People get together to eat chestnuts cooked over a fire. The *castañeiros* seem to live forever, so chestnuts are supposed to give you a longer life.'

'Does everyone collect their chestnuts this weekend?' I asked him.

'More or less,' nodded Masi. 'The *Fiesta de los Magostos* takes place when the chestnuts are ready, so it varies across the region. People like to celebrate it as close to *Todos los Santos* as they can.'

'It's not the same nowadays, though,' sighed Solina. 'In the old days everybody would be out with buckets and barrows from sunrise. We'd spend all morning going backwards and forwards between the village and the woods.'

'The kids loved to ride in the barrows,' chuckled Masi. 'It didn't matter whether they were empty or full.'

'And in the evening, we always had a party,' said Solina. 'When José Val was alive we'd all get together in your barn.'

Mónica had told us the very same story; it seemed such a pity the custom hadn't endured. As *aldea* populations dwindled, traditions were gradually disappearing. It saddened me that the time would come when they wouldn't exist anymore.

After lunch I was bagging up the rubbish when there was a knock at the door. When I opened it I was surprised to see an unexpected visitor. Hermitas was standing on the doorstep wearing her typically friendly smile.

'*Hola*, Elisa! *Qué tal*?'

'Hermitas! *Que sorpresa*! Come on in!'

'I'm not stopping,' she said. 'It's the day of the *Difuntos Fieles* so I've been to the cemetery with flowers for my mother. I'm going back to Vigo in a while, but I wanted to see you before I go. Come for a little walk with me, won't you? I've got a *castañeiro* a short distance down past the *río*. I'll show you where it is, and you can help yourselves to the chestnuts. It would be a pity to let them all go to waste.'

We hadn't walked far past the path that led up to Manolo's *finca* when Hermitas stopped. There were two chestnut trees growing close together at the edge of the path. Hermitas hesitated for a moment before she spoke.

'It's one of these two. Hold on a minute, let me see.' Eventually she nodded. 'This is the one.'

I looked at the trees. They were similar in size, and both were girdled by a dense overgrowth of bramble. If Hermitas had chosen the wrong tree, would it really have mattered? It was safe to say that no-one had been foraging here for years.

As if reading my thoughts Hermitas turned to me,

'I had to be sure that this one's mine,' she explained. 'Galicians are very possessive about their *castañeiros*; it's not the done thing to collect chestnuts from someone else's tree. They've been the cause of all kinds of trouble over the years.'

'Really?'

'Oh, yes. Feuding families have come to blows during the chestnut season.'

This weekend was turning out to be quite a revelation; it seemed there was a lot more to the humble chestnut than met the eye.

'Másimo was telling me about the *magostos*,' I told her. 'I can see why chestnuts are a symbol of long life and permanence, but I don't understand the link to *Todos los Santos*. How can chestnuts have anything to do with the dead?'

'It's an ancient ritual,' explained Hermitas. 'They say that the souls of the departed roam in dark, shadowy places, so when families go off into the woods to gather their chestnuts they're supposed to leave some on the ground so as to share their feast with their loved ones who've died.'

'Surely people don't really believe it?'

'You'd be surprised; in Galicia, many of the rural people are very superstitious. Who knows?' she smiled mysteriously. 'It might even be true.'

Later that evening Gary and I sat round the fire with beers and roasted chestnuts. It seemed an appropriate finale to what had been a truly superb weekend.

'Well,' said Gary. 'Manolo and Hermitas have done us proud with their chestnuts. It's saved having to go helping ourselves through the woods.'

'Thank God we didn't. According to Hermitas there's a time-honoured Galician etiquette when it comes to chestnuts. You can't just go pilfering from the trees of any old Juan, Javi or José – there are consequences. They've probably saved us from a fate worse than death.'

Liza Grantham

Rose in Ruins

In Vilabeira, Pete and Rose
Had bought an old stone ruin,
They couldn't move in straight away –
It wanted so much doin'.

They'd stay there for the summer months
And take a long vacation,
Returning in the early spring
To start the renovation.

The end of summer came too fast.
Rose said to Pete, 'Let's stay!
We'll rent a small apartment and…'
'Forget it, Rose, no way!'

But Rose was quite impulsive
And so keen to relocate
That despite poor Pete's insistence
She decided not to wait.

She bought a little camping stove,
A sleeping bag, a tent.
'I wish you'd change your mind,' she said
But Pete would not relent.

So, Pete went back to England,
Leaving Rose to do her thing,
'She'll give up soon enough,' he thought,
'She'll never last 'til spring!'

Rose made new friends who asked about
Her living situation:
'You've water and electrics, Rose?
You've started restoration?'

How Now, Mad Cow?

She'd look at them and, laughing, say:
'Electrics? Water? Pardon?
It doesn't even have a roof –
I'm camping in the garden.

I'd ask you round to dinner but
I have nowhere to cook it,
I'm eating mainly bread and cheese,
I'm peeing in a bucket!'

'You can't camp out when autumn comes,
The days and nights grow colder.
You'll need a little heated room,
We'll sort it out,' they told her.

'The outhouse will be just the job,
The roof will need securing,
We'll put a little woodstove in,
And proper concrete flooring.'

As soon as they began the roof
They knew they were in trouble –
The slightest banging on the beams
Reduced the walls to rubble!

The autumn nights turned bitter cold,
The new room still not finished –
All hopes for its completion now
Were totally diminished.

No way would Rose admit defeat,
Not in a month of Sundays!
She bought a thicker sleeping bag
And proper thermal undies.

Then came the storms, fierce winds and hail.
The tent was torn and tattered;
Rose stood her ground, would not lose face,
Although her nerves were shattered.

The weather worsened week by week,
Much colder, darker, wetter.
She bought a leaky caravan –
It wasn't that much better!

At last poor Rose could stand no more,
So much for sunny Spain!
She went down to the Wi-Fi bar
And booked a homeward plane.

Then Pete rang up: 'I've changed my mind –
Guess what? I'm coming over!'
'No don't!' she wailed. 'Too late!' he laughed,
'My ferry's just left Dover!'

Chapter 15

To Die For

'I can smell toast,' frowned Gary when he surfaced on Monday morning. 'I meant to tell you not to light the range this morning. It must have slipped my mind.'

'You *are* a strange one. On Saturday you were pleased I'd lit the fire. If I remember correctly, you said it was "about bloody time."'

'It was. It still is. I meant *today*. I wanted to mend the oven. I was going to stop at the *ferretería* on my way back from shopping to buy the metal sheets.'

'Well, it's too late now, the fire's been lit for hours; the oven would take all day to cool. You can still buy the stuff though and do it tomorrow, I'll remember not to light it when I get up.'

Once Gary had left for Monterroso I applied myself to preparing the lunch. Over the weekend I'd been thumbing through countless cookbooks, determined to put our chestnuts to good use. I'd found numerous recipes for soup but every one was far too convoluted; by the time I'd zested lemons, crushed garlic and faffed about with a *bouquet garni*, Gary would have been wasting away.

This morning I abandoned the cookbooks; my soup would be quick and simple, using only the ingredients that were closely to hand. I peeled and chopped chestnuts, apples and onions. I tossed them all into a pan with a good knob of butter and a handful of sage. When the chestnuts were golden and the onions caramelised, I poured in a jugful of seasoned chicken stock and left the lot to simmer until the apples and chestnuts softened. Once the soup had cooled down, I gave it a quick whizz with the hand-blender and stirred in a pot of Greek yoghurt for a rich creamy taste.

'Something smells nice,' said Gary, as he brought the last of the shopping into the passage.

'I'm glad you think so, it's the chestnut soup.'

'You found a recipe okay then?'

'I found loads, but I've not used any of them. They were all too fancy and long-winded. In the end I invented my own. Did you remember my newspaper?'

'It's in one of the bags.'

Once Gary was slurping his soup down, I opened *El Progreso*.

'Guess the number of road accidents,' Gary grinned.

'Don't be horrible,' I frowned. 'Let's see what the weather's going to do… here we go: six degrees today… eight degrees tomorrow… bloody hell, look at Wednesday – it might get up to eleven degrees!'

'Tee-shirt weather, that's the one to be with. If I'm going to mend the oven it'd make more sense to do it then.'

I turned my attention back to the paper and winced at a photo of a mangled car. Suddenly a headline caught my attention: '*LUCENSE ASESINÓ SU PRIMO POR COGER CASTAÑAS*' – surely I was reading it wrong?

'Gary, listen to this. A bloke from Lugo's murdered his cousin for picking his chestnuts.'

'Get away.'

'It says the tree was on a *finca* that belonged to their Grandad who'd not long died. The chap from Lugo claimed his Grandad had left it to him but he couldn't prove it because there was no paperwork…'

'Like the little courtyard at the side of our kitchen?'

'Yes, I s'pose so. Anyway, the cousin said that he was the only other grandson so half of the chestnuts should be his. He went to the *finca* last week and he was filling his bucket when his cousin turned up. A fight broke out and his cousin bashed him on the head with a rock.'

'Unbelievable. Is there any more of this soup left?'

'There's a bit in the saucepan if you want it.'

'Might as well finish it off while it's still warm.'

As I poured the last of the soup into his bowl I said, 'Was it alright then?'

'Alright? It's fantastic. It's more than soup, it's ambrosia. You should write some of your recipes down.'

'It wouldn't work. Nobody would be able to follow them. Imagine opening a cookbook where the standard unit of measurement is a fistful, or the recipes say, "when it looks right" and "you'll know when it's done".'

As we settled round the fire with our beers that evening, Gary suddenly broke into a grin. 'That chestnut story in the paper – it's ironic really.'

Here we go, I thought. 'Why?'

'The bloke that killed his cousin, he'll do God knows how long in prison – he won't be able to collect his chestnuts for years. Every November the family will all turn up for the *magostos* and they'll leave loads behind for the dead folks. The poor departed cousin will have his fair share of the chestnuts after all.'

On Wednesday morning I could see my breath when I went down to let the chooks out. You couldn't believe everything you read in the paper; there was no way the temperature was going to hit eleven degrees today.

'I think I might leave the oven 'til it gets a bit warmer,' shivered Gary as I passed him his cuppa.

'You bloody well won't,' I frowned. 'I've been freezing in here since six o'clock this morning. I've not put myself through abject misery for nothing. You can bite the bullet and get the job done.'

After three hours of clanking and cursing the work was finished and I was invited to look. Despite my closely guarded reservations, Gary had done a truly professional job.

By Friday evening I had bags of chestnut flour and cartons of Chestnut Ambrosia in the freezer, and preserved chestnuts in syrup and chestnut jam in jars. If that wasn't sufficient, bagfuls had been frozen whole to use at a later date in soups and stews.

'I'm starting my pantry today,' I announced on Saturday morning.

'What *are* you talking about? You've already got a pantry, it's through there.'

'Through *there* I've got a bare stone room covered in dust and cobwebs, with a chest freezer against the wall and an ever-increasing collection of bottles and jars on the floor. I'm going to turn it into a proper larder, with shelves for pickles and chutneys and jams and cookbooks, and hooks to hang bags of fresh fruit and veg.'

'Aren't you being over-ambitious? It sounds like an awful lot of work.'

'It won't be. It needs a good de-cobwebbing and a thorough sweeping out. After that I'll give the walls a couple of coats of emulsion and then I'll show you where I want the shelves.

'The shelves?'

'Honestly, Gary, weren't you listening? I shall be wanting somewhere for my chutneys and jams.'

I also had plans to extend my pantry to include the area under the stairs, but Gary didn't need to know about that just yet. The space had been crudely boxed off with planks to create a walk-in cubby hole with an ill-fitting stable door. When we'd first moved into the house, I'd given the cupboard a quick onceover with the torch beam and deemed it as good a place as any to store mops and buckets. I hadn't investigated any further – as far as I could see there was nothing in there but straw.

When I came back from the fields with Anxo, Gary was just setting out for Manolo's *finca*. As soon as he'd disappeared past the *río* I dashed out to fetch the crowbar from the barn. To my relief, I prised the planks away easily. By the time Gary came back with the chestnuts the job was done.

'I've made the pantry bigger,' I beamed, as I passed him his coffee. 'I'll show you when we've finished your fag and your brew.'

He put his mug down and eyed me suspiciously. 'Bigger? That sounds ominous. I think you'd better show me now.'

Getting rid of the cubby-hole had been a spot-on decision; the pantry had almost doubled in size.

'Bloody hell!' he exclaimed. 'That's made the world of difference. I don't envy you your next job, you'll have to sweep out all that straw.'

'I'll barrow it down to the garden and it can be dug straight into the *huerta*. It'll rot down well over winter and be great for the soil.'

Twenty minutes later the loose straw was in the barrow. Instead of the stone floor I'd been expecting there was more straw compacted underneath.

'You'll never believe it,' I sighed, as I took the pizza out of the oven at lunchtime.

'Pizza? Ooh, lovely! How did you find time to make that?'

'I didn't. I took it out of the freezer. It went in the range before you came in for coffee. The oven's a godsend as long as you plan well ahead.'

'So what won't I believe then?'

'Ah yes, the straw. After I'd swept the loose stuff out it just kept on coming. I've had to use the garden fork and I've taken two barrowloads down to the *huerta* already. No way was *that* used as a cupboard. I think José Val kept an animal in there.'

'Get away. Whatever it was must have had a pretty grim existence, it's pitch black under the stairs.'

'Listen, I'm going to carry on while you eat your pizza. I was hoping to get the first coat of emulsion on before I walked Anxo but at this rate I shall still be digging the muck out at least until tea.'

Ten minutes later I had the shock of a lifetime.

I was forking another clod out from under the bottom step of the staircase when I noticed something pale and lumpy lying amongst the gunge. In the half-light it looked like a scrunched-up ball of paper; I was puzzled – why hadn't it disintegrated after all those years? My curiosity piqued, I nipped through to the kitchen.

'Forgotten something?' said Gary, who was still tucking into his pizza.

'Found something, actually. I need the torch.'

I grabbed the torch from the telly shelf and dashed back to the pantry. Gary was hot on my heels behind. When I shone the beam onto the unidentified object I couldn't believe my eyes.

'God!' exclaimed Gary, 'What the *fuck* is that?'

'I *think*,' I said, peering more closely, 'it's a mummified rat.'

The skin, a ghastly whitish grey, clung like a shrunken shroud to the skeleton, and teeth still protruded from the ghoulish, gaping mouth. Whilst my senses swung between fascination and revulsion, Gary's response was straight down the line.

'Do something with it, will you?' he mumbled. 'I'm off to get some more chestnuts. I'll finish the pizza tonight.'

By breaktime on Sunday morning I'd given the pantry walls their first coat of emulsion. Before I went through to make the coffees, I poured plenty of bleach and hot water over the flagstone floor.

'Coffee, Gary!' I called.

Five minutes later there was still no sign of him.

'Coffee, Gary!' I called again.

When I'd drained my mug and smoked a second ciggie I went back to the pantry. I'd been in there a couple of minutes when Gary walked in.

'Have you already called me for coffee?'

'I have, it's probably cold by now.' I leaned my mop against the freezer. 'Come on, I'll make you another. You can tell me where you've been.'

I stuck the kettle on the hob and reached for my bacca. From the sheepish look on Gary's face I had the feeling this might be fun.

'Okay, prodigal husband. Fire away.'

'I was walking back from the church when I noticed clouds of smoke above the farmhouse. It seemed to be coming out of the roof of the animal pen.'

'You mean out of the chimney?'

'No, I mean *literally* out of the roof.'

'Oh dear.'

'I thought the animal pen must be on fire. I thought of all the straw and all the gases from the cow poo… does that sound stupid?'

I thought for a moment: all that body heat and methane; it didn't seem beyond the realms of possibility. 'No, I'd have probably thought the same.'

'Anyway, I rang the bell and nobody answered, and when I couldn't hear the telly I knew for certain no-one was inside. I wondered about running back to the church and ring oh-eight-oh for the fire brigade, but I thought that might be a bit hasty. In the end I ran round to the cowshed to see if anybody was there.'

'And?'

'I tramped across the farmyard and yelled at the top of my voice and Javier appeared. I shouted, "Smoke! There's smoke coming out of the roof top! Is something in fire?" Javier looked up at the roof and started laughing. "Hold on," he told me. "Wait there." He came squelching through the mud and took me back round to the house, through the door and into the animal pen.'

'And?'

'There were hams and *chorizos* everywhere, hanging from the rafters. There was a fire going underneath them…'

'Oh my God! They were smoking the meat!'

'Exactly. I felt like a prize chump, *I* can tell you. Javier's going to think I'm a fool.'

'He won't. It's the same as when I told Masi there was smoke coming out of the henhouse, remember? He didn't think any the less of me for raising a false alarm.'

'I s'pose you're right. It'll give them something to talk about later. I wish you'd been there; it was really impressive. You wouldn't believe the amount of meat.'

'Did you ask Javier where it all came from?'

'I didn't, but that's obvious, isn't it? It's the time of the *matanzas* – they must've slaughtered a pig.'

'That's why I asked you. They don't keep pigs, do they?'

'Perhaps they've been fattening one up in one of the buildings round the back.'

'I doubt it. It'd be a shame if they've had a *matanza* and we've missed it. It might have been fun.'

'I can't see any fun in spending the day staring at pigs' corpses and flinging their intestines about.'

'They don't *fling* the intestines anywhere. They need them to make the *chorizos*. I must ask Maruja how it's done.'

When I took the rubbish up to the wheelie bin I couldn't see any sign of Maruja. I wondered if she was up to her elbows in chestnuts like I'd been during the week. On the way back I was lucky; she was going into the farmhouse with a bucket of logs.

'*Hola*, Maruja. *Buenos días.*'

'*Hola*, Elisa. Isn't it cold?'

'Very,' I said.

'Gary was worried that we were on fire earlier,' smiled Maruja. 'He thought the *cuadra* was burning down.'

'He's quite embarrassed about that, you know. He's worried you'll all think he's a fool.'

'*Hombre*! We don't think that at all! We're happy to have such good neighbours. Gary wasn't to know we're smoking *chorizos* and hams.'

'He was very impressed when Javier showed him. He told me there was so much meat you must have done a *matanza*, but I didn't think so. I said I was certain you hadn't been keeping a pig.'

'You were right, we haven't. We used to buy a couple to fatten, but not anymore. Over the years the number of people in the *aldea* has grown smaller and smaller, and there aren't enough of us left to have a *matanza* now. It would mean an awful lot of work for only a handful of people – you'd be surprised by how many different jobs it involves. It's easier for us to go into Monterroso and buy a pig that's already butchered, that way we only need to do the smoking and curing ourselves.'

Yet again, another custom was gradually dying. Yet again, it seemed so sad.

'So, you hang everything from the ceiling over an open fire and leave it to smoulder?'

'Yes. We hang the *chorizos* and hams on *pallos*. Look…' She took a cow stick from the bench and held it horizontally. 'We take a *pallo* like this, but longer. We tie the meat along it, wedge it across the rafters and light a fire underneath. It's better if I show you – it's in the *cuadra*. Leave Anxo out there and come in.'

I hovered in the passage while Maruja carried the firewood through to the kitchen.

'Don't stand out there, Elisa,' she called. 'Come through.'

Maruja's kitchen was like a furnace. The intense heat and the delightful smell of something cooking hit me as I walked in. The aroma was coming from a casserole heaped with golden joints of sizzling meat.

'Rabbit,' I grinned. 'It smells gorgeous.'

'Yes,' nodded Maruja. 'I killed two this morning. That's Javier's lunch.'

'I'm going to keep rabbits next year. There's a place behind the barn enclosed with standing stones. I'm going to ask Gary to turn it into a pen.'

'That's where Tonito's dad kept his chickens,' smiled Maruja. 'José Val kept *his* rabbits under the stairs.'

She shoved an enormous log into the fire and stacked the rest in the cubby-hole.

'Right,' she said. 'Let's go and see.'

She led me through to the end of the passage and opened the door next to the pristine fridge where she kept her scrumptious home-made cheeses. We stepped down into an animal pen where a rust-coloured calf no bigger than Anxo was tottering about in the straw. To the right was a roughly hewn plank door and through it there was a smaller pen where a dwindling fire glowed and crackled in the middle of the earthen floor.

'I come in every now and then to put a new log on the fire. This has been lit for two weeks but we'll keep it going for the rest of the month.'

'So you bought the pig in cuts, but did you have to make the *chorizos*?'

'No, they came with the pig, ready-made. The filling's simple enough – minced meat scraps, chopped garlic, salt and sweet paprika – it's getting it into the skins that's a nuisance. You have to stuff them into the *tripa* with a bodger, you need at least two people and it takes ages by hand. These won't have been done that way, though – nowadays it's all done by machine.'

I gazed up at the two giant hams and countless strings of *chorizos*. 'There're so many of them, I can see why Gary was so impressed.'

'That's nothing,' she smiled. 'Apart from these, you should see what we've got in the curer – the head, the *lacon*, the *tocino*... and then there's all the fresh cuts. You'd be surprised how much meat we get from one pig.'

'Thanks for showing me,' I smiled, as we walked back through to the passage. 'It's a real education for someone brought up in a town.'

'I'm glad you've learned something, Elisa. Before you go, I've got some *chorizos* in the kitchen. They've only been smoked for a fortnight, but you should take one, they're perfect for stew.'

As Maruja handed me the dark red *chorizo* I couldn't resist a final question.

'If you ever have a *matanza* in the future...'

'I doubt it will ever happen, Elisa, but if it does, you'll be the first to know.'

'Is there any chance of a stew this week?' Gary asked me on Monday morning. 'I know you've already done the shopping list, but I fancy something hearty now the weather's turned cold.'

'No problem. I'll do you one tomorrow. I won't need to add anything to the list, I've got plenty of stuff I can use.'

Since I'd made the Chestnut Ambrosia, I'd been planning to create a soup using nothing but plants from the hedgerow. Gary's request for a stew was the perfect chance to take the idea a step further; I set myself the challenge of concocting a Hedgerow Stew. I'd use Maruja's *chorizo* – the farmhouse wasn't *too* far from the hedgerow, some windfall apples, and I'd swap spuds for chestnuts exactly as an eighteenth-century peasant would have done. With the proteins and carbohydrates taken care of, everything else would be gleaned from my natural surroundings. The only fly in the ointment was Gary. He'd refuse to eat the stew if he knew what was in it. There was a simple solution: the husband need never know.

As soon as the car disappeared round the corner, I donned a pair of rubber gloves and grabbed a bucket. It was time to pick leaves for the clandestine Hedgerow Stew.

The first and most obvious choice was nettles. They were growing everywhere in proliferation: along the lanes, over the fields, in the woodlands and, quite fortuitously, by the side of the barn. There were occasions when I'd seen the dogs cock their legs there, but it didn't deter me. I reasoned that shop-bought veg had probably been sprayed with far more offensive substances: a couple of good rinses under the tap and they'd do.

Next on my agenda were dandelions. It made sense to pick the leaves from our garden; there were hundreds of them growing all over the lawn. I added a few fistfuls to my bucket and tossed in some bits from the herb bed as I made my way back to the gate.

After the dandelions came pennywort. The shiny round leaves protruded from the gaps in every stone wall in the village. I could have filled a barrow just walking the length of the lane.

It took me the whole of the morning to gather my ingredients. When Gary pulled up with the shopping I was just coming back down the lane.

'What's in the bucket?'

I showed him.

'Ah, good thinking – green stuff for the hens.'

After lunch Gary went off to collect chestnuts. They were dwindling in number now, but there were still enough to make the effort worthwhile. He was only gone an hour, but by the time he came back he looked frozen.

'I'll peel these for you later,' he shivered. 'I need to warm up by the fire before I do *anything*. Even with these gloves on I can't feel my hands.'

The final ingredient for the stew was added to the bucket later when I came back from walking Anxo. I'd brought back a bagful of wild rocket that I'd picked from Field Four.

'Do you want these chestnuts freezing or shall I leave them out?' asked Gary when I walked into the kitchen.

'Leave them out, please. They'll go in tomorrow's lunch.'

'Smashing. I'm already looking forward to my stew.'

I was on tenterhooks when Gary came in for lunch on Tuesday. I watched as he dug his spoon in and prayed that my Hedgerow Stew would pass the test.

'It's lovely,' he said as he swallowed another mouthful. 'It's got quite a unique taste to it, what's in it?'

'*Chorizo*, chestnuts apples…'

'Ah. It must be the chestnuts – they're the secret to its distinctive flavour. I'll tell you what, Liza, this is probably the best stew you've ever made.'

Hedgerow Stew

He's told me he fancies
A stew for his dinner
(Once Autumn's upon us
It's always a winner).

I've onions, chorizo,
And chestnuts aplenty,
But what about green stuff?
The veg rack is empty!

There's no need for panic,
Alarm or confusion –
Step out through the door,
It's all there in profusion!

No need for a cookbook –
I'm feeling creative
I'll fill a small bucket
With things that grow native.

Alongside the barn
There are nettles galore,
But that's where the dogs pee,
I've seen them before.

Oh well, it won't matter –
I'll give them a swilling,
I'll just get the worst off,
The odd trace won't kill him.

Ah, dandelions – they should
Go nicely with nettles,
I'll chuck lots of leaves in
But leave out the petals.

Liza Grantham

And look, in this field
There's wild rocket to savour –
Those peppery leaves
Will be packed full of flavour.

Along the stone wall
I see pennywort growing,
It's safe for consumption
(A fact that's worth knowing).

In England it's rare
And has trouble surviving,
No worries out here though,
Prolific and thriving!

I've got what I need,
So I head home to cook it
But Gary comes past
And he peers in the bucket:

'Oh, good thinking, Liza,
Some greens for the chickens!'
I stifle a giggle
And head for the kitchen.

The stew looks the business –
Terrific aroma!
(I hope he won't choke
Or fall into a coma!)

He's slurping it down
(Good, I won't have to bin it):
'It's excellent stew, dear,
What did you put in it?'

Chapter 16

Feliz Navidad

Our first Galician autumn had been an enchanting and exhilarating experience, not to mention an unexpected education besides. Though the season had been fruitful for us, it had been less generous to the surrounding landscape; with the onset of winter, our erstwhile verdant paradise was almost laid bare. The oaks, as majestic as the chestnuts throughout summer, had been relegated to the status of poor relations; their lustrous leaves were little more than a memory and those that remained hung like rags from their scrawny branches in dingy shades of ochre and brown. The chestnuts, in contrast, had retained their regal status, their robes changing from green to gold, before cascading into a rich brown carpet on the ground.

The *huerta*, patched in dark, damp earth, lay bereft of purpose, but the composters, brimming with the casualties of the season, held an incongruent sense of optimism; decaying roots and foliage would all rot down to feed the new life planted the following spring.

As wildlife scurried back and forth preparing for their winter hibernation, the people around us were depending on Nature's bounty to fill their larders and woodstores; it was vital to eat well and keep warm now that the harsh Galician winter had arrived.

'White rabbits!' I shouted, when Gary walked into the kitchen.

'Bugger!' he yawned. 'I remembered when I went through to the bathroom. I'd forgotten again by the time I came down the stairs.'

I smiled to myself. Pennywort was renowned for improving sharpness of mind and memory. It was about time I made more of my Hedgerow Stew.

'Do you still want to go to the market?'

I knew where this was heading; not only was it market day in Monterroso, but it was also Monday. Gary had looked decidedly disgruntled when he'd realised he'd have to do the shopping *and* go to the market as well. Eventually we'd reached a compromise: I'd go to the market while he did the shopping, but the prospect of dropping me off on the main street had rattled his nerves. This morning he was clearly hoping I'd changed my mind.

'Yes, I do,' I said firmly. 'I need some long-sleeved thermals. And after the market I want to go to the hotel.'

'You're *joking*. I thought we agreed last month we wouldn't do both in one go.'

'We agreed nothing of the kind. November was All Saints bank holiday *and* the cattle market. We missed the market because of the parking as I recall. Today's completely different, folks won't be out in their hordes.'

'It's the last market before Christmas, they'll all be out doing their shopping. It'll be a nightmare...'

'Don't you *dare* say it. This isn't England, it's rural Galicia. Christmas shopping to the locals means a trip round Día chucking a few *turrons* and a load of frozen seafood into the basket. It won't be busy today – you mark my words.'

Armed with two long sleeved thermal vests and a three-pack of thermal socks, I bid the chap on the clothes stall '*Feliz Navidad*' and headed to Día's car park where Gary stood smoking by the car.

'Did you get what you wanted?'

'Yes, ta. You were wrong about the festive pandemonium anyway. The bloke on the stall looked at me like I was bonkers when I wished him a Happy Christmas. I might as well have been saying it in July.'

When we pulled up in front of the Hotel Río Ulla there wasn't a single soul outside.

'Hiya!' called a familiar voice as we came through the doorway. Rose was waving at us from a table in front of the bar.

'Hello,' I grinned as we wandered over. 'How's things?'

'Different,' she giggled. 'Pete's here. He's just nipped to the toilet and then he's under orders to fetch more coffees from the bar.'

'Hello, Rose,' said Gary. 'I think I'll do likewise. What're you having Liza? Normal coffee or large?'

'Large, please.'

At that moment a heavily built man came through the door to the side of the fag machine.

'Here he is now,' said Rose. She waved him over.

'Pete, this is Liza and Gary who I've told you about. Fetch the coffees with Gary and we can entertain them with all our terrible news.'

'Terrible news?' I said, as the men walked away from the table. 'Have you had a problem?'

'Hundreds,' Rose giggled. 'I've lurched from one disaster to another since I last saw you. I'll give you the gory details when the chaps get back with the coffees.

To cut a long story short though, I won't be here for Christmas. I'm going back to England with Pete.'

'Really?' I feigned surprise. In truth, I'd harboured doubts about whether her madcap plans would ever come to fruition. Now it seemed my suspicions had been well-founded; Pete was going to drag her away from cloud cuckoo land and plant her feet firmly back on the ground.

'So, what's happened?' I asked, once we were all sat down with our coffees.

'What *hasn't*?' laughed Rose. 'Where do we begin?'

'The builder,' said Pete, wryly. 'He umm-ed and aah-ed about taking the job on. He'd been expecting more of a renovation than a complete rebuild.'

'As a result,' said Rose, 'he gave us an astronomical quote.'

'Dare we ask?' ventured Gary.

'Put it this way,' Pete frowned, 'the roof, walls, floors, doors and windows will cost three times what we paid for the house itself.'

'But we okayed it anyway,' Rose added. She looked at Pete. 'If we hadn't, we'd have been stuck with a ruin we couldn't live in. What would have been the point of that?'

I sensed that Pete was having misgivings. Surely there must have been *some* progress? I remembered the electricity; that must have been sorted out by now.

'What about your electrics?'

'More problems,' said Rose. 'We're still not connected. Pete's brought a generator over in the van.'

'Which caused a further problem,' frowned Pete. 'I dropped the generator on my foot. It was agony – thank God there were no bones broken. That was five days ago, I'm still limping now.'

'It couldn't have happened at a worse time,' Rose giggled. 'The rain came down and it was torrential. Poor

Pete could only hobble. He was drenched by the time he got back to the tent.'

'You're not in the caravan?' asked Gary.

'We are *now*,' laughed Rose. 'But it's too cramped for both of us. When Pete arrived he said we'd be better off in the tent.'

'And we were,' Pete continued. 'Until the day of the generator incident. The rain had turned into a full-blown storm by evening and the tent got ripped in the winds.'

'What'll you do now?' asked Gary.

'I thought I told you? Oh, no, I told Liza. I'm going back to Blighty. I'll be back here for when the builder starts in spring.'

Pete sighed despondently. 'And then it'll all start again.'

The problems didn't end there: a misunderstanding with the architect, the *permisos* being refused by the council, a terrible flare-up with the neighbour... fifteen minutes later I was beginning to wonder how much more I could bear.

'We should be making tracks,' said Gary. 'Liza's still got the lunch to see to when we get home.

'I'll see you in spring then,' said Rose.

'At least you'll get a proper Christmas dinner,' grinned Gary. 'There's nothing disastrous about that.'

As we stepped out onto the terrace, Gary nudged me and pointed. Jenny and Russell were just getting out of their car.

'Hi!' smiled Jenny. 'Have you got yourself a brooder yet?'

'No,' I said. 'I'm waiting 'til after Christmas. I don't want to hatch chicks before spring.'

'That's why you need to buy one now,' said Russell. 'Think about it. A point-of-lay hen won't go broody as soon as she starts to lay. If you get one today she'll be laying by Christmas, and by springtime she should be ready to sit.'

He was right of course. I cursed myself for not thinking of it sooner. I gave Gary an entreating stare.
He rolled his eyes skywards in mock despair.

'Thanks for that Russell, It looks like we're heading back to the market. Have yourselves a great Christmas and New Year.'

Up until now all but one of Rufo's wives remained nameless. Five of the six were a burnt orange colour with no distinctive markings; even after ten months I still couldn't tell them apart. The sixth was a darker, richer shade and she was called Canela. My brooder, with her deep tan plumage and black tail would certainly stand out from the rest.

'I'm pleased with my hen,' I told Gary as we drove home from the market. 'She looks different to the others. I'll be able to give her a name.'

'That's nice.'

He might have at least *tried* to sound enthusiastic. Perhaps if I asked *him* to choose the name, he'd show more interest? It had certainly worked with Scholes.

Gary saw me pouting. 'So what *is* her name, then?' he added, in a bid to bring back my smile.

'I was hoping *you'd* choose one.'

'Isn't that a bit longwinded? "Oh lovely, I-Was-Hoping-You'd-Choose-One's laid her first egg", or…'

'Very funny. Trust you. Go on, choose her a name.'

'Okay. Have you got a theme or anything?'

'No, not especially. The names Rufo and Canela refer to their colours. That might narrow it down.'

If it had been left to me I'd have chosen Autumn or *Castaña* or Amber – something that not only described the plumage but was also evocative of the time of year. Not Gary.

'Mrs Brown.'

'Mrs Brown?'

'It fits with your colour theme. She's brown.'

And that was that.

'Javier and José Manuel are cutting the giant birch tree down at the side of the *río*,' said Gary when he came in for coffee on Tuesday morning.

'Crikey. That'll be a job and a half. It's hanging over into the water. The branches are practically touching the other side.'

'I can't see how they'll manage without standing in the water. They'd have to wear waders; it's got to be three feet deep.'

'I can't really see Javier in waders,' I grinned. 'I tell you what though, it'll give them an awful lot of wood.'

'*If* they burn it.'

'What do you mean?'

'It's something else Manolo mentioned. He said the locals only tend to burn oak and chestnut and ash.'

'Did he say why?'

'Yes, it's because they burn slowly and give out plenty of heat.'

'Pine gives out a lot of heat as well.'

'Yes, but it's gone in no time. If you're out in your *huerta* or milking cows you don't want to be coming back every ten minutes to tend the fire, do you?'

'I see. And unlike us, the folks roundabout seem to own lots of *fincas*; they can afford to be choosy. That's why Manolo said you cut down his elders, I suppose.'

'That's something I've still not got round to. What with the chestnut collecting and fixing the oven... I think I'll follow Javier's example and make a start before lunch.'

The little triangle where the elders were growing was just past the corner of the barn. Instead of shouting Gary for lunch from the doorstep I wandered the short distance to see how he was getting on. He was loading huge sections of tree trunk into his barrow when I reached him. Despite the December chill he'd broken into a sweat.

'Whooh,' he panted. 'Is it that time already?'

'It is,' I grinned. 'But I reckon I've made a cock-up. I thought you'd be glad of a winter warmer – I've made hot chilli beef and lentil broth for your lunch.'

'Don't worry, it'll be perfect. A cold beer should temper it down.'

'You've done wonders,' I said, as I surveyed the loaded barrow. 'There's a lot of wood there, how many trees' worth is that?'

'Just one, believe it or not, and there's four more to go at. I reckon I can have them all down by the end of tomorrow. On Wednesday I can start to chop them and stack them in the barn.'

When it was time to walk Anxo I decided to go down past the *río* and up into the oak woods; I couldn't wait to see what Javier and José Manuel had achieved. As we passed Mási's *hórreo* Anxo stood stock still and barked gruffly. The hackles on his neck were raised.

'What is it?' I asked him. 'What have you seen?'

I looked across to where he was staring. The thicket behind the *río* had completely disappeared.

'Oh, Anxo,' I laughed. 'You *are* funny. It won't hurt you, there's nothing there.'

What *had* been there was now lying in the middle of Dry-Your-Laundry Field. How on earth had Javier and José Manuel managed to move such an enormous tree?

'You'll never guess,' I said, as I burst into the kitchen and made straight for the range.

'I think I will,' grinned Gary. 'You're going to tell me they've dumped the tree in the middle of the field.'

'Oh,' I said, deflated. 'You already knew.'

'Because I watched them move it. It wasn't long before you took Anxo. You were down the garden, picking chickweed for the chooks.'

'I wish you'd called me. I can't believe they shifted it between them. Did they ask you to help them? Put me out of my misery, what did they *do*?'

Gary was laughing now. I pulled off my hat and gloves while I waited for an answer.

'They used the tractor, you silly moo!'

A farmer and his son; it was so obvious! I couldn't believe it hadn't occurred to me before.

'But here's the weird part. I asked Javier if they'd be chopping it up for *leña*. He laughed and said they'd be burning it eventually, but not as firewood. They were going to set fire to it right there in the field.'

'You're joking. If it's going to burn anywhere it might as well burn in our range. You should have asked him…'

'I did.'

By Friday things were looking a lot more positive on the wood front. Manolo's elders and Javier's enormous birch tree now formed three huge log pyramids in the top of the barn.

'How's your back?' I asked Gary as I passed him his cuppa on Monday morning. Even without a delivery there was a price to pay for firewood; the poor devil had been suffering throughout the weekend.

'Much better this morning. I think a couple of days of taking it easy's done it the world of good.'

'I can come with you to do the shopping if that'd be helpful?'

'It wouldn't, to be honest. You'd be dashing about in a frenzy saying, "I need to get back, I've got so much to do,"'

I grinned sheepishly. 'Alright. But don't forget the bone bag, will you? We missed out last week – you were too busy fretting about parking outside the hotel.'

Since October, opening the bone bag had become something of a ritual. As I lifted it onto the marble surface I'd feign excitement, Gary would say something sarcastic and Anxo would sit like a china dog on a mantelpiece in the hope of a meat scrap or two.

When Gary came back this morning, he was keen to get out to the *huerta*. The man in the *ferreteria* had sold him some cabbage plants that he'd assured him would give us an early crop in spring.

'Aren't you going to stick around to see what's in the bone bag?'

'Honestly, Liza, perhaps we should get out more often. How can you get so excited about pig fat and bones?'

Despite his indifference he sat down and began to roll a cigarette.

Anxo waited beautifully as I unknotted the handles. As I pulled them apart, I braced myself for the rancid smell of raw pig escaping from the bag. Much to my surprise it didn't. I bent over to see what was inside. On top there were a dozen or more chicken ankles, and beneath them a generous heap of cooked meat bits that looked as if they might be roll ends. I pulled out a chunk of luncheon meat for Anxo and noticed a white, marble-sized object underneath.

'It can't be,' I mumbled, passing Anxo his titbit. I rummaged deeper; sure enough there were more. 'Eyeballs!' I exclaimed. 'See, Gary? How can you say that's not exciting? Here, you *must* come and look!'

'What do you think it's come from?' he asked, as I proffered him an example in my palm.

'Too big for a chicken,' I frowned. 'Way too small for a pig. I reckon it's a rabbit.'

'I think you're right.'

'But why would they remove the eyeballs? Surely if they've left the head on they'd leave the eyeballs in?'

'I don't know. To be honest, I'd rather not think about it. Go on then, tell me what other gems you've found.'

'Cooked meat bits. Back in England you could buy them in Tesco for sandwiches – tight buggers. But look at these chicken bones. It seems a shame to waste them, they still look fresh.'

'They are. I watched the girl chopping them off half a dozen oven-ready chickens for the woman in front of me. The chickens looked beautiful. They must've been corn-fed – a lovely golden colour they were. Anyway, they weren't good enough for this woman, she wanted all the ankles chopping off as well.'

'I could boil them down for stock,' I ventured. I knew how Gary would have reacted to the contents of his Hedgerow Stew, so I could hazard a guess as to how he'd feel about cast-off chicken bones. On this occasion he surprised me.

'It's a good idea. And you could firk out the bits that drop off for Scholes.'

'What about the eyeballs?'

'No chance. I don't want *them* in the stock.'

'No, you daft bugger, I meant why don't I boil the eyeballs up for Anxo? He could have them mixed in with his *piensos* for his tea.'

As the days crept closer to Christmas the weather grew colder and the weak winter sunshine was frequently accompanied by bitter northerly winds. Safe in my cosy new thermals I was ready for whatever harsh blows the elements dealt me. I couldn't possibly be as cold as I'd been this time last year. I shivered as I remembered how we'd arrived, three days before Christmas, to the icebox that we now called home. Back then the terrace was open, and daylight poured in through the bathroom ceiling. It was the biggest mistake of my life when I'd tried to have a bath on Christmas day. It was a testing time, yet somehow we'd survived the hardships. This year I couldn't care less about the festivities. All I wanted to do was stay warm,

'You're leaving it late to put the decorations up.' said Gary when he surfaced on Friday morning. 'There's less than a week left 'til Christmas. Aren't you bothering with them this year?'

For the last couple of weeks I'd been wondering what to do about decorations. At one stage I'd even got as far as digging out the baubles and the lights and the tree. Gary was right, spending that first evening in the living room lit by the tree lights had been gorgeous, but the ensemble that had been perfectly acceptable in the past now seemed somehow inadequate; I couldn't see the point of plastic holly and metallic sprayed branches when Nature's floristry was right outside the back door.

'I've got something different in mind. I'd like us to take a drive into town.'

'On a Saturday? Whatever for?'

'There are some holly bushes growing along the pavement on the way out towards Monterroso. I'm going to take my secateurs and bring some foliage home.'

'Everybody'll see you if you take them from the roadside. You don't know what the laws are. I've got a better idea.'

Half an hour later we turned off by the butcher's and parked up outside the pharmacy.

'There you go,' said Gary as we strolled round the corner. To the side of the bandstand was one of the biggest holly trees I'd ever seen.

'Don't you want me to get a turkey?' asked Gary, as he inspected the shopping list on Monday morning.

'I can't see the point, can you? There's only the two of us. A leg for you, a breast for me. I won't manage a whole one so there'll be some left over for you to have cold at night.'

'I always have a leg on Boxing Day as well.'

'You didn't last year,' I grinned.

When Gary had set off for Cádiz on Boxing Day I'd made him a scrumptious Christmas pack-up. After four hours of driving he was feeling peckish. Alas, the lunchbox was still in the fridge in Cutián.

'All the more reason I should have one this year.'

'Go on then, I suppose you'd better get two.'

Once the car had disappeared round the corner I set to with the laundry. Even after a year without a washing machine the task seemed no less gruelling. I'd made up my mind this would be the final load until after Christmas; I needed a break from plunging my arms elbow-deep into buckets and carrying saucepan after saucepan of hot water to the sink from the range.

An hour and a half later I stood smoking a fag on the threshing floor, watching the clothes on the line blowing like billy-o in the biting wind. At this rate they'd be bone dry by tea-time; we wouldn't have to spend the evening in a kitchen surrounded by damp washing and steam.

Whilst I'd been pegging out, the chooks had been doing a lot of squawking. Now seemed as good a time as any to go down and collect the eggs. To my surprise there were seven this morning; Mrs Brown had laid her very first egg.

When Gary came back from Monterroso I gave him the news.

'Mrs Brown's laid an egg.'

'Never. Already? Good old Mrs Brown.'

I studied him for a moment. His expression showed no hint of sarcasm. Either his foray into civilisation had filled him with Christmas spirit or he was turning over a new leaf ready for the coming year.

'Come on then, aren't you going to show me?'

I opened the fridge and pointed to the egg compartment. 'There. It's very tiny. I thought I'd boil it for Anxo – he can have it chopped up in his tea.'

'I don't *think* so. Hard boil it by all means but it's not going in the dog bowl. I'll have it with my beer tonight.'

'You can't be serious? It's no bigger than a damson. I'll do you a proper-sized one, if you like.'

'I don't want *any* old egg; I want that one. Mrs Brown's *my* chicken. She's laid it for *me*.'

On the 24th of December the sun was shining and the sky was cloudless; the chances of snow this Christmas seemed a million to one. At the top of Field Two I paused to take in the view across the valley and up towards the horizon: I couldn't have my snow scene but there was something delightfully festive about hilltops crowned with pine.

That evening Gary brought the Christmas CDs down from the living room. He settled by the range with his wine and roasted chestnuts, Anxo chewed on a pine cone and I peeled the veg.

'This is my all-time favourite Christmas song,' I said, as Steeleye Span's *Gaudete* rang out from the CD player.

'Really? I thought it was *Fairytale of New York*.'

'That's my second favourite. You'd be hopeless on *Mr & Mrs*[12]. Go on then, what's my favourite Christmas food?'

'Marzipan.'

---

[12] 1970s British husband and wife TV quiz show

'That's my second favourite. It's smoked salmon.'

'You change your mind, that's *your* trouble. Okay, ask me one more.'

'What's my favourite gift in an old-fashioned Christmas cracker?'

'How the bloody hell would I know *that*?'

'Best of three?' asked Gary, as he pegged himself home on the crib board.

'Go on, then, but I don't really trust you. I wonder if it's genetic – Howard said your Mum cheats at crib.'

As he paused to shove another log on the fire, I thought about Christmas back in England. I couldn't help but feel sorry for poor old Rose and Pete. Right now they'd be digging in to mince pies and Toblerone in front of a telly showing time-honoured repeats. I put down my can of cheap lager and reached for another cold roast parsnip. The simplicity of our Christmas Day had been surprisingly gratifying; I wouldn't have changed it for the world.

Liza Grantham

Back to Blighty

You've come to the end
Of your lengthy vacation,
Though all's not gone well
With your house restoration.

Despite the delays,
You're not down or defeated,
You'll come back next year
And make sure it's completed.

You're bound to feel strange
When you get back to Blighty,
The changes in landscape
And lifestyle are mighty.

You won't see the hillsides
And woodlands and valleys,
Just grey concrete buildings
And dingy back alleys.

No crowing of cock'rels
As new days are dawning,
Just loud roaring traffic
And sirens all morning.

But look on the bright side
while you're reminiscing –
Just think of the goodies
We ex-pats are missing.

You'll shop when you want to –
There's not a siesta,
No random bank hols
Or annoying fiestas.

How Now, Mad Cow?

You'll go into Marks's[13]
For quality undies,
Not big nylon pants
From the market on Sundays.

You'll sit in your local,
Enjoying an ale,
While we're supping lager,
Insipid and pale.

You'll nip to the chippy
Straight after your beer
The best we can hope for
Is Menu del Día.

You'll scoff a kebab
In the taxi-rank queue,
Or dine on prawn bhuna
Or lamb vindaloo.

You might opt for tacos,
Chimichanga, burritos
But Mexican here's
Just a bag of Doritos.

You'll go to the cricket
Or maybe the bookies,
You'll pig out on Hob-Nobs
And Maryland Cookies.

There's pork pie, black pudding
and real English mustard,
And jam roly-poly
with proper Bird's custard.

---

[13] Marks & Spencer, a popular English clothes store.

Liza Grantham

And then you've got Christmas –
Mince pies and mulled wine,
You'll see the new year in
And sing Auld Lang Syne.

It's not so bad really –
Indulge and make merry.
In no time at all
You'll be back on the ferry!

Chapter 17

Fit for a King

By Monday morning Christmas already seemed far behind us. As soon as Gary picked up the shopping list I knew for certain that the season to be jolly had been and gone.

'Cava?' he frowned.

'Yes. I thought it'd be nice to toast the new year in.'

'Hmm, I s'pose so. Fair enough. *Two* bags of grapes? Are you expecting visitors? We'll never manage to eat all those.'

'It doesn't mean *big* bags, Gary, it means those little cellophane packets with a dozen seedless grapes in. You know – they get handed out to everybody just before midnight. It saves a lot of trouble if you've got a big family, or you've invited loads of guests.'

'But we've got neither. I bet you pay over the odds for them, can't I just get a normal bunch of grapes?'

'No chance. I haven't forgotten that first New Year's Eve on the island. You bought a bag of big red ones with massive pips in. I'd have ended up in an ambulance if

I'd tried to neck one of those on every strike of the clock.'

The memory seemed to lighten his mood.

'I remember,' he grinned. 'I thought I'd broken a filling.'

'As I recall we ended up eating them for ages after with crackers and that tangy Canarian cheese.'

He began to smile, but it faded quickly.

'What is it?' I asked. 'What's wrong?'

'You were so happy there that first year, weren't you? It worries me sometimes you know.'

'What do you mean?'

'Well, we moved to the island and you were over the moon. Then, in less than two years you were bored to tears. Now we've been in Galicia a year and so far everything's hunky-dory... I just wonder if there might come a time...'

'Don't even think it. There won't, I can assure you. This is completely different, it's real life. The island was like a fantasy somehow; it felt over-indulgent, hedonistic... I missed facing challenges, solving problems, experiencing successes and failures... I have to be constantly learning, otherwise I stagnate.'

'You've no shortage of problems and challenges in the *aldea*, that's for certain.'

'Precisely. Every day's an education and I'm sure that's the way it'll stay.'

'You know what your next big challenge is don't you?'

'I can't say I do.'

'Drinking your share of the cava and staying awake 'til midnight. I'm prepared to put money on it it'll be one time you *won't* succeed.'

On New Year's Day I was feeling as fresh as a daisy. I scattered a dozen seedless grapes on top of my bran flakes and was still digging into them when Gary came down the stairs.

'Nice grapes,' I grinned, sheepishly. 'Well worth paying over the odds for. *And* we've got a lovely bottle of cava left over for the night of The Three Kings.'

I couldn't wait to give Gary the shopping list the following Monday morning. I was confident there was nothing on it he could gripe about today. Come on, I willed him, as I set it down next to his cuppa. Let's see if you can be a tightarse this morning – I dare you to do your worst.

As he drew on his cigarette he was nodding his head in approval. Just when I thought I'd achieved the impossible his expression changed,

'Boiled sweets?'

'Yes. You *know* it's Epiphany on Thursday. We have to put sweets out for the Kings.'

'We didn't last year.'

'No, we didn't. I forgot all about it what with you coming back from the island and the excitement of giving you the wheelbarrow. Anyway, you won't have to pay Día's prices. Your kindred spirits in the shit shop buy them by the boxful and split them into fifty *céntimo* bags.'

Not long before lunchtime Gary pulled up with the shopping. I was busy making omelettes for the freezer; Gary had three boiled eggs every morning for breakfast, but now that Mrs Brown was laying we were getting seven eggs a day.

'Is everything alright?' I asked him. 'You've been ages. I was beginning to think there was something wrong.'

'I'm fine,' he nodded. 'I bumped into John and Jane in Farelo's. Jane says to pop round and she'll give you some bulbs.'

'Oh lovely. I can do some planters for the threshing floor; we *must* make time to call round.'

'We will. Anyway, after that I got stuck behind cows at Randulfe, and *then…*' he paused and cleared his throat. 'I procured a rather magnificent chair for the dining room.'

'Never. How come?'

'I noticed it sticking out of the wheelie bin as I drove off the main road. Come on, you'll be over the moon when you see it. I've left it upstairs in the barn.'

I folded the omelette in half with a spatula and slid it onto a sheet of foil.

'Right then, lead the way.'

On the upper level of the barn sat a rather unusual piece of solid oak furniture. It might have been a hundred years old, but there was something vaguely art-deco about the sunray design carved deep into the wood.

'That's not a chair!' I exclaimed.

'No,' grinned Gary, 'it's a kneeler. They must have been having a good clear out at the church ready for the big mass at the weekend.'

'I can't for the life of me see why they'd chuck it out, there's nothing wrong with it. The armrest's a bit tatty, but apart from that it's as good as new.'

'I'll take the padding off completely. Then I'll give it some legs and a good coat of varnish. Give me a couple of days and it'll be fit for a king.'

Two days later I was in party mode all over again.

'I don't know why you're getting so excited,' yawned Gary as I passed him his cuppa. 'You started off like this on New Year's Eve and you were dropping to sleep over the Scrabble board by half past ten.'

'*Los Reyes* is different. We don't have to try and stay up until midnight. In fact, I reckon The Three Kings are like Father Christmas; they won't deliver your presents until you're safely tucked up in bed.'

'Well don't forget to leave them the boiled sweets you insisted on. Where will you put them, have you thought?'

'Outside on the bench, I s'pose, next to the shoes.'

'The *shoes*?'

'Honestly, Gary, your memory. The shoes filled with straw for the camels, of course.'

'I'm not leaving *my* shoe outside, what if it rains?'

'It won't rain. It's far too cold and frosty. Well, if you want to end up with no presents that's your lookout. I shall certainly be leaving mine. I'll probably leave a welly – I'll be able to fit *loads* of straw in it. The Three Kings will think better of me and do me proud.'

'I bet Javier, Maruja and José Manuel don't leave *their* shoes outside.'

'They don't need to. There are rolls and rolls of silage out in the farmyard, the camels could have a banquet in there.'

'So, if your theory's right they'll all end up with a *huge* present.'

'Not necessarily huge, but something extra special. You may mock, but tomorrow you'll eat your words. Seriously though, you haven't got me anything, have you? I'm assuming we're not bothering with presents like we agreed last year.'

'But you *did* get me something. You bought me the wheelbarrow.'

'That was different, you'd have needed one anyway, sooner or later. On top of that, you were in Las Palmas when I fetched it – it wasn't just a Reyes present, it was a sort of "welcome home" surprise.'

'Did we do *Reyes* in Las Palmas? I don't mean the presents I mean... well, what did people *do*?'

'Most of the ex-pats did nothing special. They saw it as an extra day off work. For the Canarians it was much like Christmas in England. The kids opened their presents and whole families got together for a meal.'

'As in, more sea food?'

I nodded. 'More sea food. And a *roscón*, of course.'

'A *roscón*?'

'Yes, don't you remember, I made one? *That's* it – we had a party. Ron and Miranda came, so did Jan and Graham... but anyway, the *roscón*... oh Gary, it was hilarious! You had the most amazing idea!'

'Ah, something to do with baby Jesus. Tell me what happened then, it's starting to come back to me now.'

'For *Los Reyes Magos* the Spanish have a *roscón*. It's a big sheet of dough spread with a dried fruit filling, rolled up like a Swiss roll but with the ends fastened together to form a round.'

'I've got you.'

'Then it's glazed and decorated with nuts and glacé cherries.'

'I remember – it looks like a crown.'

'Right, but the important bit is what's hidden inside.'

'The baby Jesus!'

'Exactly. People used to put in a dried bean to represent him but nowadays they tend to use a coin. I decided we'd have the real McCoy, so I bought a set of plastic Nativity figures from the shit shop and I was wrapping the baby in foil...'

'That's where my stroke of genius came in. I said, "it doesn't look like Jesus, Jesus had a beard." And you said, "it's a baby, trust you." I said, "it's not Jesus unless you put a beard on him..."'

'And you were so bloody insistent that in the end I did. With black nail varnish. And we spent all night waiting for pudding time so we could watch everybody falling about laughing.'

'But they didn't, did they?'

'No, they didn't. Not one person noticed. It was Jan that won him. She unwrapped the foil and everybody went, "Ah, baby Jesus." We waited… and we waited… Gary, we couldn't *believe* nobody had noticed. I even told her to pass him round to give them a broad hint.'

'I can't remember what happened in the end. Didn't we have to tell them?'

'We did. *Then* they all fell about in hysterics. I shall remember that night for as long as I live.'

When Gary surfaced on the morning of *Los Reyes Magos* you could have knocked me down with a feather; the old softy had only gone and bought me a gift.

'There you go,' he grinned, as he passed me a blue plastic bag just like the ones from the shit shop. 'Don't say I never give you anything. It's your present from The Three Kings.'

'Ah, Gary, that's lovely.' I stood up to give him a hug. 'Thank you. I wasn't expecting it, honestly – you've already given me a gorgeous dining chair. I haven't bought you anything, I feel really mean.'

'You won't feel mean when you open it. Go on, then, have a look.'

I pulled out a pair of navy socks with big white spots on. I squidged them up against my cheek because they looked so delightfully fluffy and soft.

'They're smashing, thank you. They're too nice to go under work boots, I shall save them for best.'

'They were only a couple of euros. So much for your big wellyful of straw.'

'It was a flip-flop.'

'Pardon?'

'I remembered what you said about it raining. I didn't want to risk squelching about when I walked Anxo. I used a flip-flop 'cos they're waterproof. I stuffed a bit of straw under the strap.'

At breaktime Gary came in chuckling. 'Flip-flop or no flip-flop your theory was wrong.'

'What *are* you talking about?' I frowned.

'Your idea that you can bribe the Kings with extra straw for the camels to get a better present.'

'That's not *quite* how I worded it. Anyway, go on.'

'I've just seen José Manuel outside the farmhouse, and I asked him if he'd had anything nice off the Kings. He said none of the family bother with presents any more. He's not had a *Reyes* gift for years.'

With the festivities almost over, we were ready to look to the future. We were only just off the starting blocks when it came to self-sufficiency, but we'd learned some valuable lessons and with these in mind our thoughts now turned to the year ahead.

'I've been thinking about ways of improving our veg crop,' said Gary, when we settled with our beers round the fire that evening. 'The first year's been a bit of a flop really – the *huerta* didn't give us anything like the harvest I'd planned.'

'On the contrary, I think you've done wonders. You told me back in April not to get my hopes up, yet we've got enough courgettes and green beans in the freezer to last us for months. You mustn't think of it as a failure, it's an achievement we'll be able to build on. Jenny and Russell have given us loads of pointers; this year things can only improve.'

'I hadn't thought of it that way. You're right though. I'll be sowing acclimatised seeds for a start off, and we'll have a heck of a lot more compost - the apples from the cider pressing alone have been a huge boon.'

'And don't forget you've thrown in all the old bean plants – they're full of nitrogen. They'll do the soil the world of good.'

'I'm going to build a couple of raised beds to sow the carrots and beetroots in. It says in the gardening book that root veg benefits from a greater growing depth – I s'pose that's obvious really, but it also says raised beds are great for soil drainage as well.'

'It's a brilliant idea. It'll make better use of the compost. You'll be digging it into a contained area instead of spreading it out in the surrounding soil.'

While Gary had been reflecting on vegetables, I'd been pondering on our meat situation. We now had a hen that would go broody and, unless we were very unlucky, we could expect to have a few chickens in the freezer by the end of the year. It was a start, but it certainly wasn't enough to meet the needs of two omnivorous adults; this year I was going to introduce the rabbits that had always been part of our long-term plan.

In contrast to his misgivings about chickens, Gary had raised no objections when I'd first suggested keeping rabbits; when he was a child, his father used to breed New Zealand whites for meat. As far as he could remember, they'd been low maintenance and cost-effective – all they'd needed was food and water and a thorough cleaning out once a week.

With this in mind, I decided that now was as good a time as any to broach the subject. I took a deep breath and grabbed the bull by the horns.

'I want to buy a couple of rabbits at the February market. It'd be nice to have baby bunnies bouncing about in spring.'

'Not to mention sizzling away on the barbecue in summer. It's a great idea. I was wondering when you were going to mention it. I was beginning to think you'd changed your mind.'

'Not at all. It's just been a matter of timing, really. Now that the chickens are ticking along nicely a couple of rabbits should slot easily into the daily routine.'

'So, you'll be wanting me to build a couple of hutches. That should be simple enough. I'll use some of the window frames in the barn for the structure and get some planks from the wood yard – it'll work out quite cheaply that way.'

'Brilliant. And what about the pen?'

'What pen?'

'The pen that the rabbits will be able to run about in. I told you ages ago – I won't have them confined to a hutch.'

'I hadn't forgotten. I still don't think it's necessary. I was hoping you might have changed your mind.'

'I haven't. No pen, no rabbits. Full stop.'

Gary went silent. I watched as he stubbed out his cigarette and drained the last of his beer. I was beginning to think we'd reached an impasse when at last he let out a sigh.

'It can go against the barn where the standing stones are – it'll be cheaper if I only buy wire for three sides.'

I was on tenterhooks as I waited for Gary to come back from shopping on Monday morning. He'd be calling at the *ferreteria* and the woodyard on the way home. I lit a cigarette and paced the kitchen as I braced myself for the impending diatribe. I'd abandoned the idea of ducks in the future; after rabbits there would be no further livestock. There was only so much animal housing a marriage could stand.

On Tuesday morning I was pickling hard-boiled eggs in chilli and garlic vinegar when Gary came into the kitchen. He usually waited 'til I called him for coffee; I must have been running behind time.

'Oops,' I grinned. 'I've only just stuck the kettle on. It'll only be a minute. You look pleased about something, are the hutches coming on well?'

'They are. But that's not what I've come in for. I went up to check the phone five minutes ago. José Manuel's bottle-feeding a pair of baby calves out in the lane. If you nip up now you should still catch them. Make haste or you'll miss it. I'll see to the brew.'

I dried my hands on the tea towel and dashed up to the farm. José Manuel was sitting on the bench holding a wine bottle from which a tiny calf was suckling hungrily, while another calf beside it was trying to nudge its way onto the teat.

'*Hola*, Elisa,' called Maruja who was standing on the doorstep.

'*Hola*,' I smiled. 'When Gary told me about the calves I had to come and see.'

'They're *gemelos*,' smiled José Manuel, proudly.

'Twins?' I said. 'Is that quite rare?'

'Not really,' said Maruja, 'we've had them before. It's much rarer to have triplets, but they can be hard work because they tend to be smaller. It's common for one to die.'

'So, you're bottle feeding these two to supplement their mother's milk?'

'No. A cow will produce plenty of milk for two calves. The stuff in the bottles is rice milk. It's to settle their stomachs because they both have diarrhoea.'

Even as she spoke, there was a splutter from the rear-end of the calf who was suckling. I could see in an instant why they were being fed in the lane. When the bottle was drained, José Manuel stood up to fetch a re-fill and the calves tottered after him.

'They're so tiny,' I smiled.

'They were born on *Los Reyes Magos*,' smiled Maruja. 'A gift from The Three Kings.'

By Wednesday lunchtime Gary had finished the hutches. He'd built them exactly as I'd wanted. Each had a solid wooden door which opened outwards for cleaning, and a ramp that dropped down like a drawbridge for the rabbits to come and go as they pleased.

'They're perfect,' I said. 'And from what I've seen of the blueprints you'll make a fantastic job of the pen.'

Gary's attitude towards the rabbit pen had done a complete U-turn since Monday. After a couple of hours doodling in the barn with a notepad and pencil he'd emerged well and truly inspired. The pen would have a wooden framework enclosed with sturdy galvanised mesh. It would be divided down the middle by a two-foot-high mesh partition so that the buck and the doe would have company without invading each other's space. There would also be an escape run inside the entrance, lest either of the rabbits should try to abscond. Gary would use the tiles we'd stored in the animal pen to make a sloping roof complete with guttering, but the sun would still pour in through the wire during the mornings and afternoons. If all went to plan, the pen would be weather-proof, fox-proof and Anxo-proof. All I had to do now was cross my fingers and wait.

Happy with Gary's plans, I turned my attention to the pen's forthcoming inhabitants. They'd need hay in the hutches for bedding, and a bowl each of rabbit pellets and fresh water every day. With no access to grazing, green stuff would be a regular ration of kale. In addition they'd be given a monthly powdering with a herbal insecticide to keep mites and lice at bay.

The pen took almost a week to build, but the outcome was even better than I'd envisaged. As I opened the door and stepped into the escape run, Gary announced that the luxury complex would be known as Warren Place. He'd pinched the name from a famous racing stable, but that didn't matter; the title was perfect for a pair of bunny bungalows set in their own grounds. The inhabitants, however, would receive no such moniker; they weren't pets, they were livestock, and as such they would never be given a name.

On the 31st of January we were tucked up in bed by ten thirty. I was beside myself with excitement at the prospect of our trip to market the next day.

We couldn't have been in bed more than an hour when, down in the kitchen, Anxo issued a long, drawn-out growl. Seconds later, he began to bark and I wondered what had caused him to raise the alarm. It couldn't be Carmen; she tended to pilfer by daylight. It couldn't be one of the farm dogs; Anxo wouldn't have growled. Reasoning that nothing of any consequence could have disturbed him at this time of night I snuggled deeper down under the duvet and waited for him to settle. Seconds later he began to bark again.

'Gary?' I whispered.

'Uh.'

'Are you awake?'

'Uh.'

I eased myself out of the bed and crept over to the window. Pushing the curtain aside, I peered out into the lane. There was nothing there. Whatever had set Anxo barking must have gone on its way. As I turned away from the window I heard a thud, then another. There was no doubt about it, something or someone was moving about in the barn. As I strained to listen, the bedsprings creaked loudly; Gary had stirred.

'For God's sake. Liza, what are you doing?' he mumbled through the darkness.

'Shh, I'm listening. I think there's somebody in the barn.'

'Don't be ridiculous. I bet it's Posster. Perhaps he's chasing a mouse or something. Just close the curtain and come back to bed.'

Gary was right. I hadn't thought of Posster. Of course, he must be mousing – he'd made the thudding sound when he'd pounced. Satisfied that we'd solved the mystery, I closed the curtain. As I stepped away from the window I heard a metallic clink.

'There! That wasn't Posster! Surely you heard it; there's somebody poking about in the barn.'

'You were probably dreaming. If you want me to be up early tomorrow, you'd better come back to bed.'

When the Cows Met a Camel

The cows plodded home from the pasture,
They'd grazed and they'd gossiped all day,
Belén shouted, 'Look over yonder!'
A strange cow was heading their way.

'My God!' shouted Luz, 'She's a hunchback!
And yet she's incredibly tall...'
Belén said, 'but where is her udder?
She can't be a cow after all.'

'She's wearing a saddle,' mused Clara,
'I think she's a weird kind of horse.'
'She's got a long neck,' smiled Dolores.
'She must be a donkey, of course.'

Belén cried, 'Oh crikey, she's seen us!'
'Hush, now,' said Dolores, 'stay calm.
Stand back and let me do the talking,
I'm sure that she means us no harm.'

The stranger began to plod forwards,
She'd finally caught sight of the herd,
'I do hope the locals are friendly,
But where are their humps? Oh, my word!'

'Hello there! My name is Dolores,
That's Clara, that's Luz, that's Belén.'
The stranger replied, 'I'm Delilah.
I've lost my two mates and three men.'

'We wondered if you were a donkey,
You seem like a strong, sturdy beast...'
Delilah laughed, 'No, I'm a camel!
I've walked all the way from the East.

Liza Grantham

'That star overhead is our signpost,
It works if the firmament's clear,
But cloud cover makes it a nightmare –
I seem to get lost every year.'

'You ought to get fitted with Sat Nav –
Your trek would be simpler by far.'
'Our journey is steeped in tradition –
It's vital we follow the star.'

'I expect,' said Dolores, 'you're hungry,
Back home we've no shortage of hay,
You must sleep tonight in our cowshed –
Your plight will seem brighter by day.'

'You're awfully kind,' smiled Delilah,
'I'd be glad to get out of the rain.'
So they all plodded home to the farmyard,
Where a figure stood out in the lane.

Cried Cruz, 'It's a chap in a helmet!
And a nightie that drags on the ground!'
'My master! Hooray!' cried Delilah,
'That "helmet", my dear, is his crown!'

Chapter 18

The Best Laid Plans

'White rabbits!' shouted Gary as he came into the kitchen on Tuesday morning.

'I hope not,' I grinned, as I passed him his cuppa. 'I don't want white, I want brown.'

'I should have seen that coming. Still, at least you're back to normal – God only knows what was up with you last night. You must have been dreaming, you were adamant there was an intruder in the barn.'

'I'm still convinced this morning. I had a quick look when I went to let the chooks out. I didn't see anything out of place, but I had the distinct sensation there'd been somebody there.'

'You've got an overactive imagination, that's *your* trouble. You were over-excited about the rabbits, and it brought on a nightmare. You'd have slept a lot better if you'd stayed calm.'

Gary wasn't going to believe me and there was no point in trying to convince him otherwise. Besides, if I wanted to be at the market early, it was time for Anxo's walk.

When we came back, Gary was wearing a sheepish grin.

'What's up with *you*?' I asked suspiciously.

'I owe you an apology. I was wrong about your nightmare. I've been doing a bit of sleuthing – there *was* somebody poking about in the barn.'

'I *told* you, but you wouldn't have it. So, what did you find that's caused you to change your mind?'

'It's not what I found, it's what I *didn't* find. Paul's key's not on the hook where I left it. I have a sneaking suspicion our English neighbour returned in the night.'

'Good God. I didn't think he'd be back 'til springtime. I'm surprised you haven't been round.'

'I have, but there were no signs of life, and I didn't want to wake him. I'd be surprised if he surfaces this side of lunchtime. It must have been nearly midnight when Anxo raised the alarm.'

While Gary was driving the car out of the barn, I went into the garden for one last inspection of Warren Place. Satisfied that everything was ready for the impending arrival of the bob-tailed duo I picked my way cautiously over the threshing floor, avoiding the slimy mosses and lichens that clung to the stones. I was almost at the gate when I heard footsteps. Sure enough, Paul was coming down the lane.

'Morning,' I called. 'What brings you to this neck of the woodlands?'

'Morning,' he smiled. 'I've come back to sort out the ridge tiles. Are you going to Monte-roh-soh? I flew in yesterday, especially to get to the hotel today.'

'We are,' I nodded. 'But we're only going as far as the market.'

I waited for Gary to turn off the engine and get out of the car.

'Morning Paul,' grinned Gary. 'You want to be careful. Liza thought you were an intruder. She was all for coming down and clubbing you over the head.'

'Ignore him, Paul – he's trying to be amusing.' I turned to Gary: 'Paul was wondering if we were going into Monterroso, and I was explaining that we won't be going to the hotel.'

'We could drop you off at the hotel first,' said Gary. 'But we're off hunting rabbits so we won't be able to bring you home.'

'Don't worry, I'll cycle. I had an email off Luc about doing a short house-sit while I'm here.'

'That's strange,' I frowned. 'He must know your time's at a premium. Tom did it in August – why didn't he ask him again?'

'There are issues,' said Paul. 'Luc says that Tom's pinched some of his tools. Apart from that, Luc and I have more in common. We both drink the same kind of wine.'

It was exactly a year since we'd been down to the livestock section of the market. We'd come away empty handed; I wasn't prepared to pay ten euros a piece for bog standard hens. We'd ended up at the agricultural store round the corner, where, for only forty-two euros we'd walked away with Rufo and his six wives. Today there *was* no alternative. The *agro* shop didn't sell rabbits; we'd be buying them from the market and, whether we liked it or not, we'd be paying the going rate.

We eased our way through the crowds, past stall upon stall of village pinnies, big knickers and nylon slacks. As we passed the entrance to the market hall Gary paused momentarily. 'Do you want to go in and sample some cheese?'

I shook my head. On any other occasion it would have been my first priority, but this morning was different; all I wanted to do was buy my rabbits and go home.

We wound our way down to the green where the livestock were on sale. The stall holders shivered as they hovered beside cages crammed with chickens and turkeys and ducks. Tied by its leg to a garden chair was a cockerel the image of Rufo; he was crowing raucously and beating his wings.

'There,' said Gary pointing over to an oak tree, where a couple were setting two cages of rabbits down on the ground.

'*Hola*,' I said. '*Buenos días*. I'd like a pair of rabbits, ready to breed.'

'A male and a female?'

I resisted the urge to say, 'two males'll be fine, I believe in miracles.' Instead, I nodded, '*Si, muy bien*.'

The woman opened the cage next to her and pulled a young brown rabbit out by its ears.

'The female,' she said, holding it up for our approval.

The doe seemed a good size and in excellent condition. I nodded, and the unsuspecting creature was duly deposited into a sack.

Meanwhile the man had taken another brown rabbit from the cage in front of him. Holding it up by its ears he now inspected the underparts. He frowned and showed it to the woman who promptly shook her head. The man placed the rabbit back in the cage and this time he pulled out a grey one. He peered at the tackle and nodded his head.

With both rabbits safely in the sack, it was tied tightly with string.

'That's fourteen euros,' said the woman.

I turned to Gary. 'That's nice and cheap.'

'Are you English?' asked the woman.

'Yes,' I said. 'We live near Antas de Ulla. We've been here just over a year.'

'We live quite a distance away,' said the man. 'We're in an *aldea* close to Guntín.'

'We know Guntín,' nodded Gary. 'We drive through it on the way to Lugo. We bought our cooker there.'

'There's an English couple in our village,' said the woman. 'You'll know them I suppose.'

I smiled to myself. There seemed to be a commonly held assumption amongst the Spanish that all the English knew one another. I'd often noticed it when we lived on the island; it was as if they thought England was no bigger than a town.

'It's possible,' I said. 'What are their names?'

'Rossel and Henny.'

The names sounded more Dutch than English. I looked at Gary quizzically. Like me, he didn't have a clue.

'Henny,' the woman repeated. 'You must have seen her. She comes here for the market. She's got short hair and glasses like you.'

Henny... Short hair and glasses... suddenly it clicked. 'Ah, *Jenny*.'

'Yes, Henny. So you know them?'

'We do,' nodded Gary, grinning broadly. 'Rossel and Henny are our friends.'

'Tell them you met their neighbour María, won't you? They'll be ever so pleased.'

'We're lucky to have a grey one,' I said as I lifted the buck gently into his run. 'Even *you* won't get them mixed up.'

'I won't be getting involved so it makes no difference. I'm veg, you're animals – that's what we've always agreed.'

'Until it comes to eating them,' I grinned. 'Right, now for the doe.'

Once both rabbits were safely inside their enclosures, I stood back to admire them. 'Aren't they lovely?' I smiled.

'They're smashing,' agreed Gary. 'No names, though, remember? They're not pets, they're meat.'

'No names,' I nodded. 'But we'll need to refer to them somehow.'

'That's easy. They're the buck and the doe.'

Within minutes the rabbits were exploring their new surroundings. It wasn't long before they were sniffing one another though the wire.

'That's good,' I smiled. 'By the time I put them together for mating they'll be used to one another. I'm glad it's all going to plan.'

'When *are* you going to mate them? I was serious about having barbecued rabbit in summer – make sure you don't leave it too long.'

'I'd like to give them a couple of weeks to settle. That'll give us baby bunnies in the middle of March.'

'That sounds good. So you'll put the buck in with the doe and leave them to it?'

'Apparently does are very territorial – you're supposed to do it the other way round. The doe goes in with the buck for a day of unbridled coney passion, then at night she goes home with a bunny in the oven, so to speak.'

'Shall we let Anxo out to see what he makes of them?'

'To be honest I'd rather be here to keep an eye on him to start with. I'm going to start the lunch in a minute, he can stay in the kitchen for now and meet them in the afternoon.'

Half an hour later I was putting a pan of spuds on when Gary came into the kitchen.

'I think you might want to check on the rabbits.'

My heart skipped a beat. 'Shit, what's happened? Tell me nothing's wrong?'

'They're fine, don't panic, but I still think you should go and look. Put it this way, Liza, I've a feeling you might have to revise your master plan.'

I dashed out of the door and up into the garden; it was time to pay an impromptu visit to the residents of Warren Place. To my surprise, I wasn't the only one who'd decided to go calling. The buck had invited himself into the doe's run and it seemed her hospitality had extended to more than tea and cake. The hostess was reclining in a corner while her guest sat in the middle of the floor, licking his bits and bobs.

'Do you think they've mated?' asked Gary, as he came up behind me.

I frowned at him. 'Given that *he's* washing his willy and *she's* lying there dazed...'

'There's no need to be sarcastic. Ooh, hey up, it looks like they're going to do it again.'

'This'll be interesting. He's meant to squeal and fall off backwards. Let's see if he does.'

We waited and watched.

In a matter of seconds, the buck gave a high-pitched 'hick' like a drunk on helium and slid off to one side.

We looked at one another and burst into laughter.

'That's it then,' I spluttered, as I struggled to regain my composure. 'We can look forward to baby rabbits on...' I paused to do the calculation. '...the fourth of March.'

After lunch, Gary added another sheet of wire to make the divider higher. However randy the buck was feeling, he wouldn't be scaling a three-and-a-half-foot fence. With the minor hiccup resolved it was finally time to let the dog see the rabbit. The second Anxo caught sight of the new arrivals he was thrown into a state of delirium. Gripped by bunny-mania he spent the entire afternoon charging up and down along the front of the pen. The buck's run put a good distance between the rabbits and their hairy marauder, and they seemed undaunted by his antics. Tomorrow, however, might well be a different story; the honeymoon would be over, and the buck would come face to face with Anxo through the wire once he was returned to his own run.

That evening, when Anxo had been walked and the chooks were safely to roost, it was time to shut the rabbits into their hutches. I scooped the buck up and carried him through the escape run and back into his own enclosure. To my amazement he lolloped straight into his hutch and began to nibble the hay. Back in the doe's pen my task wasn't quite so simple; she scampered around the run for a couple of circuits before I finally managed to steer her towards the hutch and push her in.

'Well?' said Gary when I came back into the kitchen.

'They were fine. The buck was straightforward, but the doe was a little bit skittish. I'm sure she'll be calmer tomorrow; I reckon the rabbits are going to be a doddle compared to the hens.'

Next morning, I was dreading taking Anxo into the garden; I was certain the buck would be terrified when Anxo ran to the pen. When Anxo saw the buck he barked and pawed at the wire, while the frightened rabbit thumped his back feet hard on the ground. It wasn't long before Anxo realised that the pen was impenetrable and lay down with his nose to the wire. The buck, satisfied that he wasn't in imminent danger, jumped up on top of his hutch and began washing his paws.

By Thursday I was hoping that Anxo might have shaken off his rabbit fixation. On the contrary it seemed that his obsession was well and truly setting in.

'I've been watching Anxo and Buck,' said Gary when I came into the garden to peg out the laundry.

'Come on, I'll show you. It sounds crackers, but I think Buck's playing a game.'

I abandoned my pegging and went over to join him at the side of Warren Place.

Anxo was running up and down along the front of the pen and the buck was doing exactly the same inside his run. To begin with it seemed that the poor rabbit was fleeing, but on closer examination it was hard to work out who was actually chasing who. The pair ran to and fro for several minutes, until the buck stopped to rest in the corner, pressed up against the mesh. As Anxo pushed his face against the wire, the buck showed no signs of agitation. The way he sprawled on his side suggested he couldn't care less. Eventually he stood up and hopped across the pen. When Anxo followed, the buck began to run again.

'You're right,' I nodded. 'The buck really *is* doing it on purpose. I think he's goading Anxo into chasing him, as unlikely as it might seem.'

'He's doing more than goading him,' said Gary. 'If I didn't know better, I'd say he's giving Anxo the run around. I reckon our Buck's got a sense of humour – it's his way of taking the piss.'

Although I'd planned to sweep the rabbit pen out once a week, by Friday a sizeable pile of droppings had already amassed in both runs. Armed with a brush and dustpan and a builder's bucket I went in to clean up the poo. When I went into the doe's run, I was taken aback to discover the beginnings of a burrow hidden away on the far side of the hutch. Not only had she been digging but her progress was extremely disconcerting. In the space of four days she'd made significant inroads into tunnelling her way out of the pen.

'Poor Doe,' said Gary. 'Perhaps she's scared of Anxo. I think it's too early for her to be making a nest.'

'I don't think it's anything to do with Anxo. She's a rabbit – it's her instinct to burrow, it's as simple as that. Anyway, I've filled the soil back in and I've wedged a heavy stone on top of it. We'll have to keep an eye on her tomorrow, just in case she starts to dig another one somewhere else in the pen.'

When Gary came in for lunch on Saturday, he brought bad tidings.

'Doe's been digging again.'

'Bugger. I could kick myself for not thinking of it when you drew up the blueprint. You'll hate me for saying it but we're going to have to pave the floor.'

To my surprise, Gary didn't go off at the deep end. Instead, he simply shrugged and smiled.

'At least it won't mean a trip to the builder's yard or the *ferretería*. The rabbits are easier on the bank balance than the chooks if nothing else. I can't believe old Doe was planning on doing a runner. Not very grateful is she, after all the hard work I've done?'

The way Gary had laughed about the doe's ingratitude and the buck's sense of humour gave me the distinct impression that he was becoming rather taken with the rabbits. I made up my mind I'd mention it subtly when I had an opportunity – it was Gary's idea in the first place that our rabbits wouldn't be pets.

As we settled round the fire with our beers that evening, I looked at Gary squarely. 'Who's been trying to burrow out of Warren Place?'

He frowned for a moment. 'Is that a trick question? You know who it is, it's Doe.'

'And who's been giving Anxo the run-around?'

He frowned again. 'Is there a point to this? It's Buck.'

'Just as I thought then – you've reneged on our agreement. Unless I'm very much mistaken you've given both of our rabbits a name.'

On Sunday morning it was all hands on deck for Operation Crazy Paving. As a matter of urgency, we needed a quick-fix, cost-free floor in Doe's half of the pen. Leaving a somewhat disgruntled Anxo in the kitchen, we slogged away in the bitter February cold. Given that time was of the essence we opted for a division of labour: I spent the next three hours filling the wheelbarrow with large rocks from along the track and depositing them at the side of the pen, while Gary used a trowel to make hollows in the compacted soil and sink them in. Every time I wheeled the barrow past the kitchen, I'd nip in to throw another log on the fire and try to placate a frustrated Anxo by telling him that we wouldn't be long. By lunchtime, Gary and I, though exhausted, were safe in the knowledge that Doe wouldn't be giving birth to our barbecue fodder out in the back of beyond.

While we'd spent the last six days having fun and games with the rabbits, Paul had been busy adding the ridge tiles to his roof. With so many higgledy-piggledy sections his task hadn't been easy, but Paul had dug deep, and we were genuinely impressed when he finally finished the job.

On Sunday evening, he turned up on the doorstep. 'I'm sorry to bother you – I know you're always so busy. Could I possibly buy a couple of eggs?'

''Course you can,' I laughed, 'but wouldn't you rather have half a dozen?'

'I only want enough for tonight,' he explained. 'I'm going to Luc's tomorrow. He'll be picking me up around ten.'

'Is he off back to Belgium?'

'No. He isn`t going anywhere. He wants me to stay for five days until his wife gets back from Tenerife.'

'His wife? I didn't know he was married.'

'Really? You must have met her at the ex-pats get-together, her name's Angela.'

The name rang a bell. 'Ah, yes, I've met her. She's always with Tracey. Apart from me and Rose I think she's the only woman who smokes.'

'This might sound a daft question,' said Gary. 'But weren't you supposed to be doing a house-sit?'

'I thought so, but apparently this is a practice. They want me for a week in summer and Luc knows I haven't got much experience when it comes to animals. He wants me to get to know the dogs, and he's got a few jobs for me to do as well,'

'How long are you here for altogether?' I asked him.

'Three weeks. When I get back from Luc's I'll be sorting out the guttering and the wood treatment. I'll be going back on the twenty-second, but I'm hoping to move out permanently in May.'

On Monday Gary looked pleased with himself when he came back from shopping.

'You look jolly,' I said, as he came into the kitchen. 'Either you've made some savings with the Día club coupons or Man United have managed a win.'

'Neither actually. Sometimes you make me sound so shallow. I'm smiling because of the bone bag. It looks too knobbly to be pig fat. I reckon it's chock full of bones this week.'

The bone bag had become a bit of an anti-climax since the ankles-and-eyeballs indulgence back in December. Most Mondays we'd had nothing but pig fat, with only the occasional meat bits or bones.

'Fetch me the bag then. We'll see if you're right.'

As Gary went through to the passage, Anxo followed. Instead of sniffing out the bone bag he sat in front of the back door.

'There you go,' said Gary as he deposited the bag onto the marble surface. 'You can tell me what's in it at lunchtime. I stopped off at the builder's yard and bought a couple of dozen breeze blocks. I want to make a start on the raised beds.'

'Please yourself, spoilsport. Come on, Anxo, it looks like it's just us.'

'It looks like it's just *you* from where I'm standing. Have you seen him? He wants to get out to his rabbits. He's staring at the door.'

'Oh, Anxo,' I sighed. 'Do you want to see your rabbits?'

Anxo barked and pawed at the door.

'I'll take him with me, then, shall I? Come on Anxo, let's leave your Mum to her bones.'

Once the party-poopers had left to pursue more alluring pastimes, I turned my attention to my prize. Here and there, pieces of bone jutted out through the plastic as if the bag, though huge, was barely big enough to contain the goodies inside. I unknotted the handles and sniffed cautiously; to my relief there were no traces of pig to appal me today. The bone at the top was smooth and bloodied, with pieces of pinkish-red flesh still attached. It was certainly what I classed as 'a good one'; now it was time to see what lay underneath. I ran my hand over the top of the slimy surface and down the side, feeling for a ridge or protrusion on which to get a firm grip. Eventually my fingers poked into a hole in the cold, hard surface. I pulled upwards, but the bone didn't shift. I stuck my other hand in and yanked hard, heaving the bag and its contents from the marble surface. It seemed that whatever was shrouded inside the plastic was one gigantic bone. Setting the bag back down again I began to work the sides downwards until the colossus was finally exposed. It was remarkable, to say the least.

'Alas, poor Daisy,' I giggled, as I hoisted the cow's skull up into the air.

The skull was a truly magnificent specimen; I must have spent an age examining the teeth and the jaw. Once I was satisfied that I'd studied every inch of the bovine cranium I carried it proudly out to the lane.

'Gary,' I called. 'Are you down the garden?'

'No,' came the answer. 'I'm up here in the top of the barn.'

Whilst my own reaction to the *objet d'art* had been a literary parody, my husband's response was far less cultured.

'*Fucking* hell!'

'So what shall we *do* with it?' asked Gary, when he came in at lunchtime.

'I thought you could take the axe to it. You know, chop it up into manageable bits.'

'I had a feeling you'd say that. I'll do my best.'

'How did you get on with the raised beds?'

'I put the breeze blocks in place, then I stopped for a fag and a read of *Marca*. I'm going to start filling them this afternoon.'

'I was thinking about that. I was wondering about the rabbit poo. Instead of tipping it into the composter it could go straight into the beds.'

'Good idea. Perhaps we should do that with the chicken shit as well.'

'Apparently not. I remember reading somewhere that it's too potent to start with. You're supposed to let it rot down for six months or more. Saying that, the amount they give us is pitiful. What we get from six chickens and a cockerel is nothing compared to what the rabbits are giving us. They won't just be good for meat – they'll be a fantastic source of manure.'

As I stood at the sink washing the lunch pots, I could hear Gary bringing the axe down on what was left of poor Daisy in the barn. I was drying my hands on the tea-towel when I realised that all had gone quiet. Seconds later, Gary came in through the kitchen door.

'You've not taken the rubbish up yet, have you?'

'I was just about to, why?'

'You might as well take that bloody cow's skull with you. It won't be any good for Anxo. It's breaking up into splinters. There were bits of bone flying about everywhere when I was chopping. I'm not joking, I nearly lost an eye.'

'That wouldn't do, poor Anxo. Here, shove it all into this bin bag. I'll roll a fag and then I'll be on my way.'

'I don't think it's worth calling Anxo to go with you. He's just taken a plastic sausage over to the rabbit pen for Buck.'

Up at the farmhouse Maruja was out on the doorstep. Luna and Pastor were lying beneath the kitchen window dozing, while a strange, tousle-haired dog, no bigger than Buck, was dashing around in circles in the lane. She hadn't mentioned that they were having another dog; perhaps they were minding him? Surely they'd got enough on their hands with Luna and Pastor and Res?

'*Hola*, Maruja.' I called. 'Have you got a visitor?'

'*Hola*, Elisa. He's not visiting, he's ours.'

I looked at him for a moment. Though tiny, he wasn't a puppy; they certainly hadn't had him to work with the cows.

'He was a surprise to me as well,' she smiled, registering my confusion. 'A friend of José Manuel found him in the *campo*. José Manuel thought he'd be company for me in the house.'

'He's very hairy,' I said.

'He was a terrible mess when he arrived. His coat was all tangled. I've bathed him and taken the scissors to him to cut out the knots.'

'Bless him,' I said. 'What's his name?'

'Fleepel.'

Flea-pelt, I thought. It couldn't have been more appropriate.

'Fleepel,' I repeated. 'That's a nice name.'

Back in the kitchen, I gave the latest news to Gary.

'Another one?' he frowned. 'They'll be shelling out a fortune for food.'

'He's only tiny. Think miniature mophead, that'll give you an idea.'

'What's his name?'

'Fleepel. Or at least, something that *sounds* like Fleepel. I can't have got it quite right 'cos I'm sure there's no such word.'

'Perhaps it was Felipe?'

'I doubt it. I think it's frowned upon to give dogs the names of saints.'

'It might have been Free-something. Sometimes "r" can sound a bit like "l".'

'I hadn't thought of that. There might be an "r" at the end then. Freeper? Fleeper? That's it –it's Fleeper! Of course.'

Gary looked none the wiser.

'Flipper, like the dolphin in the movie. Remember how the kids on the island loved all the American box-office movies? *Toy Story, Sponge Bob, Ice Age*? *Flipper* would have been as popular in Spain as it was in England…'

'And that's how you'd pronounce it if you were Spanish. Of *course*.'

I thought of how the excited little dog had been leaping about like a playful dolphin. I could see how he'd earned the name, but somehow it didn't quite suit him. As far as I was concerned, he was Flea-pelt. It fitted him to a tee.

'Isn't it about time we paid a visit to John and Jane?' I asked as I handed Gary his cuppa on Tuesday morning. 'If I'm having those bulbs off Jane they'll want to be going in soon.'

'I s'pose so,' yawned Gary. 'I'd like to do some more on the raised beds this morning, but we could have a drive over this afternoon.'

After lunch I nipped upstairs to put an extra layer on under my jumper. If John and Jane lived in an old stone house like ours, I wasn't leaving anything to chance. The temperature outside couldn't have been more than a couple of degrees above freezing. I hoped they'd have a decent fire going; I needed to keep warm.

'So, where are your directions?' I asked Gary as we took the turn-off for Barreiro.

'I haven't got any. Apparently we have to keep an eye out for a nameplate. It's got their surname on it – you know, like Masi and Solina's? It's done in ceramic tiles stuck on the outer wall.'

'And what *is* their surname?'

'I can't honestly remember. Just look out for something English, on a plaque on a wall.'

We passed two or three small houses but judging by the dogs and the kale the inhabitants were definitely Galician. Eventually we turned a bend and sure enough I spotted a strip of five white tiles on the end of a stone wall.

'Major!' I shouted. 'Look! That's English!'

'Calm down,' frowned Gary. 'How many times have I told you not to wave your arms about when I'm trying to drive?'

He pulled onto the verge and turned off the engine.

'John Major,' I grinned. 'Well I never. Honestly, Gary, only *you* could've forgotten a name like that.'

John and Jane's house was beautifully renovated. The upstairs was a mezzanine with an incredibly well stocked library. Radiators running off the back boiler behind the roaring log fireplace meant that the whole house was sumptuously warm.

For an hour or so we chatted and drank freshly brewed coffee, but outside the sky was turning an ominous shade of steel. When Jane collected our coffee cups, I declined a refill.

'I think it's time we made tracks,' said Gary. 'Liza keeps looking out at the sky.'

'I do,' I admitted. 'It looks as if it'll get dark early and I don't trust the foxes. I can never settle 'til I know the rabbits and chickens are away.'

By Wednesday afternoon the rabbits were long overdue for their second clean out. I wasn't impressed when I discovered that Buck had been digging a burrow under his hutch.

'You didn't have any plans for tomorrow, did you?' I asked Gary as I added the rabbit droppings to the soil he was shovelling into the raised bed.

'Only what I'm doing now, unless there's something more pressing.'

'There is, as it happens. Buck Rabbit's put a request in – he'd like Operation Crazy Paving extending to his half of the pen.'

When we settled down with our beers and the crib board on Friday evening, I felt deeply contented. Despite the bitter February weather we'd achieved so much in the garden in only the space of a week. The raised beds were finished and there were daffodil, tulip and crocus bulbs planted in pots on the patio and beneath the kitchen window. Most importantly, Warren Place now had a state-of-the-art, burrow-proof floor.

'Well,' said Gary as he pegged me two holes short on the crib board. 'Paul should be back tomorrow. He'll notice the difference in temperature. I bet it's been nowhere near as cold in Escairón.'

'His heels,' I frowned, moving my matchstick two places forward. 'You're right, and the way it's looking at the moment, he might yet be arriving to snow.'

'Robbing a bank?' laughed Gary as I pulled on my balaclava on Saturday morning.

'I *knew* you'd say that – you're so predictable. If Anxo's to have a full hour, I need to make sure I won't freeze.'

'Once you get out over the fields you'll be in your element. You enjoy the walks just as much as Anxo – some mornings you seem keener than him.'

Gary was right. I'd enjoyed walking ever since I could remember, but out here in Galicia the breath-taking landscape made every outing a pleasure beyond belief.

'Anyway,' Gary continued. 'Jane told us they've forecast snow for the weekend. I bet when you look out to the distance the hills will be white.'

Out in the *campo* I stuffed my gloved hands into my pockets and quickened my pace against the biting wind. At the top of Field Two I gazed across the valley towards the horizon. Sure enough, the hillside was covered in snow.

'You were right,' I said, when Gary came in for his coffee. 'The snow's settled up on the hilltop. I think it's only a matter of time before it finds its way over to us.'

'Paul'll be pleased then. Luc dropped him off while you were walking Anxo. He can't wait to see a flurry of the white stuff. He's half Swiss, so he told me, and he loves being out in snow.'

'He's bonkers. It`s nice to see it from a distance but being out in it's a different matter. It's my absolute most loathed sort of weather. Rain, wind, thunder – bring 'em on, but snow…' I paused to feign a shudder. '…urgh, no thanks.'

'Paul's pet hate's anything sticky or slimy, apparently.'

'Really? How do you know that?'

'He started the wood treatment round the edge of the roof half an hour ago. He managed about two metres then gave up 'cos it kept dribbling down his arm.'

'You're joking? What a wimp. Perhaps he'll fare better with the guttering. All he's got to do is clip it in.'

When Gary came in at lunchtime he was smiling.

'The guttering's not a goer either, I'm afraid.'

'Go on, amaze me.'

'It's a waste of time – it won't catch the rain. When he put the tiles on, he didn't allow an overhang. The tiles fall shy of the guttering, so the rain'll just roll off down the wall.'

On Sunday morning the whole village was white over. It was my worst nightmare, yet I trudged dutifully over the fields for an hour; Anxo, like our deluded neighbour, was completely smitten with the snow.

By mid-morning the snow showed no sign of abating. It was falling in flakes the size of old pennies and I'd yet to clean out the rabbits and the hens.

When Gary came in for coffee, he was grinning. 'I bet I can make you smile.'

'Unless you've hired a snow plough, I doubt it. Go on then, you might as well try.'

'Paul's gone for a walk up the *alta*.'

'The *alta*? Where's that?'

'It's what he calls the hills in the distance. He reckons he's walking all the way to the top.'

'He's *what*?' The very idea was preposterous. I reached for my tobacco. It made sense to roll a fag.

'He set off about half an hour ago, he reckons it won't take more than two hours to reach the peak.'

'I'll bet you a euro to a *céntimo* he won't make it as far as the main road.'

'He's not going the roadway. He's going across country.'

'Oh dear. That's *not* so amusing. The snow might be four feet deep up there – he's out of his mind.'

'I tried to tell him, but he was having none of it. He was all wrapped up in his ski jacket and he assured me he'd be fine.'

'But he's putting himself in danger. It's a wilderness up there and he won't get a mobile signal. He could lose his way or fall or anything... Crikey, Gary, does he know there are wolves?'

By the time I set off to take Anxo at teatime, Paul still hadn't come home.

'Right,' I frowned as I zipped up my jacket. 'It's five o'clock now, I'll be less than half an hour. If he's not back by six, we'll ring the Old Bill.'

As I grabbed Anxo's lead I looked at Gary. There was no mistaking his anxiety; it was written all over his face.

'Hey,' I said. 'Don't worry. He's a seasoned pilgrim, remember? I'm sure he'll be fine.'

By the time we reached Field Two I felt like a snowman. Even Anxo looked frozen; it was time to cut our losses and head for the warm.

Back in the kitchen, Gary was smiling.

'Number ten's got the lights on. The Alpine hiker's come home.'

Paul didn't surface until after lunchtime on Monday. He was the first to admit he'd had a narrow escape. He'd had no trouble finding his way up to the *alta*; although the landscape around him was an indiscernible white blanket he'd kept his eyes firmly focussed on his target far up ahead.

On the way home it had been a different story. Any familiar landmarks had disappeared beneath the continuous heavy snowfall and for a while he'd trudged round in the same circle three or four times. In desperation he'd taken a turning in the opposite direction and, after walking for twenty minutes across supposedly unknown territory, the jangling of cowbells had finally guided him home.

Whilst the first half of February had been so typical of a harsh Galician winter, the second half turned suddenly and most agreeably into an early spring. There was still a light frost on the ground in the mornings, but the biting winds had subsided and there was a surprising amount of warmth cast by the sun in the afternoons. The welcome change in the weather brought with it the promise of new life in the world around us. Nevertheless, I was surprised when Maruja told me that one of her hens was already broody; she'd be expecting her first clutch of chicks only a week into March. I took a deep breath when I broke the news to Gary; anytime now we'd be needing a nursery unit for Mrs Brown.

By the last weekend in February, a neat little hutch was added to the far corner of the chooks' pen, enclosed within a concertinaed fence of hinged window frames covered with closely woven wire. All our maternity wing lacked now was an incubator. I was pinning all my hopes on Mrs Brown.

To be A Pilgrim

There once was a hiker
Who loved the outdoors,
And he'd trekked over hillsides
And mountains and moors.

This year he would try
Something daring and bold –
He'd walk the Camino,
Like the pilgrims of old.

He'd carry a gourd
And a staff and a shell,
And when he got home,
Oh, the stories he'd tell!

He'd fill up his gourd from
The crystal-clear fountains,
And fend off the wolves as
He passed o'er the mountains.

He'd spend every night
Sleeping under the stars,
With no need for hotels
Or hostels or bars.

He'd take an old compass –
No need for the signs,
As he wove though the oak trees
And chestnuts and pines.

As summer drew closer
Folks tried to deter him,
But he remained steadfast,
His drive was unerring.

Liza Grantham

He'd cope with the dangers,
His nerve would hold steady,
The day came at last
And, by Jove, he was ready!

He set out at daybreak –
It brought him such pleasure
To wander through woodland
And fields at his leisure.

He ambled so freely,
No heed for time passing,
'Til the sky became darker
With rainclouds amassing.

The drizzle came first,
Then it started to pour,
And he sensed that he'd passed
Through this forest before.

He opened his compass,
His fingers now numb –
He was walking the very same
Way that he'd come!

He'd wandered around
In a circle for hours,
Now perished and soaked
By the terrible showers.

If wolves didn't eat him
He'd freeze on the ground,
And it might be a year
'Til his body was found!

How Now, Mad Cow?

He shivered and stumbled,
His strength disappearing,
About to collapse when
He came to a clearing,

He spotted the roadside
And lights from afar,
He dragged himself onwards
And flagged down a car.

'Er, do you speak English?
I can't find my way –
I'm meant to be heading
For Palas de Rei...'

He felt such a fool 'cos
His trek could have killed him –
Take heed if you've thoughts
Of becoming a pilgrim!
.

Chapter 19

Expectant Mothers

On the 1ˢᵗ of March the lawn glistened with dew drops; for the first time since December there had been no frost in the night. The air was crisp, the sky was blue and the world brimmed with vernal promise. Leaves were unfurling on the fruit trees and the birds, undeterred by the chill of the early morning, were already busying themselves building nests – unlike Doe. With only three days to go before the baby rabbits were expected, Doe seemed to be doing nothing to prepare. I shoved another armful of hay into the hutch as she shuffled down the ramp and into the run. She looked heavier, there was no doubt about it, but she was devouring the hay in her hutch as fast as I could replace it: if the truth be told, I was beginning to wonder if she really *was* going to become a mum.

'Doe's still showing no signs of nesting,' I sighed as I handed Gary his cuppa. 'She's not behaving like an expectant mother, if anything I'd say she was blissfully unaware.'

'I'm sure she knows what she's doing,' said Gary. 'Stop worrying about it, you'll know in three days' time. Anyway, you'll have a nice distraction this morning; meeting Jenny and Russell will take your mind off it for a while.'

'I'm looking forward to it,' I nodded. 'It seems an age since we've seen them.'

'It *is*,' he laughed. 'It was way back in December. Crikey, where does the time go? We haven't seen them since last year!'

When we walked into the Hotel Río Ulla, we were greeted by cheery 'good mornings' and smiling faces; perhaps the ex-pats' icy clique was thawing with the onset of spring? We nodded and smiled our 'hellos' to the regulars, before joining Jenny and Russell who were sitting drinking coffee at the bar.

'It's lovely to see you both,' smiled Jenny, handing Gary a jiffy bag. 'I'll give you these now in case I forget later. It's a bumper selection of our tried-and-tested Galicia-grown seeds.'

'Thank you,' he nodded, gratefully. 'It's good of you to remember – they'll be a godsend this spring.'

'They will,' I agreed. 'We've thought a lot about where we went wrong with the *huerta*, and Gary's already started to make some changes. We're determined to have a better harvest this year.'

'There's so much to learn though,' said Gary, 'I'm still not sure about the best time for sowing. Last year it was quite confusing – I went by what it said in the veg book and I reckon I sowed too soon.'

'And I did the opposite with the plants,' I laughed. 'I was hanging on until the end of May to be on the safe side, but the neighbours had already put everything in.'

'It's not an exact science,' explained Russell. 'More's the pity. If it's an English gardening book I wouldn't pay it too much heed, to be honest. Nor would it be much use to go by what's worked for us. Galicia's known for being a region of micro-climates – when it's summer in Ourense it might still be spring up on the north coast.'

'Our rule of thumb is to watch what the neighbours do,' said Jenny. 'They seem to know exactly when the time's right for sowing and planting. Follow their lead and you won't go far wrong.'

'We've certainly been feeling more optimistic,' said Gary. 'With these seeds, and plenty of extra goodness in the soil we're bound to see *some* improvement.'

'And don't forget the raised beds,' I reminded him. 'They're filling up nicely with rabbit poo and…'

'The rabbits!' said Gary. 'Sorry to interrupt you, Liza, but let me tell Jenny and Russell, before I forget.'

'Rabbits?' grinned Russell, 'I'm all ears.'

Jenny and I looked at one another and groaned.

'We bought them from two of your neighbours at the market last month. It seems you're quite a legend in these parts, the woman was certain we'd know who you are.'

'And she was very insistent we should tell you we'd met them,' I added. 'María – that was her name.'

'Right,' grinned Russell. 'That doesn't do much to narrow it down.'

'There are five Marías in our *aldea*,' explained Jenny. 'There were actually *six* when we moved in, can you believe it?'

I thought of the Manolos in Barreiro.

'Actually,' I said, 'I can.'

For the next two days I was almost as obsessed with the rabbits as Anxo. More precisely, I was keeping an overly watchful eye on Doe.

'I don't know why you can't leave her to it,' frowned Gary. 'You're up and down every ten minutes. I'm worn out just watching you – you're like a cat on hot bricks.'

By Thursday afternoon I was starting to worry. The babies were imminent, but Doe still showed no signs of making a nest.

'She should've been pulling her fur out by now,' I told Gary at tea-time.

'Perhaps she won't bother – you seem to be tearing your hair out enough for two.'

'I'm serious. The book says the doe will pluck fur from her dewlap up to two days before the babies are due.'

'There you go then. *Up* to two days could mean an hour, or even ten minutes. I don't think old Doe's the type to hurry, she's too much of a big lazy lump.'

That evening I put the rabbits to bed half an hour earlier than usual; all I could do was wait to see what Friday would bring.

I was up with the lark on Friday morning. After two cigarettes and a mug of strong coffee, I peeled some potatoes and cleaned out the fridge. In the bedroom above me, I could hear Gary snoring. I didn't half envy him; *he'd* have no trouble filling two hours before the sun finally rose.

Before descending on Warren Place, I went down to the chooks' pen. The logistics of my routine seemed ironic; I'd waited all this time for daylight but now I was saving the best 'til last. Once the chooks were out and Buck was eating his breakfast, I moved over to Doe's enclosure. I put down food and fresh water, then squatted nervously in front of the hutch. Inside there was no hint of shuffling or squealing, only the sound of Doe thumping impatiently as she waited behind the door. When I eased down the ramp, I couldn't believe it; she bounded out without a care in the world. When she was safely out of the way and munching her breakfast, I opened the side door a fraction and peeped in. To my amazement the floor of the hutch was covered in a dense blanket of fluff. I was about to close the door when I noticed the slightest quiver of movement. Perhaps Doe had given us baby bunnies after all.

When I came back into the kitchen Gary was up and making his cuppa.

'Morning,' he yawned, 'Any news?'

'Yes. There's a layer of grey fluff on the floor of the hutch and something seemed to move ever so slightly underneath.'

'That's it then, she's had them. Thank God for that.'

'I *think* she's had them. I'm not a hundred per cent certain, the movement could easily have been a mouse. Still, we should know soon enough by her behaviour – if she *has* had them, she'll keep going in to give them a feed.'

I couldn't waste another day pacing about by the rabbit pen; there was housework and laundry and cooking to be done. Leaving Gary to keep an on-and-off vigil, I crossed my fingers and hoped for the best.

On Saturday morning I was a nervous wreck when I finally went out to the garden. Gary hadn't been much of a lookout; he hadn't once seen Doe go in to her young. Maybe he'd been unlucky and missed her, but there was a distinct possibility that the babies had gone ten hours without a feed. When Doe bounded out as large as life I peeped anxiously through the doorway. I needn't have worried; the nest was stirring like a furry grey sea.

Gary was already drinking his cuppa when I came into the kitchen.

'The babies are alive!' I beamed.

When Gary surfaced on Sunday I was already back in the kitchen; now that I trusted Doe to take care of the babies, I could relax back into the normal routine.

'Morning,' I smiled, as I handed him his cuppa.

'Morning,' he yawned. 'I take it there's news?'

'There is, as it happens. I've seen five noses this morning. Doe's babies are going to be fine.'

'That's good then. I was starting to have doubts about you breeding rabbits. A bloke shouldn't have to get up in the morning and make his own brew.'

Later that morning I took chickweed down to the chooks' pen; thanks to the baby bunnies it was almost a week since I'd spent any quality time with my birds. The hens descended on their treat clucking away like old women at a Bingo; all except Mrs Brown.

'Mrs Brown's acting oddly,' I told Gary when he came in at lunchtime. 'She won't let Rufo anywhere near her and – this'll sound silly – she's started to sing.'

'Sing?'

'I know, I told you it'd sound silly. She's making a sort of warbling noise – it doesn't half sound strange.'

On Monday morning only six hens and Rufo flew out of the hen house. I looked at them for a moment; the missing chook was Mrs Brown. When I looked inside, she was sitting on the nest box. I felt a shudder of excitement; could it be that she was ready to brood?

By lunchtime, Mrs Brown still hadn't left the henhouse. There was no mistaking her position; she'd flattened herself like a pancake over the nest.

Over the next week the fur in Doe's hutch became sparser, and the five little noses had become a thriving litter of nine. At ten days old the bunnies' heads still looked too big for their scrawny brown bodies, but with their eyes wide open it wouldn't be long before they were venturing out from the nest.

Mrs Brown had been moved, along with her six warm eggs, gently into the maternity unit. In a fortnight's time, Gary would probably be making his own cuppa again.

'Well,' said Gary, 'what with the chicks and the bunnies, I reckon that's as good a reason as any to start building a barbecue, don't you?'

'Just bunnies,' I said firmly. 'You're tempting Providence. Don't count your chickens until they're hatched.'

'Of *course* they'll hatch. She's been sitting on them for almost a fortnight, and she's barely left them. You said yourself you didn't think she was getting up often enough to eat.'

'You're right,' I nodded. 'But you know how I worry. Anyway, in answer to your question, I think it's a great idea, even if it does seem a bit soon.'

'I'm not suggesting we *use* it yet – I'm thinking of the weather. You know how it always rains in April; it makes sense to do it while it's still fine.'

'True. Where were you thinking of putting it?'

'I thought I'd build it at the edge of the threshing floor, against Carmen's wall.'

'Sounds good. We can put chairs out in summer, and you can make some more tables. Now the ex-pats are friendlier we might hold a bash.'

'Brilliant. I'll get some bricks from the builder's yard on my way back from shopping tomorrow.'

'Bricks? I hope you're joking. It'd be an out and out eyesore, it wouldn't be…'

'In keeping? Aesthetically pleasing? Trust you. If you'd let me finish, I'll need bricks to build the framework. Afterwards I'll clad it completely in stone.'

'Sorry. I should have known better. I won't say another word.'

'Good. I've had an ingenious idea for the grill part. Remember the metal cupboard that was in the bathroom when we moved in?'

I nodded.

'I'll use that for the tray. It'll slot into the top, so we can take it out for cleaning. For the griddle, I'll put an old oven shelf on top.'

'I didn't know you'd *got* an old oven shelf.'

'I've got two actually. Remember Carmen's old cooker that's still lying in the woods past Sacrificial Stone?'

I giggled. 'How could I forget?' During our first summer we'd let Carmen have José Val's dodgy butane cooker; somehow, she'd managed to dump her even dodgier one all the way up in the woods. 'I'd never have thought to look inside it. Good for you.'

'See, I think of everything. Okay, I reckon that's covered it – what d'you think?'

'I think there needs to be a worktop.'

'A worktop?'

'You know, a surface at the side where you can put the burgers and stuff. We don't want Anxo running off with the grub.'

'Good thinking. There are some tiles in the barn that look like they were left over from the kitchen. It'll save buying if we make do with those.'

On Monday afternoon Gary started on the brickwork. Yet again I went off down the track with the barrow to collect an assortment of flat stones. By Tuesday lunchtime the framework was finished. The structure was already starting to look like a barbecue, and Gary was eager to start the cladding that same afternoon.

After half an hour, he returned to the kitchen smiling. For a man who'd been so keen to get cracking, he hadn't been out very long.

'What's up?' I frowned. 'You've never run out of stones already?'

'Don't be daft, there'll be plenty there to finish the job. It's Carmen. She's worried about the barbecue. She thinks it might set fire to her animal pen.'

'Never! That's ridiculous. You're building it against a two-foot-thick stone wall.'

'That's what I told her.'

'And?'

'She pointed out the gaps between the stones.'

'For goodness' sake!'

'*Well*, if you were building a roaring fire, I s'pose it wouldn't be beyond the realms of possibility…'

'But we're not. It's a barbecue. The charcoal doesn't have flames, it… well… it sort of smoulders and glows.'

'I told her that as well.'

'You managed all that in Castilian? I'm impressed.'

'I didn't go into that much detail. I just told her, "*No hay lamas*". She knew what I meant. Anyway, she wasn't convinced. She said I'd have to fill all the holes in with *mortero* – basically she wants me to point the wall.'

Carmen's wall was bigger than the area of our house and the annexe put together. She had to be having a laugh.

'Bloody hell, Gary! It'd take you *weeks*.'

'She didn't mean the *whole* wall, just the surrounding stonework. A couple of feet above it and the same to each side.'

'I see. D'you know what? I think that might look quite attractive.'

'Aesthetically pleasing, even. Yes, I thought so as well.'

'You agreed then?'

He nodded.

'And she was happy with that?'

'*Oh*, yes. If anything, she seemed elated. She scurried off whispering "*Muy bien, muy bien*".'

Once Gary had returned to his cladding, I sat down with a pile of cookbooks. Using cigarette papers as post-it notes, I started to earmark ideas for the barbecue season ahead. I was reading up on relishes when Gary burst into the kitchen.

'I've got a problem,' he sighed.

I couldn't for the life of me think what had happened. Ten minutes ago he'd told me everything was fine.

'What sort of problem?'

'This.' He tossed a fifty euro note onto the marble surface.

'Where the heck did that come from?'

'Guess.'

'Shit, Gary. Not Carmen?'

He nodded.

'We can't possibly keep it. We'll have to give it her back.'

'Easier said than done, I'm afraid. I told her I didn't want it, but she shoved it into my hand. I think she was telling me it's to pay for the *mortero*. I told her cement's only two quid a bag.'

'Here,' I said, shoving it into the pocket of my pinny. 'I'll go round and make her see sense. I'd feel like we'd robbed an old lady if we kept it. We're English, for God's sake, it's not the way things are done.'

Ten minutes later I was back in the kitchen.

'Well,' said Gary, 'how did you get on?'

I held up the fifty euros in answer. 'She made me accept it, Gary. She was so insistent – I swear I had no choice. I explained that it'd only cost a couple of euros to fill the wall in, but she said it was to pay you for your labour. She told me, "Your husband works hard, Elisa. He's such a good man."'

By Thursday breaktime the cladding was finished and Gary had started the pointing. It looked fantastic; far from being an eyesore our barbecue would be practically camouflaged against the wall.

Just before lunchtime, the latch on the back door rattled. It had to be Carmen. I thought of the fifty euros and hoped she'd come to tell me she'd changed her mind.

'Carmen,' I smiled. 'Come in.'

'No, Elisa, I'm not stopping. I only wanted to give you these.'

She handed me a blue carrier bag. It was same as the ones I'd seen Maruja bringing away from shop van. The contents clinked ominously as she handed it over; it was a safe bet the bag was full of booze.

'*Gracias*, Carmen,' I said, feeling embarrassed. I was about to tell her it really wasn't necessary. That we were neighbours and that the fifty euros alone was above and beyond a fair payment for Gary's work. Carmen, however, was quick to second-guess me.

'*De nada*,' she whispered, before scurrying off up the lane.

On Monday morning I didn't quite know what to expect when I went down to the chooks' pen. I eased the panelled fence aside and opened the door of the hutch. Mrs Brown was still sitting on her eggs.

'Morning, Mrs Brown,' I smiled. 'No babies yet?'

Mrs Brown shuffled and pecked at the straw in front of her before tucking it underneath her chest.

I squatted down and poked my head forward towards the nest box.

As Mrs Brown made an angry 'bwaak' in protest I could make out another sound coming from underneath her. There was no mistaking the high pitched 'peep, peep, peep'.

'Oh, Mrs Brown,' I gasped. 'You *are* clever. Can we see?'

I reached into the hutch, but Mrs Brown was in no mood for visitors. She leaned forward and jabbed me hard on the hand.

'Okay,' I grinned. 'I get the message. Keep it up, then, you're doing a grand job.'

'Well?' said Gary, when I walked into the kitchen.

'Result,' I grinned. 'I definitely heard one go peep.'

'*One*?'

'There might be more, but no way was Mrs Brown letting me look underneath her – she's every bit the protective mum.'

'Ta-da!' announced Gary, as he dumped the bone bag onto the marble surface on Monday morning.

'Hooray, you managed to get one. What do we say, Anxo? It's about bloody time.'

We hadn't had a bone bag since the cow's skull adventure. Many of the rural Galicians had dogs so the bone bag was a popular commodity; for the last seven weeks Gary had been pipped at the post every time.

'I wouldn't get too excited,' said Gary. 'It feels really squidgy. I s'pose we're back on pig fat again.'

I hovered over the bag and sniffed hard. There was definitely a trace of pig in there somewhere, but I couldn't detect the usual stench of blubber…

'Hmm,' I frowned. 'It's definitely not pig fat, I think it's bones.'

'Bones?'

'Yes, pig bones. There's a porky smell, but it's not obnoxious like the fat.'

He stood beside be and sniffed.

'*I* can't smell anything.'

'You won't do. I've told you a thousand times, you're…'

'Old-factory-challenged, I know. At least I've not got a terrible memory as well.'

'Smart-arse. Are you going to do a runner like last time or are you going to wait and see what's inside?'

'Go on then, open it up.'

I undid the handles only to find another knotted bag inside.

'Crikey,' I giggled. 'It's like pass-the-parcel. I hope there's not another one underneath.'

'For God's sake, Liza, just see what's inside.'

I untied the second set of handles and peered in.

'Bloody hell, Gary, you've done us proud this morning. Have a look at this!'

I plunged both hands into the bag and lifted out an enormous pig's liver.

'It's as fresh as a daisy,' I marvelled. 'Here, have a whiff.'

He leaned forward and sniffed cautiously.

'Gorgeous. That would've made me a lovely dinner. It's a crying shame to have to feed it to the dog.'

'We don't *have* to.'

'What do you mean?'

'Well. there's no label saying, "not fit for human consumption", is there? If it was left to me, we'd be eating it, but what with you being so faddy…'

'Hey, hold on a minute. I'm not faddy, I'm cautious. If you had your way, you'd be feeding me stuff from the hedgerow. This is different. It's come from a quality butcher's, and we know for a fact the bone bag's always fresh.'

'So you're saying you'd be prepared to risk it?'

'I don't see why not.'

'That's it then, tomorrow I'll do liver and onions and you can enjoy a top-notch free meal. Don't worry, Anxo, I'll boil some up for you.'

'I've seen them!' I shouted, when Gary came into the kitchen on Tuesday morning.

'Them?' he yawned. 'I thought you said she'd got one?'

'I said I'd *heard* one. But now I've seen them *both* – there're two! Mrs Brown was sitting there as good as gold and there was a peep-peeping coming from underneath her. All of a sudden the peeping got louder, and a beak popped out of her chest.'

'A beak?'

'Yes. The tiniest beak you've ever seen. And then another little beak popped out. Oh Gary, I'm over the moon!'

When I went to shut Mrs Brown away that evening, I couldn't believe it; *three* beautiful little chicks were pecking about in the hay.

'Oh, Gary,' I sniffed, dabbing my eyes with a tissue. 'They're beautiful. Three tiny ginger miracles. I was so overcome with emotion I couldn't help but cry.'

Gary sighed. 'And this is the woman that's raising meat for the table? I'd lay money on it we'll still be buying chicken from Día this time next year.'

Liza Grantham

The Barbecue

She's baking to death
In the afternoon sun,
The lager is warm
And the meat's underdone.

It's black on the outside,
The middle's still red,
There are wasps in the relish
And flies on the bread.

Against better judgement
She sits down to eat
And the sweat sticks her legs
To the cheap plastic seat.

She eyes with suspicion
Her beefburger bap,
And groans to herself:
'God, this party's so crap!'

She wonders what's taking
Her hubby so long,
As a greasy-haired man makes
His way through the throng.

He looks round the table
For somewhere to sit,
The next chair is vacant,
She mumbles 'Oh shit.'

The chairs are packed tight,
So she can't make a dash
From his white socks and sandals
And porn-star moustache.

How Now, Mad Cow?

He plonks himself down
With a lecherous grin,
And she balks at the ketchup
Smeared over his chin.

He says, 'Hi, I'm Gerry,
D'ya fancy a dance?'
'No thank you,' she smiles,
Thinking 'No sodding chance!'

She's filled with relief
When her hubby appears,
'God, what the hell kept you?
He's bored me to tears!'

He says 'I was stuck in
The queue for the loo,
That chicken was dodgy –
It's passing straight through.'

'Fantastic!' she beams,
And he gasps, disbelieving,
'You've given us both
A good reason for leaving!'

She grabs his hand firmly
And says, 'Come on, quick!'
And makes for their host
Who's bent down being sick.

'It's been a great party,'
She says, as he's throwing,
'Had a wonderful time
But we have to be going.'

Liza Grantham

He's wiping the drool from
His face with his sleeve,
As he says 'It's a pity
You both have to leave.

You'll come to the next one?'
She nods with a grin.
'That's great, it's next weekend,
I'll pencil you in!'

Chapter 20

One Man's Meat

Though March had come in like a lamb *and* gone out like one, April was coming in like a lion. Not outside in the *aldea*, or even across the valley; but *inside*, upstairs in the house. With ages to go before sunrise I was filling the kettle for a second cup of coffee when the pans hanging from the ceiling began to jiggle fitfully; there was some kind of commotion going on in the bedroom above.

'Scholes!' came Gary's voice.

Even through the ceiling I could detect a tone of exasperation. I wondered what on earth poor Scholes could have done. The bedsprings clanged, but there was no sound of Gary's feet thudding on the floorboards. Whatever Scholes was guilty of, it wasn't serious enough to stir Gary into getting up.

Satisfied that all was well I sat down with my coffee and began to roll a ciggie. Within seconds the pans began to jiggle again. All of a sudden there was an almighty crash and a clatter; Scholes seemed to be charging about like a delinquent kitten up there.

'Scholes!' shouted Gary.

'Is everything alright?' I called.

'Put the kettle on. I'm getting up.'

The bedsprings clanged and this time I heard heavy footfall across the bedroom. Five minutes later, Gary came down the stairs.

'Morning,' I grinned, as I passed him his cuppa. I couldn't resist ribbing him: 'You're up early, couldn't you sleep?'

'What do *you* think? Oh, *I* see, you're trying to be funny. I've just been rudely forced from my bed and I'm not in the mood for humour.' He took a swig of tea. 'Ah, that's better.' He reached for his bacca. 'Scholes had a mouse.'

'Bless him. Is it dead?'

'It is *now*. It wasn't ten minutes ago. That's what all the ruckus was about. He was going crackers chasing it about.'

'What was the loud crash then?'

'He knocked the alarm clock off the bedside table. The back fell off it and the battery rolled out.'

'That's clever, jumping onto the table to get a good vantage point. Shrewd and strategic, that's Scholes.'

'It was bugger all to do with strategy. He jumped on the table when the mouse shot across the bed.'

I giggled. 'No wonder you yelled. He caught it, then, eventually?'

''Course he did, I told you – it's dead.'

'Good. Have you chucked it out of the window?'

'No, he's eating it under the wardrobe. Last seen, it was missing its head.'

'White rabbits,' I laughed when I called Gary in for coffee. 'With all the kerfuffle this morning I forgot all about it when you got up.'

'Crikey, so did I. It doesn't seem like the first of April somehow, I wonder why.'

'I'll tell you why. It's 'cos we've not gone into Monterroso for the hotel or the market. I wouldn't want to do it every month, it'd get a bit samey. It's nice to give it a miss for a change.'

'*I* know why you're not bothered about going – you don't want to leave the bunnies and the chicks.'

It was true. Doe's babies were adorable, and highly entertaining. At two weeks old they'd ventured down the ramp and into the run. From there onwards it had been all systems go. At first, Doe could often be seen lying on top of her hutch, grabbing a well-earned break from her maternal duties, but the bunnies were agile and inquisitive; they'd encroached on her haven within a matter of days. Now, at four and a half weeks old, they spent hours on end bombing about the enclosure, leaping on and off the hutch and chewing for all they were worth on the slats of the barn. They were eating like gannets and pooing accordingly. I was cleaning them out twice daily and the raised beds were filling up a treat. If I was gladdened by their voracious appetite, Doe most certainly was not. If any of the venturesome tykes attempted to snatch a top-up from the milk bar, she'd kick them away and give them short shrift. There were five males and four females, and all had brown ticked fur just like Doe. One of the nine stood out from the others; he had a strip of white running from his forehead almost down to his nose. Against my better judgement, I named him; he was Blaze.

Whilst Doe had assumed a nonchalant attitude to motherhood, down in the maternity wing Mrs Brown was every bit the fussy and overly attentive mum. The chicks were only four days old, yet she was bringing them out into the little enclosure, already encouraging them to scratch at the earth and forage for grubs. If any of the other hens ventured too close to the wire, Mrs Brown would squawk them a warning and send them on their way. Rufo seemed to know instinctively where he wasn't wanted; when I opened the house in the mornings, he'd cast a cursory glance in the direction of the nursery pen before strutting over to harass his other wives. Alas, for the last two mornings, he'd also begun to harass *me*. I wasn't *overly* worried; despite his apparent lack of involvement with the chicks he was clearly being a protective father. I assured myself he'd stop jabbing at my wellies once he realised that I wasn't a threat to his young.

On Saturday morning there was cause for celebration. Scholes, the tactical hunter and mouse decapitator *extraordinaire*, was three.

'We should have bought him something for his birthday,' said Gary when I reminded him at breaktime.

'A toy mouse, for example?' I grinned. 'Look at him though, he's made a beautiful cat – he's so well-grown and sturdy-looking, it's hard to believe he used to sit in your shoe.'

'Crikey, he did, didn't he? I'd forgotten about that.'

'I bet you've not forgotten where we were when Barbara sent the text to say the litter had been born?'

'Now, *that's* something I'll always remember. Not many people can say they've met the famous *bombo* that drums for Spain.'

After four years on the island without a cat I was desperate for feline company. When our friend Barbara had told us her cat, Lily, was expecting kittens I asked her to keep one by for us. Gary and I were on holiday in Valencia when the litter was expected. On the day that Scholes emerged into the world we were sitting in the bar of Manolo, the mascot of the Spanish football team, famous for rousing the crowd as he beat on his big bass drum.

'I wish we'd taken a photo,' sighed Gary wistfully.

'We did.'

'We didn't. You said people that had their pictures taken with celebrities were sad.'

'I *actually* said "puerile and sycophantic". Anyway, I thought you meant a photo of Scholes. I'll dig it out later, it'll be nice to reminisce.'

Once I'd peeled a pan of potatoes and put a steak and onion pie in the oven, I nipped upstairs to look for the photo of Scholes. I rummaged about in the cupboard, peering now and then into bags and boxes that had been there so long I couldn't remember what was inside. Eventually, I unearthed the album I was looking for, revealing a carrier bag of fabric oddments underneath. I pulled it out, hoping to find some scraps of denim amongst the offcuts; it was high time I sewed some much-needed patches onto Gary's jeans. I emptied the contents onto the bed and stared in horror at the sight that lay before me. Nestled on top of the fabric was a huddle of pink, squirming baby mice. For a moment I stood there, flummoxed and saddened; I'd spent the last month marvelling over chicks and bunnies and now the fate of the tiny lives before me lay squarely in my hands. For a brief moment I wondered whether Gary had been right when he'd teased me about my aptitude for meat production. If my resolve faltered over disposing of a litter of vermin, what chance would I have when it came to killing the livestock I'd so tenderly raised? It was time to dig deep; I'd been adamant that I could cope with a self-sufficient lifestyle, and I was still determined I was going to pass the test. At length I scooped up the entire bundle and shoved it hurriedly back into the bag. I'd take it up to the wheelie bin later, for now it could wait in the barn.

'We're going to have to buy some mousetraps,' I announced when we settled down with our beers that evening. 'I found a nest full of babies in the cupboard upstairs.'

'That's gross. Did you kill them?'

'No. They weren't much bigger than maggots; to be honest I wasn't quite sure what to do. In the end I dropped them into the wheelie bin when I took the rubbish. It was a bit of a cop out really; they'd perish naturally, but it took the final outcome out of my hands.'

'That's not a cop out. It was good thinking on your part. There was a time you'd have been looking for a surrogate mother and asking me to build a cage for them – it's another step in the right direction, you should be proud.'

'We've had a text message off Rose,' announced Gary when he came in for coffee on Sunday morning. 'She's back in Galicia, she landed last week.'

'Ooh, that's exciting,' I said, reaching for my tobacco. 'Let me roll a fag and you can read me what she says.'

'Hold on then.'

After what seemed an age of tapping and cursing, he cleared his throat. 'Ready?'

I nodded.

'Got back Thursday. Hoped to see you at market. Got help-exes for two weeks. Be good to see you later this month. Rose, m, w, a. What's that?'

'It's a kiss. It's the noise it makes. Mwa, see?'

'That's daft.'

'I knew you'd say that. I think it's nice.'

'Must be a woman thing. I wonder what she'll have the help-exes doing – it's not as if they'll be able to rebuild the house.'

'It's not impossible. Okay, your average help-ex – or workaway, for that matter – might not necessarily be a specialist in a particular area. They might be young folk with a sense of adventure who want to travel on a limited budget, or middle-aged gappers, or... well, just normal people like us. But then there are others with a trade behind them, so you could be lucky enough to bag yourself an electrician or a joiner or whatever – d'you see what I mean?'

He nodded. 'I s'pose so.'

'I'd like one, to be honest. I think it'd be cool.'

'But we wouldn't have any jobs for them. I don't need help with the logging and the garden, and you're *far* too proud to have somebody else doing the laundry or cleaning the house.'

I grinned. 'You're absolutely right, which is why I've never suggested it. It's a shame though, I bet we'd meet some really interesting folks.'

'We'd probably attract the weirdos – it'd be just our luck.'

I giggled but stopped abruptly. I'd had an uncomfortable thought. 'The text didn't mention Pete, did it?'

'No, why?'

'So Rose is here on her own.'

'Yes?'

'Well, she's living in a caravan in the middle of nowhere and she's having complete strangers over to stay.'

'I shouldn't worry. I'm sure everyone's thoroughly vetted. I don't think she'll come to any harm.'

'I hope you're right. Anyway, what did you reply?'

'I didn't. I was leaving that up to you.'

'I'm off to clean the rabbits out as soon as I've swilled the mugs through. You could do it this once, surely? Be a love.'

'Go on then, what d'you want me to say?'

'How about we invite her over for dinner in a couple of weeks, say Saturday the twenty-third?'

'Okay, she'll probably want to stay over, though – she likes a drink.'

'No, problem. In fact, suggest it – it'll be fun.'

As Gary went out through the door, I stubbed my fag out and went over to the sink. Suddenly I heard Maruja calling me from the lane.

'Elisa!'

'*Momentito*!' I shouted. I went through to the passage and opened the door.

'Would you like some milk?' she asked, while Flea-pelt ran in circles round her legs. 'There's a litre and a half here. It's all fresh from this morning's milking. I've got more than I need.'

'Don't you want it for cheese? I asked her.

She shook her head. 'I'm making five a day at the moment. There's only the three of us, and I'm not really supposed to have it – the doctor wants me to lose some weight. Solina and Másimo take a few at the weekend, but if I make any more it won't fit in the fridge.'

I could remember the first time I'd gone round to buy a cheese from Maruja. It was the height of summer and, at first, she wasn't sure if she could spare one; she'd told me the cows weren't producing much milk because the *campo* was dry. Last year we'd had rain in summer, and the effect on the fields around us was remarkable. The pasture was dense and lush and growing like crazy. When I'd walked Anxo this morning, my joggers were drenched from the dewfall; in places the grass was already well above my knees.

'Is it because of the *campo*?' I asked.

She nodded. 'The pasture's usually good in spring, but this year it's exceptional. The cows are eating far more than normal and turning it all into milk.'

'If you're sure, Maruja, I'd love it, thank you,' I smiled.

When Maruja had gone, I took the lid off one of the bottles. I sniffed the contents with interest; the milk had a distinctive creamy, earthy smell. I didn't usually drink milk on its own, but I took a mug from the cupboard, eager to give it a try. It was deliciously rich and slightly tangy. I drained the mug and poured in some more.

When Gary came in at lunchtime, I showed him our gift.

'It's really kind of her to think of us,' he said surprised. 'What will you do with it all?'

'I'll bake us a custard tart this afternoon. And I was only going to do eggs and chips for lunch tomorrow; I'll chop up some ham and peas and mint and do a luxury creamy risotto instead.'

'That sounds good. But surely that won't use all of it?'

'It won't. I'll have some on my bran flakes tomorrow for breakfast, and of course you can have it in your brew.'

'Perhaps you could give some to Scholes? A belated birthday present. He'd love it, I'm sure.'

I wasn't a great believer in giving milk to cats; it wasn't good for them. I knew that Scholes adored it and at times I took advantage of the fact, using it to lure him out if he'd snook into a cupboard or under one of the spare beds. Still, a chance like this didn't come every day, and it *had* been his birthday... I opened the back door.

'Scholes!' I called. 'Milk!'

Scholes appeared from under the barn door and came trotting into the kitchen wailing. As I poured a tiny amount into an empty Philly pot he butted the bottle, causing it to splash on the floor. I wasn't in the least concerned; once he'd cleared the contents of the tub, he'd lap up the spillage in no time at all.

'Happy birthday for yesterday,' I told him.

To my amazement he sniffed at the milk and walked away.

On Monday morning I poured a generous helping of cows' milk over my bran flakes. It had been lukewarm when I'd tried it yesterday; it tasted so much nicer chilled, straight from the fridge, today.

'How were your bran flakes?' yawned Gary as I passed him his cuppa.

'Gorgeous. The milk's better chilled. I could get used to it. In fact, I might have bran flakes again tonight instead of a sandwich for tea.'

'Bran flakes for *tea*?'

'Yes, why not? It's a luxury and I don't want to waste it. Think of all the goodness in it – I'll be blooming with health.'

At bedtime I poured the very last of the milk into a mug and drank it to the very last drop. When I snuggled down under the duvet, I felt deliciously wholesome. I was packed with country goodness; this was the life.

When I awoke in the early hours of Tuesday morning my stomach was in agony. As I shook off the throes of sleep, I realised that I needed the bathroom; and soon. As I eased myself up from the mattress, I recognised the urgency. I shot out of bed and made a dash for the door.

Three hours later, I awoke again in daylight. Once more I eased myself from the mattress and my stomach felt decidedly sore. This time I plodded listlessly through to the bathroom, tracing the glistening trail of bleach across the living room and dining room floors.

An hour later, revived only slightly by strong black coffee and a cigarette, I stepped groggily out into the world. Over in Warren Place, the bunnies descended on their breakfast with gusto; it was no wonder they were growing at such a great rate of knots. For the moment they still had plenty of room to charge about in the enclosure, but even now it was clear they'd be vying for space by the time they were eight weeks old.

As I shuffled down to the chooks' pen, I wondered if today would be the day that Rufo would give up on his warning jabs. Once Mrs Brown and her chirpy trio had hopped out into the sunshine, I strolled over and opened the hen house door. Rufo strutted out and pecked half-heartedly at my wellies, then suddenly jabbed hard at my knees. As I tried to ease him away with my toe, he jabbed even harder. I shrieked as his beak punctured my skin.

'I'm going to have to revert to the waterproofs,' I told Gary. 'Rufo's not satisfied with pecking my wellies; his jabs have progressed to my knees.'

'You're back to square one then. Jenny and Russell warned you it'd happen. You wouldn't have it. You were adamant he was cured.'

'He is. This is different. It's only since Mrs Brown's had the babies, he'll quieten down once he sees I'm no threat to the chicks.'

Over the next week, Rufo's aggression showed no signs of abating; some mornings he'd attack viciously with his beak *and* his claws. The waterproof trousers no longer served to deter him, but they afforded me some protection at least. My legs, though bruised, weren't scabby and I was becoming resigned to my fate.

'I really think we should neck him,' said Gary, on Monday evening. 'It's alright saying you can cope when you're wearing the waterproofs, but that doesn't solve the problem. Anyway, there's another reason. Chook food's gone up one euro forty a bag.'

On Tuesday morning I was scowling when I marched down to the chooks' pen. Gary's gripe about the price of chicken feed had really made me see red. If the truth be told, I'd begun to give tentative consideration to the option of killing Rufo, but after those miserly comments I'd pushed the idea firmly to the back of my head. When I entered the run there was a riotous clucking coming from the henhouse. I'd have to let the hens out quickly; I didn't want them trampling on the freshly laid egg.

As they scurried, jostling and squawking, over to the feeder I looked down at Rufo who was launching himself at my leg.

'Ungrateful brute,' I told him. 'If only you knew.'

Once he was satisfied that I'd been chastised enough, he swaggered off to join his wives. Paying him no more heed, I bent down to open the fence to Mrs Brown's enclosure. My punishment wasn't over; Rufo jabbed hard at my head.

As Rufo lay on the marble surface, a wave of guilt ran through me. Stripped of his opulent plumage, he didn't look a great deal bigger than his thriving chicks. I'd have to do plenty of extra veg and a mountain of roast potatoes if he was going to make a decent meal for two hungry peasants and their guest.

I wrapped his legs carefully in fatty Galician bacon, then covered each one with a layer of foil. I laid him on a trivet in the roasting pan and gave him a generous dousing of stock before covering the whole assemblage with foil. He'd cook slowly at a low temperature and the steam from the stock would keep him tender and moist. I'd remove the foil for the last fifteen minutes to turn him a lovely shade of gold.

'There,' I told him, as I closed the door of the oven. 'That's shown you. Bastard in life, basted in death.'

Once Rose, Gary and I were seated around the table, Gary picked up the carving knife ready to do the honours, while I poured cava into our flutes.

'Breast for me and Rose,' I reminded him.

'No problem,' he grinned. 'That means I'll get both of his legs.'

When we'd all helped ourselves to roast spuds and vegetables, Gary was ready to dig in.

'Wait,' I said. 'I think *I* should be the first to try him. He was my nemesis after all.'

I cut off a small piece and put it slowly into my mouth. I chewed deliberately, while Gary and Rose looked on.

'Well?' said Gary.

'Superb,' I smiled. 'Good old Rufo. Go on, Rose – see what you think.'

Rose waved her fork in an exaggerated flourish before spearing a sizeable slice of white meat.

'Mm,' she nodded, chewing eagerly. 'Delicious. It melts in the mouth.' She picked up her glass of cava. 'I propose a toast…'

'Not so fast,' grinned Gary. 'I've not had my turn yet.' He sank his teeth into the drumstick he'd been holding impatiently above his plate. His brow furrowed and he tugged hard with his fingers and thumb. 'Bastard!' he frowned.

'What's up?' I asked.

'He's very crunchy. Is he overdone?'

'He most certainly isn't. His legs were wrapped in bacon. He's crispy that's all – I browned him off for a while at the end.'

'He got off lightly then, didn't he?'

'What d'you mean?'

'He's browned *you* off for months.'

'Trust you. Anyway, get him down you – I'm sure he'll be more succulent underneath.' I turned to Rose. 'So how did the help-exes get on?'

'The first ones were fantastic. A young couple. They cleared bramble and shifted rubble and even built me a little shower cubicle behind the van.'

I nodded, my mouth full of Rufo.

'The next one was disastrous. A bloke in his fifties, on his own.'

'What happened?' asked Gary, pulling a crispy bit out of his teeth.

'He propositioned me.'

I swallowed. 'He *what*?'

'It's a long story. He didn't like the work or the accommodation. He knew in advance he'd be camping – I've patched up the tent. He was ever so pleasant about it – said he was really sorry, but he'd have to be off in the morning. To make up for letting me down he took me into town that evening for a meal. He even drove so that I could have a drink. Anyway, it was a pleasant enough evening, but he wasn't the most stimulating company. I was relieved when he suggested we come home.'

'And that's when it happened?'

She nodded. 'He asked if he could spend the night in the van. I was slow on the uptake and said it was no problem, I'd kip in the tent. He told me he meant he wanted to spend the night in the van *with me*.'

'Shit,' I frowned. 'What did you do?'

'I told him I was a happily married woman and if he didn't retract his suggestion I'd report him to the help-ex website. He turned all sorry and scuttled off to the tent.'

'Crikey, Rose. You weren't half lucky. What if he'd been persistent, or ...?'

'I know, I know. I've learned my lesson. Couples or women only from now on.'

I glanced over at Gary, who was now gnawing manfully on the second leg.

'Bastard,' he said.

Gary fell strangely silent as Rose began to regale us with the plans for her garden. Finally, he spoke.

'I'm sorry, Liza, if I finish this leg I'll have no teeth left. I'm going to have to have some of the breast.'

I stifled a smile as Gary lifted the plate towards him.

All that was left were Rufo's ribs.

It's April and the early morning drizzle threatens a downpour typical of Galician spring. Scholes flattens himself amongst the wildflowers to stalk a blackbird that pecks beneath the fig tree. Anxo paws at a slug sloping languidly through the damp clover. Staccato raindrops patter on Warren Place, rolling down the tiles, into the gutter and cascading onto the lawn. An extraordinary silence hovers over the chooks' pen, where the breeze sways the damson trees, yet the chestnut with its majestic strength remains still.

I peer out from beneath my umbrella and gaze upwards into a sky which promises patches of blue to the north. Here in paradise, we remain as optimistic as that sky, and Fate continues to lead us, hoping, trusting, believing, here in Galicia, our home.

Liza Grantham

Another Year

Another year has passed so soon –
Twelve cycles of the silv'ry moon,
One orbit of the golden sun,
Four seasons, merging into one.

Through winds and snow and sun and rain,
The wheel of time has turned again,
And from the dark, decaying earth
There springs the promise of new birth.

From old to new and new to old,
The wonders of our world unfold.
From every sorrow, joy will come
Before another year is done.

Life's carousel spins round so fast,
No time to dwell on what has passed.
Appreciate its every turn,
Be sure to live, to love, to learn.

Four seasons, merging into one,
One orbit of the golden sun,
Twelve cycles of the silv'ry moon,
Another year comes round so soon.

Liza Grantham was born in 1965 in the East Midlands brewery town of Burton-on-Trent. She worked for over twenty years as a primary teacher in England and Gran Canaria before moving to rural Galicia where she continues to live, love, and learn.

How Now, Mad Cow? is the second book in the Mad Cows in Galicia series. The other books in the series are also available in paperback and e-book from Amazon stores, or as a free download on Kindle Unlimited.

If you love reading or writing memoirs, join us!
http://www.facebook.com/groups/welovememoirs/

Printed in Great Britain
by Amazon